ECONOMICS AND COMMERCE

economics
and
commerce
THE SOURCES OF INFORMATION
AND THEIR ORGANISATION

ARTHUR MALTBY
BA FLA FRSA
SENIOR LECTURER AT LIVERPOOL
SCHOOL OF LIBRARIANSHIP

LONDON
CLIVE BINGLEY

FIRST PUBLISHED 1968 BY CLIVE
BINGLEY LTD 16 PEMBRIDGE ROAD
LONDON W11 SET IN 10 ON 12 POINT
PLANTIN AND PRINTED IN GREAT
BRITAIN BY THE CENTRAL PRESS (ABER-
DEEN) LTD COPYRIGHT © 1968 ARTHUR
MALTBY ALL RIGHTS RESERVED
85157 011 9

CONTENTS

PREFACE

WHEN I FIRST read, and mentally endorsed, the statement in the preface to Lewis' *The literature of the social sciences* that 'detailed bibliographical studies (in social science fields) are needed', and that 'there is clearly plenty of scope for individual specialists . . . to contribute to the control of the literature', I certainly did not imagine that I might attempt to provide librarians with a more extensive guide to a major social science discipline than was possible in his excellent conspectus. My experience, however in preparing students for the Library Association part II paper, the bibliography and librarianship of economics and commerce, from its inception in 1964, convinced me that an introductory guide to economics literature was needed and this work attempts to meet that need.

The primary aim is to provide a suitable text for the LA examination, but it is hoped that the book will also be of use to librarians other than students who work, or intend to work, in the commercial or social sciences and, in part, to those with a subject interest in the elements of economic science. The overlapping between disciplines has led me to cover management information sources in addition to those relating to economics and commerce, but as management is becoming increasingly well covered in other guides, I have considered some of its bibliographies and organisations much more briefly than those on pure and applied economics.

The emphasis throughout is on description rather than upon evaluation of material as it is hoped that if the book is to be used in library schools, it will serve to eliminate much of the listing of titles that so often takes place in lectures on systematic bibliography. I have, no doubt, left out some publications and organisations of significance—especially from overseas countries—but enough items have been included to indicate the potential of the various kinds of information sources. The inevitable proliferation of titles will prove well worthwhile if it genuinely permits a greater proportion of class time to be devoted to tutorial work and the vital task of examining and appraising the chief bibliographies.

7

My first chapter is designed to offer to librarians who have no subject background a short basic account of economics and economists. It is provided to encourage the reader to seek more information about the character of the subject field and to learn enough to be able to use the bibliographical materials intelligently. Chapters two to ten deal with economics bibliography, reviewing in turn the various categories of reference material. I have not attempted to list textbooks on the various branches of economic activity, as these are enumerated in several of the pamphlet bibliographies and any such list quickly becomes dated. Then, in the remaining chapters, I have reviewed the work of librarians in this province before describing the major economics and commercial organisations and libraries. The presentation of the bibliographical chapters according to form of material rather than subject has led to some distribution of related items and a certain amount of repetition. However, some entries under major subject themes are included in the index and the reiteration of certain important points should prove helpful to the student. References are given to other literature which, unfortunately, is often scattered in pamphlets and journals; these references could be expanded by students, particularly with regard to the library literature of the USA. Finally, it should be pointed out that the growth of social science and commercial literature is increasing the demand for good librarians in this province. I sincerely hope that this volume contributes to the meeting of that demand by revealing something of the most valuable and often absorbing work that is carried out in appropriate libraries.

I wish to record my debt to a number of librarians with extensive experience in commercial information work for the advice which they have, directly and indirectly, given to me. I am especially grateful to Mr P R Lewis of the School of Library Studies at Queens University Belfast, who read my manuscript and provided many helpful comments and suggestions. Any errors or inaccuracies in the text are, of course, my responsibility alone. My thanks are also due to my wife for her help in checking some details in the text and in proof reading.

July 1967   ARTHUR MALTBY

CHAPTER ONE

THE SCOPE OF ECONOMIC AND COMMERCIAL ACTIVITY

WHAT IS ECONOMICS and in what way is it related to commercial matters and management problems? There are several definitions of economic science and many possible ways of showing its links with commercial activity. However, for our purposes, the latter part of the above query can best be answered by means of a diagram indicating the chief segments of the subject field (see page 10).

It must be pointed out immediately that the diagram is merely a sketch and that the subject field could be arranged, not only in much more detail, but also in different ways. The classification may serve, however, as a simple guide for the purpose of the student of economics librarianship, and an attempt has been made to illustrate the overlapping between categories by placing each subject category next to the one with which it has most in common. Thus applied economics, for instance, shades off gradually into commercial activity and the latter often merges with certain aspects of management practices.

THE CHARACTER OF ECONOMIC PROBLEMS

But the question remains, what is economics? It is not easy to answer this readily; one is always tempted to give the evasive sounding retort offered by one professor and say that economics is what economists do! Fortunately, although there are conflicting definitions, it is possible to be more precise than this. Economic choice is involved in any situation where there is a need or wish for particular objects, but a scarcity of resources (or time) with which to obtain or pursue them. Thus, if I have a limited amount of cash at my disposal and I must decide whether to spend it on an evening at the theatre or on a textbook, my problem (whatever its eventual solution) is an economic one. Economic science, then, naturally involves the study of demand and supply, both at the individual level and on a national and international scale. It is concerned with the factors involved in the production and consumption of goods, and attempts to formulate laws based on its findings, although these laws, as is

9

THE MAJOR DIVISIONS OF ECONOMICS AND COMMERCE

Economic and commercial history	Principles of economics	Applied economics	Commerce	Management
Development of agriculture, industry, trade and social conditions. The history of economic thought and the evolution of scientific management techniques — although really pervasive of other categories — should be considered here also.	The theory of economic science as it affects population, production, value, distribution, money and banking, and international trade.	The application of these principles to the analysis of contemporary problems in production (eg the economic size of firms), trade (including marketing and exporting), labour, money, taxation, and aid to developing countries.	Is concerned with the complex task of ensuring that goods are efficiently distributed. It involves retail and wholesale trading, company organisation and services such as transport, insurance, advertising, accountancy, banking practice and many aspects of overseas trade.	The science devoted to the achievement of efficiency in industry. It includes the application, in factory, or office, of the principles of financial production, sales and personnel management, and techniques and work study. The decision-makers and risk-bearers in a business enterprise are sometimes called ' entrepreneurs '.

the case with many of the human sciences, are not as exact as those of pure science. At the national level, economics is the servant of political science (hence its old name—political economy), but fundamentally it is concerned with every situation in which varied needs and limited means or time necessitate choice.

Economic theory deals with the hypothetical situations of individuals and nations, in order to determine for our future benefit in actual situations the probable consequences of various alternative courses of action. Applied economics is simply the application of the principles which theory has developed. So, if economic theory convinces us that firms can grow too large in a particular industry, we may find an appropriate body, and in Britain this would be the Monopolies Commission, taking steps to investigate the work of the largest firms in that industry to ensure that they are not abusing the advantages which accrue from size. It may be stressed, nevertheless, that economists are not concerned with value judgments—in their professional capacity they do not comment on the ethics of having large firms, but simply on the economic consequences of firms being too large or too small to produce their goods efficiently. There is a school of thought, known as welfare economics, which argues that economic data should in itself provide objective evidence to justify certain moral decisions involving human welfare, but most economists deny this; they have good reasons for believing that their science is detached from ethics and that the two subjects must join hands before these moral judgments can be made.

COMMERCE, MANAGEMENT, ECONOMIC HISTORY

A further insight into economic activity could be gained by exploring the nature of the work of economists in advising companies, preparing data for governmental policy and programmes and conducting independent research into, for example, likely future trends in the growth of a particular industry. Such exploration might partly serve to vindicate the apparently vague remark that ' economics is what economists do '. Yet it is clear that economics is fundamentally concerned with the problems arising from the production of goods and the demand for them. Commerce, on the other hand, is essentially involved with their distribution and the various processes and services, mentioned briefly in the diagram on page 10, which make distribution fully efficient. But while the economist may study the reasons why one method of distribution can be more advantageous than another, the allied activities of commercial enterprise deal with the way in which distribution is actually achieved. That is, the commercial student examines what *is* done (in retailing, transport in its various forms, advertising and so forth), rather than what *might* or should be done if economic gain is to be maximised. As one modern writer puts it, ' Commerce . . . has no place for theory. It takes economic facts as they are . . . he (the student of commerce) is more concerned with the how than the why of economic activity.' (J L Hanson *The structure of modern commerce* 1965 *pp* 7-8.)

Management too is severely practical, although for many years it has been possible to base management procedures on a sound body of established theory, and many economic principles find an important practical outlet in modern managerial techniques. This is a subject with many facets and, in the USA especially, it has been developed tremendously in recent decades. It has links with both commerce and applied economics, but has also problems and techniques which are all its own. Planning the structure of a firm's organisation, job evaluation, time and motion study, budgeting, industrial relations—these are a few striking examples.

The historical side of our subject field should certainly not be neglected. The industrial revolution, which gathered impetus in Britain from 1770 onwards, wrought many drastic changes; it transformed, for instance, the nature of the working-class life, and so developed manufacturing industries and the factory system that, at one period in the nineteenth century, it was justifiable to regard this country as the world's workshop. There were also sweeping changes, of course, in agriculture and transport and, in the long and drawn out period in which the nation was adjusting to these radical alterations, there was much social hardship and injustice that was only slowly alleviated by appropriate legislation. Themes such as the short and long term effects of the corn laws; the reasons for the rapid development of railways; the coming of limited liability for companies; the growth of trade unions; the problem of the unemployed ablebodied; the expansion or decline of individual industries; and the steady increase in the level of taxation and government expenditure in the twentieth century; these and many others in the story of modern industrial progress demand from the economic or social historian careful investigation.

Finally, with regard to the subjects mentioned in our diagram, it may be pointed out that the history of economic doctrines can be a fascinating study in its own right for those who like to trace the evolution and interplay of ideas. Likewise management history has its great names—Frederick Winslow Taylor (the father of scientific management), Henri Fayol, Frank B Gilbreth (the originator of time and motion study), and Mary Parker Follett, for example—these illustrating the point made previously that modern management practice is supported by sound principles, yet the management pioneers are few in number when compared with the great economists. In part this is due to the fact that the effective history of management has been relatively short, whereas the doctrines of economics can be traced back clearly for at least two centuries, and, indeed before this, if one considers the contribution of the French school of economists known as the physiocrats. Although the historical part of our subject is no more important than the rest, the outline account of the lives and work of some great economists which follows is necessarily longer than the information given to elucidate the other sectors of the diagram on page 10. (See, too, the table provided by Lewis in *The literature of the social sciences pp* 20-21.) This is because, although only a few very important economists are considered here, it is impossible to be extremely concise without failing utterly to give a tolerable idea of the status and achievement of the men concerned.

Adam Smith (1723-1790), a learned professor with a brilliant intellect, must be considered first of all in any chronological survey of great British names in economics since 1760. His *Wealth of nations,* 1776, virtually summed up all the vital ideas in the field that had gone before and provided a panoramic survey of what was to prove a rapidly developing subject. Many of his sayings have remained justly famous: it was Adam Smith, for example, who first described Britain as a ' nation of shopkeepers '. Smith believed in private enterprise and his principal work on economics shows how individuals working for their own profit can satisfy society by meeting the demand for goods and services. He also showed the great advantages that could be won by intensive specialisation of labour, each man concentrating on a relatively small but important task and making his skills in the chosen sphere, acquired over a number of years, available for the benefit of all. Smith's subject had originally been moral philosophy, but this work won him renown throughout Europe and, with the development of commerce and industry and the consequent boost given to interest in the market system and the factors determining the price of goods, he rapidly became a political economist of the very highest rank.

Hard on his heels chronologically, and perhaps in stature, are *David Ricardo* and *Thomas Robert Malthus*. Malthus (1766-1834) is best known for his *Essay on population*, first published anonymously in 1798. This was originally designed as an answer to the idea of a future human utopia which had been advanced by the eighteenth century writer, Godwin. Malthus contended that the growth of population would always increase more rapidly than the ability of man to provide food for the extra mouths. Only war or severe disease, Malthus thought, could prevent this. His prognostications might well have proved accurate but for a number of varied factors which he was unable to anticipate. Certainly, however, these views were unpopular to his contemporaries and were later distorted by others to provide an excuse for keeping down wages, on the grounds that higher pay for the working classes was more than offset by the resulting increase in the size of their families. Malthus, by profession a minister of religion, became known as 'the gloomy parson' and his writings, and possibly those of Ricardo, led Thomas Carlyle to brand economics as 'the dismal science'. Yet it is not only for his grim views on population that Malthus deserves recollection; his *Principles of political economy*, 1823, was an important work and one which appreciated the possibility of under-employment through a deficiency of spending. Malthus, alas, was never able to express his views clearly on this particular point and, as a later economics classic (J M Keynes *General theory of employment, interest and money p 32*), put it 'the great puzzle of effective demand with which Malthus had wrestled vanished from economic literature', not to be revived until the twentieth century.

Ricardo (1772-1823), a wealthy stockbroker with a keen and analytical mind with which to attack economic problems, was more pessimistic and cynical than Smith. He contributed many ideas to economic thought, not only in his books but in his voluminous correspondence with contemporary economists (especially his friend Malthus) also. His chief work is *Principles of political economy*, 1817, and his writings have often been regarded as being of especial importance for the effort which Ricardo made to explain the concept of economic rent, although his reference to it as the reward derived from 'the original and indestructible powers of the soil' is certainly dubious from a modern standpoint.

Karl Marx once described Ricardo and his British predecessors as 'the classical economists', but it is usual to apply this term also to the younger Mill and, possibly, to Alfred Marshall. *John Stuart Mill* (1806-1873) was an infant prodigy who later became a brilliant, prolific and versatile writer. His outstanding work on economics, again entitled *Principles of political economy* was published in 1848 and was produced remarkably rapidly—it was, as the biographer R L Heilbroner expresses it, 'as if he had accumulated thirty years of knowledge and then spewed it out in one effortless act'. To a certain extent Mill consolidates the work of Smith and Ricardo, but he lays great stress on the links which economics has with the production of goods as distinct from their distribution.

Karl Marx (1818-1883) together with his bosom companion and loyal fellow-worker *Friedrich Engels* are the only men to be mentioned here who are not British economists, and the contribution of Marx to economic thought has been so differently interpreted by various critics that it is almost impossible to do it justice. One can only briefly state that, while some of his views on the future of capitalism seem odd to many critics, he certainly exposed the flaws of the contemporary scene in a free enterprise economy. His work, as seen in *The communist manifesto*, 1848, and *Das kapital*, four volumes 1867-1910, seems to reveal him as destructive rather than constructive with regard to the provision of tenable economic theories.

Alfred Marshall (1842-1924) is very different again. He produced many books on economic science, but by the time his magnum opus, similar in scope to those of Ricardo or Mill, appeared the term 'political economy' was beginning to lose favour; this work of 1890 is therefore called *Principles of economics*. Marshall tended to be very conservative in his views and is probably best thought of as the last of the classical economists and as one who took as his primary task the problem of gathering together and clearly expounding the writings of his predecessors in the history of economic thought. He does, nevertheless, introduce new expressions into the terminology of economics; the phrase 'elasticity of demand'—used to explain how the change in the price of a product may not lead to an exactly proportionate change in demand for it—is one of Marshall's.

When we turn to twentieth century economics, a number of names naturally compete for attention, but one is outstanding and it is fitting that we should consider a great economics personality from the present century in rather more detail than Marx or any of the classical economists. *John Maynard Keynes* (1883-1946) was the friend and pupil of Marshall, and his father—John Neville Keynes—was an economist of no little importance. J M Keynes' outstanding works are the *Treatise on money,* two volumes 1930, and *The general theory of employment, interest and money,* 1936; the tremendous success of the latter has possibly meant that the earlier work has not received, from contemporary economists, the attention it deserves. Keynes (pronounced to rhyme with 'rains') found himself writing in an age of severe economic depression. He wrestles, therefore, with the problem of trade fluctuations and unemployment. The classical economists had, for the most part, thought of unemployment as a temporary phenomenon which would right itself in the long run, but Keynes, with his maxim that 'in the long run, we are all dead', was determined to provide a more speedily attainable solution. This he does by a discussion and clarification of a nation's aggregate expenditure, saving and investment, in his 1936 volume. His theory is not merely for depressed times; it is truly 'general', whereas classical economics always tends to assume that full employment exists.

Keynesian principles are concerned with the economic problems of a nation rather than those of an individual; they examine prices, wages, employment and investment in aggregate. This approach is sometimes spoken of as *macroeconomics,* in contrast to the *microeconomic* situation, which is concerned with the study of the individual consumer's wants and his place in the market system. The teaching of *Keynes' General theory* has been expounded in a number of more recent and simpler texts and is generally accepted as valid. Indeed, we still encounter appeals to Keynesian doctrines when the current economic situation becomes very difficult. (See, for example, *The Sunday telegraph* 18th September 1966 p 14.) More noteworthy perhaps is the influence of Keynes on government policy; his writings suggest active government measures, such as increasing the level of investment to cope with economic recessions and, since the second world war, economic planning of this kind has become the norm in many countries. It can confidently be said that no economist since Smith's time has been more influential than Lord Keynes. His obituary in the *Economic journal* emphasised this arguing that, with his death, Britain lost ' the chief architect of economic policy . . . the brain which, more than any other, was shaping her economic future '.

There are, naturally, many other great economists of the present and previous centuries, and to do full justice to them and to the management pioneers would demand a great deal of space. The reader who so wishes can discover more about the men considered, and about others such as *Say, Walras, Pareto, Edgeworth, Schumpeter, George,* and *Jevons,* or *Pigou* (as a leading ' welfare ' economist), in encyclopedias and biographical works of reference. One could also include among any select band of economic stalwarts the nineteenth century genius, *Robert Owen;* or, from a later age, the cynical American *Thorstein Veblen,* who argued that much of what we purchase is simply bought to impress others and coined the phrase ' conspicuous consumption ' to describe this process. There are many prominent names among modern economists, and judgment for posterity in this respect may still be premature, but the name of the American economist *J K Galbraith* is certainly of great significance. In chapter ten, however, we shall reconsider the important economists, whose lives have been discussed in such a fragmentary fashion here, and indicate important sources of biographical or bibliographical information relating to them.

If this chapter has stimulated the wish of student librarians to pursue readings in order to enlarge their knowledge of the subject background, it will be profitable to suggest some appropriate works for possible further study. From a multitude of introductory texts of great merit on economics, the present writer would recommend J L Hanson's *Economics for students,* fifth edition 1963, or *The approach to economics,* by H Croome, eighth edition 1965, while a good picture of the pattern of economic life in Britain can be found in C D Harbury's *Descriptive economics,* third edition 1966. On commercial themes, an excellent text by Hanson has been cited earlier in the chapter, and H R Light's *The nature of management,* second edition 1960, gives a sound basic account of management techniques and problems. A useful sketch, in tabular form, of economic development since the industrial revolution is given at the end of the *Economic history of Britain,* by H Croome and R J Hammond, second edition 1953, but far more could be learned by examination of a work such as Pauline Gregg *Social and economic history of Britain (1760-1963),* fourth edition 1964, or at least by dipping into the relevant sections of the Pelican four-volume edition of G M Trevelyan's *Illustrated English social history.* On economic doctrines, a most readable volume is *The great economists,*

1955, by R L Heilbroner and P Streeten, while *The readers guide to the social sciences*, by B Hoselitz, 1959, has a useful chapter, with a strong bibliographical emphasis, on the nature of economics and the development of economic thought.

The task of the student librarian is not, of course, to become proficient in the field of economics and commerce, or in the historical aspects of these topics, but to know the chief sources of information well enough to use them intelligently and to appreciate the major objects of librarianship in commerce and the social sciences; the rest of this book is concerned with the various kinds of reference material needed and with library problems. There is, without doubt, a case for maintaining that the librarian or information worker ought to have at least sufficient subject knowledge to use the sources intelligently so as to help the reader extract the detail that he needs; yet it must be admitted too that many subject specialists, in this and other disciplines, have an ignorance of the potential of reference books, journals, and other material and methods for the dissemination of information. The answer here must surely lie in greater co-operation and understanding developing between librarians and the specialists they serve.

Our specialist readers may differ greatly in that, while an industrial library may be providing a commercial information service for management or for market research workers, a university library will be serving the research workers in various advanced branches of economics and its undergraduates. The public library will possibly serve a whole host of varied commercial and economic interests, ranging from economists, statisticians, exporters and students of economics, to professions such as banking, accountancy, advertising and law. The subject field is thus very wide and is constantly affected by modern activities—changes in export regulations, the emergence of new management techniques or, on the theoretical aspect of economic studies, the application of mathematics to the formulation of economic principles as manifested in the developing science of econometrics. That the area of knowledge is a dynamic one and is relatively broad as well as being specialised should not deter the librarian; he is all the more likely to find the work absorbing, if he is prepared to capture the atmosphere of the subject and labour to obtain a sound first-hand acquaintance with the appropriate types of reference material and other important information sources.

These sources and the problems associated with their efficient exploitation are the theme of later chapters, and some readings on economics bibliography and librarianship are given at the end of various chapters to which they relate. Several of them virtually apply to many or all chapters in the book, and these readings of a pervasive nature are stated below, in the hope that the reader will be assisted by having a note of them at the outset of his studies.

SUGGESTED READINGS

1 Bakewell, K G B: *How to find out: management and productivity*, Pergamon, 1966, 354 pp. (A thorough and modern outline of management bibliography and documentation and of the work of major corporate bodies in that sphere.)

2 Davinson, D E: *Commercial information: a source handbook*, Pergamon, 1965, 164 pp. (Already becoming a little dated in some respects, but a useful general picture of commercial information work and its tools. Like Bakewell's volume, it is not chiefly directed towards librarians, yet it will be found especially useful reading with regard to its chapter on exporting, and because of the information given on commercial societies and institutions.)

3 Lewis, P R: *The literature of the social sciences: an introductory survey and guide*, Library Association, 1960, 222 pp. (Chapters 1-4 and chapter 6 are especially relevant. An excellent birds eye view; the annotations of bibliographical items are understandably brief on account of the very wide range of material surveyed.)

4 Mallaber, K A (editor): *Conference on librarian-statistician relations in the field of economic statistics*, Library Association, 1966, 138 pp. (Contains the papers presented at the 1965 conference and the subsequent discussion. Some of these papers are cited individually at the end of relevant chapters in the present work.)

The books by Lewis, Davinson and Bakewell are described in a later chapter on guides to economics literature; they can be read with profit after many of the chapters in this volume, especially when other readings are not provided. To support them we might use:

5 White, C M and others: *Sources of information in the social sciences*, Bedminster Press, 1964, 498 pp. (An excellent guide to United States bibliographies and reference material.)

or the now very dated

6 Lamb, J P: *Commercial and technical libraries*, Allen & Unwin, 1955, 315 pp.

CHAPTER TWO

ENCYCLOPEDIAS AND DICTIONARIES

IT IS FITTING to begin an examination of the bibliographical apparatus of economics with the consideration of dictionaries and encyclopedias, for these are heavily used quick-reference works in many libraries, and the more detailed encyclopedias are often the starting point in the search for information which is necessary to satisfy some of the more difficult enquiries. In our specialised field of activity it will be necessary to use encyclopedias covering economics or management, and commercial libraries will also frequently need dictionaries which explain terms and abbreviations used in commerce and trade. Many of the latter could well be bilingual and are heavily employed to assist businessmen who are engaged in the export trade. In this chapter, the use of encyclopedias in libraries which specialise or have strong interests in the social sciences will first of all be considered; a brief survey will then be made of some works of this nature which cover management topics and of the dictionaries which are utilised in public or special commercial libraries.

ECONOMICS DICTIONARIES AND ENCYCLOPEDIAS
The value of an encyclopedia or an encyclopedic dictionary lies most often in the range of information which it contains on a vast number of topics, rather than in the depth of knowledge it affords on any one subject, or aspect of a subject. Such works are, therefore, often employed merely to explain and define a theme, or to provide a limited amount of information upon it. Yet, when a more complex enquiry is received, the librarian may often refer the reader to an encyclopedia article, confident that the enquirer can extract some relevant data from this while a search is made for more detailed or specialised sources of information. Some of these sources may well be indicated by the bibliographical references which often follow the articles in the encyclopedia itself. Perhaps equally important in a specialised subject field is the fact that the encyclopedia article can clarify the nature of the enquiry in the reader's own mind, or help the

librarian to comprehend what is really required; this in itself serves to point the way to other appropriate items in the library's stock.

The librarian needs both encyclopedias which cover all knowledge and those which are limited to a special field and, as the late A D Roberts once pointed out, the most detailed encyclopedia account of a specialised topic is not always found in the work which is restricted to the special field concerned. Many students of librarianship, while they appreciate that encyclopedias can be general or special, often fail to realise that these are essentially relative terms. An encyclopedia of economics is obviously specialised in relation to the *Americana* or *Britannica,* but it is itself general when compared to, say, an encyclopedia confined to terms and personalities concerned with the labour movement. A social science dictionary or encyclopedia like-wise stands as an intermediary between completely general works and those serving as reference tools on economics, political science or law. Thus in considering the subject field of economics (and its close relatives—commerce and management), it should be appreciated that there are not two simple categories of encyclopedia, but many and sometimes rather subtle gradations, ranging from the work which covers the whole range of human knowledge down to the one that is restricted to a single specialised branch of economic activity. Some-times, too, it is difficult to be dogmatic in distinguishing between an encyclopedia and a dictionary, for there are certain publications which must be examined that carry the word ' dictionary ' in their title, but which are encyclopedic in character.

What are the qualities which a good encyclopedia for the econo-mist should possess? To some extent, of course, these will be the attributes that we would look for in a completely general encyclopedia. The work, unless it is clearly simply a dictionary, should certainly give long authoritative articles. These should, ideally, be signed, for the specialist user of the encyclopedia may know and respect the authority of certain great modern writers on economics, or he may be aware of the viewpoint from which a contributor is likely to regard his topic. Bibliographical references enhance the value of the encyclo-pedia, making it truly an introduction to more specialised reading and, especially in the realm of applied economics and commerce where change is often as rapid as in the natural sciences, it will be most advantageous if our work is up-to-date. It can certainly be a more useful tool also if, in addition to dealing with terms and phrases in the subject field, it gives information about important organisations in modern economics and great economists of the past and present. Another point of importance concerns the arrangement of the encyclopedia. If it is classified, it must be supported with a very full alphabetical index; if, as is more likely, it adopts an A-Z arrangement of articles, it must offer adequate cross-references between them, and will still need an index to show those related themes which have been widely scattered in the main body of the work. The arrangement of each individual article will also be of consequence; it may well be profitable for the larger encyclopedic works to begin each article with a definition or basic treatment of a theme and then to proceed to the more specialised ramifications of that theme.

Economics has forged strong links, not merely with commerce and managerial problems, but indeed with many of the other social sciences. The modern economist may therefore appreciate an encyclopedia that adequately covers marginal themes that may touch upon law, politics, or sociology, in addition to economics itself. Finally, in considering these criteria, we may note the importance of diagrams in encyclopedias; these can be particularly valuable for obvious reasons in foreign language encyclopedias, but they will always be useful in illustrating certain topics—particularly in the realm of economic theory. Likewise, the provision of statistical data lends solid factual support to the comments and assertions made in certain encyclopedia articles.

It would be injudicious to expect any single work completely to satisfy a critical test based on the full range of desiderata mentioned above. Nevertheless a consideration of these attributes should assist us in our efforts to describe and examine critically the major reference works of this type. The encyclopedias which cover the whole range of knowledge will not be described here; obviously the *Encyclopaedia Britannica, Chambers's encyclopaedia* and the *Encyclopaedia Americana,* among others, can be consulted with profit when we are searching for basic information on very broad economic themes. Very often, however, we must turn to more specialised works such as an encyclopedia which concentrates upon the social sciences. Outstanding among such works is Seligman, E R A and Johnson, A (editors): *Encyclopaedia of the social sciences,* fifteen volumes, 1930-1935.

This American encyclopedia, which was reprinted in 1957, is of very great importance in our studies. It has long signed articles, is generous in the provision of advice for further reading, and follows an alphabetical arrangement with appropriate cross-references. There is an international emphasis in the articles; the one on 'Poor laws', for instance, ranges over the situation in Britain, the USA, Italy, France, Germany and other countries. A full index in volume 15 brings together allied themes dispersed throughout the encyclopedia. This truly excellent work, despite its age, remains 'a repository of facts and principles'; it cannot, of course, be relied upon for up-to-date information, but on historical themes and on topics which do not date too quickly its detail makes it outstanding. It is extremely useful also for the way in which it encourages the inter-disciplinary approach to the social sciences. The economist will find that many important social science themes which are on the margin of his own specialist studies are fully dealt with and, with the boundaries between these disciplines becoming increasingly nebulous, this is an important factor to consider. It should be noted that a new edition of the encyclopedia is now being prepared.

A more modern work which covers the social sciences in one volume is Gould, J and Kolb, W L (editors): *A dictionary of the social sciences*. Published in 1964, this encyclopedic dictionary is also useful for its treatment of themes of marginal interest to economists, in addition to its discussion of major economic topics and terminology. It was produced by the Tavistock Press under the auspices of UNESCO and has signed articles which often indicate briefly further possible reading. This is a work which proves particularly helpful with regard to the elucidation of terms used with varied meanings by different social scientists. A most interesting feature is the method of division within each article. Firstly, in section A, there is given a definition or concise account of the topic under consideration. Section B within each article offers further discussion or provides historical detail on the theme. Some important articles have further sections.

The work, naturally, lacks the detail of *Seligman*, but it is often profitably consulted for an authoritative account of a recent subject in the economics field, to clarify the precise way in which a term is used, or to seek information which is on the boundary of the economist's territory.

But economists and the librarians who serve them must naturally be also interested in encyclopedias devoted to economic science. Of these the best known in the English language and, in many ways, still the most important is Palgrave, R H I (editor): *Dictionary of political economy*. This British work first appeared in 1894; the latest edition, edited by H Higgs was published over the years 1923-1926 in three volumes. It is truly encyclopedic, with long initialled scholarly articles. Alphabetically arranged, it is extremely helpful with regard to older economic themes, although we would of course turn to it in vain for articles on, say, 'Keynesian economics', or economic planning'. Its bibliographical references too, although good, are very much dated. The introduction to a large extent recognises these limitations, stating that 'a compendium of this character should aim at permanent service. It cannot with advantage discharge the function of supplying the latest statistics'. Yet for historical matters, for articles on the older great economists, or for economic 'schools' of thought, the librarian may find that there is no encyclopedic work to equal *Palgrave;* it is also valuable in that it contains excellent long accounts of some themes that are too specific to find their way into *Seligman.* Some of the first class articles on economic history or classical economic theory prove very helpful to the modern student and the biographical sketches include accounts of people, such as Charles Kingsley, whose links with economics could appear to be rather tenuous.

For more up-to-date information on economics, or on commercial themes, we must necessarily use *Gould and Kolb,* or turn to modern dictionaries of economics, most of which are one volume works. American reference books of this character include Horton, B J and others (editors): *Dictionary of modern economics,* 1948; Sloan, H S and Zurcher, A J: *Dictionary of economics,* fourth edition, 1964, *McGraw-Hill dictionary of modern economics,* edited by D Greenwald and others, 1965. Nemmers, E E: *Dictionary of economics and business,* 1966.

Of these, *Sloan and Zurcher* offers rather longer definitions than those to be found in *Horton,* although the latter includes some good biographical sketches. Nemmers provides about 4,000 entries, while the *McGraw-Hill* volume is almost encyclopedic when we consider the length of some of its definitions; the second part of this volume is devoted to a useful description of economic organisations. The emphasis on the United States economic scene in all these dictionaries, and the predominance of American material in their bibliographies is apparent, but the date of the McGraw-Hill work and its liberal use of diagrams and statistical tables make it a worthwhile source of reference in many British libraries.

Worthy of mention also is the French encyclopedic dictionary, Romeuf, J and others (editors): *Dictionnaire des sciences économiques,* two volumes, 1956-1958. The problem of language leads some British librarians to shun works of this kind, but some of the longer definitions and accounts (such as the ones on monopoly or social security), or the biographical sketches may be of service despite this obvious difficulty. A list of contributors is given in each volume and there are a few biographical references. Diagrams are frequently provided to illustrate articles and there are some first rate sketches of the life and work of great European economists.

It does not seem very long since the writer was bewailing, in his lectures, the lack of a modern British dictionary devoted to economic terms yet, within the space of some twelve months, four such works appeared. They are Gilpin, A: *A dictionary of economic terms,* 1966; Hanson, J L: *A dictionary of economics and commerce,* 1965; Seldon, A and Pennance, F G: *Everyman's dictionary of economics,* 1965; Taylor, P A S: *A new dictionary of economics,* 1966.

These are all much slighter works than *Palgrave* or even the *Dictionnaire des sciences économiques,* but they can be very useful as a source of reference when a brief definition, or a short account of a new topic or new British economic organisation, is sought. It would be invidious to single out any one of these single volume works as an obvious best: the student of economics bibliography should examine them critically for himself. In contrasting them, he will find, for instance, that *Hanson* offers only concise definitions with no references to further reading. It is truly a dictionary rather than an encyclopedia, but it may prove useful on account of the clarity of the definitions; its frequent use of diagrams to explain terms such as 'indifference curves'; its description, albeit brief, of organisations; and, above all perhaps, because it gives due emphasis to commercial as well as to economic terms. *Taylor's* dictionary is virtually a replacement for the once useful *Dictionary of economic terms* by J R Winton. It has no diagrams to support the concise definitions which it offers. However, it gives good accounts of recently formed national and international organisations as well as definitions of terms, and frequently supports its statements by means of useful references to government white papers issued during the last few years. *Gilpin's* work offers definitions of varying length and some diagrams, while the *Everyman* dictionary gives fewer definitions and articles than the others, but it is strong on economic theory and economic history (although it omits some important themes relating to social history) and some of its articles are quite long. Its lack of diagrams may be considered a drawback but, of the four, this is the reference work which is nearest, in character and in the treatment of our subject, to the approach we would expect from a larger, encyclopedic, reference tool. All four dictionaries follow an alphabetical sequence of articles, but the compilers of the *Everyman* dictionary have provided a novel feature, which they describe as a series of ' related subject indexes '. These gather and list in thirteen subject categories, at the beginning of the dictionary, related articles which are distributed in its A-Z sequence and give, for each category, a helpful guide to further reading on the themes within it.

One volume dictionaries such as the above are naturally chiefly of use for definitions or concise explanations of terms or abbreviations employed by economists. Sometimes, however, we need to consult more specialised works than any we have considered so far, for there are some encyclopedias and dictionaries which are confined to one important branch of economics and which seek to serve as a major source of reference with regard to concepts, abbreviations or organisations within this comparatively narrow field. An excellent example of such a work is *Thomson's dictionary of banking*, eleventh edition edited by F R Perry and F R Ryder, 1965.

This first appeared in 1912 and is yet another example of a one-volume reference work of this kind; it is alphabetically arranged with a liberal use of cross-references. Its definitions vary in length and are on a wide range of commercial and economic themes, but the longest ones are naturally on topics of major concern to the banker. Appendices deal with banking matters relating specifically to Scotland and Ireland.

So far our description of dictionaries and encyclopedias has focussed attention on those which deal with economics, or with a related field of greater or smaller extension. Many librarians, particularly in special libraries or in the commercial department of a large public library, may argue that, while these are very useful, it is frequently necessary to consult dictionaries which give more attention to management problems and commercial terms than the titles discussed above. This may well be true, but before describing some works with a stronger commercial emphasis, it is profitable briefly to summarise what has been said about the value of these economics encyclopedias and dictionaries.

For brief or introductory information on some item of current, or recent, importance we must turn to a work such as *Gould and Kolb*, *Taylor*, the *Everyman's* dictionary, or that of *McGraw-Hill*. Yet it should certainly be appreciated that the older and larger works can still be of tremendous value for the detail which they contain relating to economic history, the history of economic thought, or the older branches of economic theory. If, for instance, we want a long article on ' monopoly ' and are not unduly concerned with its recent developments, we shall be better served by *Seligman* or *Palgrave* than by most of the more modern tools, although *Gould and Kolb* is also strong on this subject. Likewise, if we consider a more specific older theme such as ' the origins of the Austrian school of economists ', it will be discovered that *Palgrave* is by far the best of the reference books we have considered here. But for short articles on, say, ' National Economic Development Council ' or an article or definition concerning ' econometrics ', we must turn to more modern sources of reference.

COMMERCIAL AND MANAGEMENT DICTIONARIES

It was noted that two of the small modern dictionaries, those of *Nemmers* and *Hanson*, deal with commercial as well as economic terms. Often, however, librarians in this field must employ a dictionary which deals exclusively with definitions of commercial phrases and expressions. Indeed, in a busy commercial information library, a dictionary or encyclopedia of commercial and management terms is more heavily used than one confined to economics. The value of these reference books of a commercial character has been perceived for many years; one may cite J R McCulloch's *Dictionary of commerce and commercial navigation*, 1882, as possibly the best example of an older work of this kind. Two British examples of much more modern guides to the meaning of business terms and phrases are Pullan, A G P and Alcock, D W: *Commercial dictionary*, 1953; *Pitman businessman's guide*, thirteenth edition, 1957; and modern examples from the United States include *Prentice-Hall encyclopaedic dictionary of business and finance*, 1960; and Clark, D T and Gottfried, B A: *Dictionary of business and finance*, 1957.

It should be observed that, in the above examples, the British works tend to offer only short explanatory definitions of terms, while their American counterparts provide some descriptive articles also. The *Pullan and Alcock* volume is a good example of a useful one volume work of the purely dictionary type and is a development of an earlier Australian publication; now, more than the other three examples cited here, it is in need of some revision. The *businessman's guide,* it may be noted, gives in addition to definitions, the equivalent phrases in French, German, Spanish and Italian for many of the terms indexed.

At times too, in the commercial information library, the reader may need an encyclopedia or encyclopedic dictionary of management topics. An excellent example of such a reference work is Heyel, C (editor): *Encyclopaedia of management,* 1963. This one-volume American publication gives some three hundred long definitions, with the occasional use of diagrams and several references to other information sources. There is a guide provided to ' core subject reading ', and this suggests the most helpful sequence in which entries from the encyclopedia may be read on some broad basic subject such as ' the management pioneers '. The work is very full for the themes covered; certainly much fuller than the commercial dictionaries previously referred to. If the reader examines articles in *Heyel,* such as the one on ' new product planning ', he may be able to assess the potential of this reference volume as the starting point for the answering of many queries demanding management information.

A smaller work of this type which gives concise definitions of management terms only is Benn, A E: *A management dictionary,* 1952. While *Heyel* concentrates on important themes, *Benn* covers about four thousand terms with a strong emphasis on personnel management; the latter is, nevertheless, a much less useful work and is becoming dated.

With commercial and management topics, as in the field of economics, we sometimes come across much more specialised reference works which cover one specific branch of the subject area only. *Thomson's dictionary of banking* has already been mentioned; commercial works of this highly specialized kind include Kohler, E L: *Dictionary for accountants, third edition,* 1963; De Kerchove, R: *International maritime dictionary,* second edition, 1961. The first of these is American and *De Kerchove* is more likely to be encountered in British commercial libraries. It is an excellent example of a specialising dictionary explaining British nautical terms, giving their French and German equivalents, and providing diagrams liberally to make the verbal explanations more comprehensible.

Many works have already been mentioned in this initial bibliographical chapter, but it would be inappropriate to conclude without a brief description of the value of the bilingual or multilingual dictionary of economics or commerce. Many of the items described up to this point have been encyclopedic in character, although certain of them are essentially dictionaries which offer only brief definitions and explanations of terms. Economists and business executives will certainly need encyclopedias, yet they must consult the less ambitious dictionary too and, if the businessman is dealing with overseas companies, or the economist has been confronted with a document or statement in a foreign tongue, they may well need a reference tool that enables economic or commercial terms to be quickly translated without elaborating upon the history or full significance of these terms. An excellent polyglot dictionary for economists is Paenson, I: *A systematic glossary of selected economic and social terms*, 1963. This is a one volume work which gives economic terms in English and supplies, in parallel columns, their equivalents in Spanish, French, and Russian. It has been published in loose leaf form and can thus be kept up-to-date readily and the work is extremely well indexed. A feature is the inclusion of short accounts of the work of the great economists as well as definitions of phrases. The publisher of this dictionary (Pergamon Press) hopes to produce companion volumes covering the kindred fields of law, statistics, and the economic aspects of industry. Students of economics bibliography who are unable to see *Paenson* may use as an example instead Smith, R E F: *A Russian-English dictionary of social science terms*, 1962, which offers translations of words from a wide number of disciplines including sociology, politics, economics, accounting and public administration—or one of the two Elsevier works Ricci, J (compiler): *A banking dictionary*, 1966; Thole, B L L M (compiler): *Lexicon of stock market terms*, 1965. The first of these gives equivalents of English terms in French, German, Dutch, Italian and Spanish, while *Thole's* volume does likewise as far as the French, German and Dutch tongues are concerned.

Commercial bilingual dictionaries are equally or more important for the exporter or businessman who has received a message from associates overseas; such men may use libraries to have a reliable translation of certain business terms in the foreign language with which they are unfamiliar and works such as Motta, G: *English-*

Italian commercial dictionary, 1961; Servotte, J V: *French-English commercial and financial dictionary,* 1963; Von Eichborn, R: *German-English commercial dictionary,* two volumes, 1962; and Zavada, D: *Czech-English commercial dictionary,* 1958, must be used if such enquirers are to be assisted effectively.

Other works of reference are dealt with in chapter three, but it is clear that, within the sphere of encyclopedias and dictionaries alone, there are many volumes of interest to the economist and business man. These volumes range in coverage from very general works to items as specialised as *De Kerchove* or *Thomson.* They vary greatly in their intention and treatment; we thus have the contrast between the simple dictionary like *Hanson,* or the polyglot dictionary of *Paenson,* and the detailed account of various facets of economics activity found in *Seligman* or *Palgrave.* The emphasis placed on a particular encyclopedia or dictionary differs from one library to another, depending upon the functions and clientele of the institution concerned, but it is evident that all these works can be heavily used in the task of assisting readers. The translator, importer, or exporter consults bilingual dictionaries; the businessman or company director needs a commercial dictionary or management encyclopedia; the professional economist or student is aided by *Palgrave, Seligman,* or one of the smaller one-volume works. In the latter case, indeed, the encyclopedia article may prove self-sufficient, but it might only prove a starting point, its information or bibliographical references directing the enquirer to other information sources and preparing him for a thorough and systematic survey of an important theme in economics.

CHAPTER THREE

THE VALUE OF DIRECTORIES AND SIMILAR WORKS
OF REFERENCE

IT IS THE INTENTION here to consider the use of directories and other tools that are heavily employed in meeting the needs of readers demanding recent commercial data and information, along with certain reference books that we need in both social science and commercial libraries. In addition to the encyclopedias and dictionaries that have just been described, there are many other volumes that can be used to satisfy the enquiry of the quick-reference type, or sometimes to provide what might be described as ' core ' or basic information while the librarian turns to more detailed sources. Indeed in reviewing directories and like works here, we cover quite a wide subject range of publications; the student of librarianship should already be familiar with some basic reference material and it is necessary to concentrate in this chapter upon the function of yearbooks and directories within the specialised province of our studies, rather than listing items of a very general character.

There are, for Great Britain, a large number of town directories, most of them published by Kelly's Directories Ltd; a complete set of alphabetical telephone directories, plus classified telephone directories for the more industrialised regions; and a host of trade directories, many of them restricted to a particular industry or group of industries. In addition, it is possible for libraries to acquire a good selection of overseas trade and telephone directories and the well developed commercial library will certainly have done so. Directories are very important as a category of bibliographical material in our field, but they will naturally loom larger in the work of a commercial information library or department than they do in most social science libraries. Yet, while this is undoubtedly so, the possibilities of employing directories for retrieving information other than current commercial intelligence should not be overlooked. They are usually used, it is true, to provide us with the names of firms making a particular product, lists of exporters and importers, the users of a particular brand name, a company's address and, perhaps, its financial status and much more important commercial data; yet they can be, and sometimes are, employed in the study of the economic character of a particular region, and are thus of value to economists studying the structure and spread of British industry, or to market research workers attempting to gauge the potential demand in various areas for new products. The back numbers of town and trade directories can also be of value to research workers in economics who are investigating the industrial history of a town or the expansion or decline of a particular industry. Hence, when we consider the utility of directories, we should not neglect their potential as source material in fields like advertising, marketing and industrial history through regarding them solely as vehicles of current commercial information.

TOOLS FOR TRACING DIRECTORIES

The most useful bibliography of the directories of our own country is Henderson, G P and Anderson, I G: *Current British directories*, fifth edition, 1966. This is divided into four parts, dealing respectively with local directories; specialised directories; international directories; and directories of the British Commonwealth and South Africa. The present edition is dated for 1966-67 and it is hoped to revise it every two years. Henderson, it may be noted, is also producing a bibliography of overseas directories, the volumes of which are slowly appearing. It is the *Reference manual of directories: an annotated guide to directories of all countries*, Canada, Australasia and India being among the countries covered to date. We have several other good guides to directories also; as an example for the United States, there is the detailed and valuable Klein, B: *Guide to American directories*, sixth edition, 1965, a bibliography which serves to emphasise the very wide range of directories on different trades and professions which exist, and the variety of information that can be obtained from them.

Within this chapter, it is only possible to examine the scope of a few of the directories that are used in commercial and, to a much lesser extent, social science libraries. The titles described are merely representative of the type of work that will be needed; in fact there are few categories of material where the need to make the examination of bibliographical works a literal one is as acute as in the case of directories. One cannot quickly capture the full knowledge of them that is necessarily acquired by appropriate experience, but a number of visits to a well stocked commercial library will do much to promote an understanding of the importance and variety of the information yielded by directories, annuals and other quick-reference volumes.

DIRECTORIES OF IMPORTANCE IN COMMERCIAL INFORMATION WORK

Among British publications, the commercial librarian must certainly use alphabetical and classified telephone directories and directories of individual towns; the latter will include many large volumes in addition to smaller works, such as those issued by Kelly's in the ' buff book ' series. The better town directories usually provide us with four distinct sequences, these being: an alphabetical list of residents; a list of householders arranged under an alphabetical sequence of roads; an alphabetical list of firms and organisations; and a classified list of firms. The first of these sequences is necessarily very selective. Such directories are employed quite heavily but, for our purpose, it is more important to consider British directories which deal with British industry or with one particular segment of it. Most of these, like the town directories, are published at regular intervals, often annually.

Beginning with directories that cover the whole of Britain's manufacturing industries, we may note the well known and frequently used *Kelly's directory of manufacturers and merchants,* which is published annually in two volumes. Volume 1 deals with Great Britain and provides an alphabetical list of firms with their addresses and also a useful classified list—London firms appearing in distinct alphabetical and classified sections from those covering the rest of the country and separate sequences again being provided for firms from Ulster, Eire, the Isle of Man and the Channel Islands. Because it does attempt to cope with all industries and trades, it is heavily used in commercial libraries, but it naturally has great difficulty in providing us with a truly comprehensive list of firms and their addresses, and it needs to be supported by a number of more specialised directories. The selective nature of the directory is even more apparent in volume 2, which did not appear for many years and has only rather recently been revived. This second volume deals with overseas countries and, especially, with the listing of important manufacturing and exporting companies in Europe. It mentions over 100,000 manufacturers and exporters while volume one offers, for Britain, half as many again.

The above directory can now be supported by the information that is to be found in the *Kompass register of industry and commerce,* which is now published for a number of European countries. The register for the United Kingdom is in three volumes covering company information—directors, products of the firms, number of employees etc; products and services—where a useful distinction is made between manufacturers, wholesalers and distributors; and indexes to the arrangement. The latter are provided in volume 1. There is also a separate volume covering trade names used in the United Kingdom. This directory demands a little patience if its arrangement is to be mastered, but it will yield a great deal of information not easily obtained elsewhere. Its publisher is to be congratulated on the progress made in extending the scope of the directories and the number of countries covered. The volume of trade names referred to above was first published in association with Thomas Skinner Ltd, in 1966; it is indicative of the attempts made by Kompass Register Ltd to further improve their services.

Another useful directory for British industry, although more restricted in scope, is one which is not published as a regular annual. It is *Rylands directory* and it deals with the coal, iron, steel, tinplate, engineering and foundry industries. Its latest edition is that for 1966-1967, published in two volumes. For the subjects covered, it provides classified, alphabetical and regional lists of firms and it often indicates brief financial information about the firms listed. Like many other trade directories it has a section on brand names. It is clear that this directory gives some very useful company information; it is certainly an invaluable work of reference for ascertaining information relating to firms in the engineering and allied trades.

There are many other directories, many of them more specialised than *Rylands*, which can be called upon to supply the addresses of British firms, a list of manufacturers of a particular commodity, the user of a certain trade name and similar details. Some of them also give information concerning important firms overseas. Examples that may be cited are the *Shops and stores retail directory;* the *Directory of the brush and allied trades;* the *Electrical trades directory;* the *Food trades directory and food buyers yearbook;* the *Cabinet maker's directory; Laxton's building price book; Skinner's wool trade directory of the world; Skinner's cotton and man-made fibres directory of the world; Sell's British exporters register* and *Sell's directory of registered telegraphic addresses.* There are many more, and the student is advised to examine a good selection at this stage and revise them later in conjunction with the comments given on commercial library practice in chapter eleven. The directories that are restricted to a single industry, or group of industries, can profitably complement the information given in those which are more general in scope, especially if they devote a section to overseas firms; they may well be the best source for tracking down the name of a company making a specific kind of product or using a particular brand name. Many British industries are served by directories of this kind and, in addition, we need those which provide information of a rather different kind, such as the telegraphic addresses of firms.

For information on companies overseas, we cannot rely solely on sections devoted to foreign nations in the directories of the kind listed above. Businessmen engaged in importing and exporting will naturally require information that can only be found in directories that are published abroad and which specialise in the industry of the country of their origin. A well developed British commercial library will have a good number of these; typical examples include *Thomas' register of American manufacturers*, which is published annually in four volumes, the first three providing a classified list of products while the final volume gives an alphabetical list of firms and American trade names; the multi-volume *Bottin* directories which cover France and French territories; the *Deutsches bundes adressbuch; Fraser's Canadian trade directory; The West Indies and Caribbean yearbook* and there are many more. With experience and patience, the library staff will be able to extract a good deal of information for their enquirers from such works of reference. The arrangement of the information naturally differs from work to work, and the language difficulty can be a problem. Nevertheless, many readers will want facts relating to some problem that they have with regard to overseas trading; it is these directories which often hold the key to details such as a list of importers in Western Germany, the French exporters of various types of garment, Italian manufacturers of milling machinery and so forth. The value of these directories is well summed up in the introduction to one of them, the *American register of exporters and importers*, as being ' to provide information which will enable foreign firms to select individual sources (in this case in the USA) . . . where they may obtain particular materials, products or services '.

The size of the library and the stress placed on commercial intelligence must determine the number of directories that are housed; a good collection of trade directories of the above kind can be seen in any large public commercial library or in a specialising library like the Statistics and Market Intelligence Library of the Board of Trade. We must not neglect, however, directories which act as reference tools for a particular large branch of economic or commercial activity. If a reader wants basic facts about this subject, or activity, annuals and directories must often be called upon to support the data offered in special encyclopedias. It is a profitable exercise to examine works relating to one particular segment of economics and commerce, both for developing one's interest in that field and for learning to appreciate the functions of directories and similar reference books apart from the obvious ones of tracing the names and addresses of manufacturing and other firms. Two appropriate segments of the field are shipping and financial economics and some of their major reference works, as far as British libraries are concerned, are considered below.

REFERENCE WORKS ON SHIPPING

The shipping industry is served by a number of important annuals and directories which show the fleets of various shipowners, indicate the charges levied at individual ports, give details of the construction of individual vessels and yield much other useful information. Many commercial libraries hold newspapers which report on the current movements of British ships, but there is a considerable demand also for background information pertaining to the industry. We have already mentioned the *International maritime dictionary* of De Kerchove, which explains the meanings of nautical terms. More heavily used than this, however, is the large *Lloyd's register of shipping*, which is published annually in several volumes, and is of great use to those wanting details of merchant vessels. It provides an alphabetical list of ships together with the names of their owners, their builders and the date when they were made, in addition to indicating construction details such as tonnage and the dimensions of the vessel. Lists of shipowners and shipbuilders are also given and the register is kept up to date by means of cumulative monthly supplements.

Lloyds register can be supported by reference tools such as *The directory of shipowners, shipbuilders and marine engine builders*, which gives the fleet of each shipowner listed and many other details; *Ports of the world*, which shows the accommodation and facilities provided at each port; and the similar volume *Ports, dues and charges* .... Several directories are published in conjunction with periodicals and *Ports of the world* is a good example of one of these, since it is issued annually by *Shipping world* magazine. It is reinforced by a sister volume, *International shipping and shipbuilding directory*. If we use works such as the directories mentioned above wisely, we will be able to answer a great many queries relating to British and overseas ships—their owners, size, age, and the charges levied on them by various ports, plus other information such as lists of dry docks or trade associations relating to shipping and marine engineering.

REFERENCE WORKS ON MONETARY ECONOMICS AND COMPANY FINANCE

Very different is the subject field of financial economics, and by the use of this term we mean money, banking, and the details of British companies that are likely to be sought by the investor. Once again, it must be pointed out that some of the works described in the previous chapter are reference tools that would be relevant when searching for information on this theme. The economics dictionaries give a good deal of information on monetary matters and we also have *Thomson's dictionary of banking,* or possibly a tool like the German work *Handbuch der finanzwissenschaft* to consider at a more specialised level. Directories and similar reference works are mainly concerned with the financial details of companies. In this country, under the 1948 Companies Act and other legislation, public limited companies which have their shares quoted on the stock exchange, must make their financial details readily available. Many of them can be found in the *Stock Exchange official yearbook* which has been published annually for many years in two volumes. Volume 1 gives details of firms under classified headings—railways, banks etc—while the second volume covers firms that do not readily fall into any of the classified categories, and it also contains the alphabetical index to the two volumes. The type of information provided includes the names of the directors of each public company, the amount of its authorised capital and a summary of the information provided in its last annual report; there is also a note of each firm's subsidiary or associate companies and brief details of its capital history. The first volume gives a list of brokers who are members of the stock exchange.

The information provided by this yearbook can be brought up to date in many respects through consulting extracts from recent company reports and current share prices that are to be found in *The financial times, The economist, Investors chronicle* and like journals, but it is also supported by that given in other financial directories.

Prominent among these is Dun and Bradstreet: *Guide to key British enterprises*, third edition, 1965. This lists over 11,000 firms and is particularly valuable because it gives information on private limited companies as well as public ones.

The firm of Dun and Bradstreet arrange their directory in four sections. The first deals with firms in an A-Z order, and an attempt is made to indicate the approximate size of each firm by stating the number of employees; section two is a trade classification, while the third section deals with products and services and offers an index to the classification of industries. The final section concentrates on showing groups of companies and inter-company affiliations.

These links between companies are made even more evident in another prominent work of reference *Who owns whom*, tenth edition, 1967, which has some 62,000 entries and indicates parent and subsidiary companies in the United Kingdom, and United States firms with British subsidiaries or associates. This volume, which is published by Roskill Brothers and uses a letter classification to show the principal industrial or trade interest of companies, can reveal many interesting links between British firms as the results of the mergers which have become so prevalent in recent years. It is supported by a continental edition.

Such works are very extensively used by those who wish to find out background information about a public limited company or a prominent private one; those who need them will include investors, prospective employees of a particular firm who want some preliminary information about its work and background and many others. Additional information can be found in an annual like the *Directory of directors*, a more general directory like *Rylands*, or in the *Investment handbook* produced by Moodies Services Limited. G P Henderson has compiled a useful reference book entitled *European companies: a guide to sources of information* 1966 and the American Special Libraries Association work *Directory of business and financial services*, edited by Mary A McNierney, sixth edition 1963, may also be utilised. The first of these volumes, perhaps from our viewpoint the most important, lists alphabetically some 35,000 British company directors, giving their qualifications and the names of the companies (some of these being private companies) on the boards of which they serve; it is complementary to the *Stock Exchange official yearbook*, in that it is impossible to tell from the latter title of which companies a particular man is director. Tools like the *Anglo-American yearbook* may also be helpful for tracing links between British and American companies, while the *Bankers' almanac* is a mine of information on the addresses and capital of banks throughout the world.

A first hand examination of these and allied works of reference will reveal their potential for supplying information on financial economics and the status of British and overseas companies. Between them, the titles singled out here will give a vast range of facts about the large British public company and, although information about the large private company may prove more fugitive, it can sometimes be traced through them also. Like the reference works on shipping, these books yielding company and other financial information form an essential part of a commercial library's quick-reference stock and this is the reason for singling out some of their more prominent titles for discussion within this chapter.

OTHER REFERENCE BOOKS

Apart from directories in the strict sense of the term, there are several annuals and other works of a reference character which must, of necessity, be frequently consulted in a social science or commercial library. *Whitaker's almanack, Statesman's yearbook,* and the American works like the *World almanac* or the *Economic almanac* (the latter being published every two years by the National Industrial Conference Board), will be employed for basic information of a very varied nature; there are also many statistical annuals which we shall consider in a later chapter. Information on various countries must be extracted from tools like Europa services various loose-leaf volumes, while that published in the general newspapers can be retrieved through the use of *Keesings contemporary archives* and the American equivalent, *Facts on file.*

Returning to works that are restricted to our field of interest here, there are many other directories and yearbooks that merit examination. Many of these, like the *Advertiser's annual* or M K Adler's *Directory of British market research organizations and services,* 1965, deal with a specialised branch of economic or commercial activity. Another valuable type of directory is the one that gives addresses of organisations rather than firms. Probably the best British example is Millard, P: *Trade associations and professional bodies of the United Kingdom,* third edition, 1966. This consists of an alphabetical list of associations, a geographical key to them, and details of the UK offices of overseas chambers of commerce and international organisations. Mrs Millard's work is all the more valuable because many of the associations do not appear in the *Ministry of Labour's directory of employers' associations* ... , in similar directories or in appropriate specialising trade directories, and because, as the geographical section proves, many of them are not located in London.

Between them these directories and similar works will answer very many queries of a varied character but most of them are indispensable for commercial intelligence and, as suggested at the beginning of the chapter, they can be used for economic research purposes also. They are bound, therefore, to be utilised heavily as reference works in the social science library, although their cost and serial nature pose certain problems with regard to their acquisition. All reference material demands examination and scrutiny if its potential is to be grasped, but it is worth repeating that this is perhaps particularly true of the British specialising directories and those which deal with manufacturers, exporters and importers in overseas nations. The treatment of these works here may serve to act as a guide with the aid of which the librarianship student can approach a good representative collection of trade directories and study their features. The variety of readers who will need directory information of one kind or another—manufacturers, exporters, advertisers, investors, market research workers, those studying the economic character of a particular region and many others—should be constantly kept in mind. Many economists and businessmen are not yet fully utilising the valuable commercial information that can be speedily acquired from directories and, in this as in other matters, the librarian should do much to make his reader aware of the potential of the vast store of facts contained in directory resources.

SUGGESTED READINGS

1 Davinson, D E: *Commercial information: a source handbook,* 1965, *pp* 29-30. (Short account of value of directories within a business firm and of some guides to published directories.)

2 Manley, M: *Business information: how to find and use it,* 1955. (Chapter 5 of this United States literature guide deals with directories.)

3 Smyth, A L: ' Trades, professional and official directories as historical source material ' *Manchester review,* Autumn 1966, *pp* 39-58.

CHAPTER FOUR

GUIDES TO THE LITERATURE OF ECONOMICS AND BUSINESS ADMINISTRATION: BIBLIOGRAPHIES IN BOOKLET FORM

WE BEGIN, with this chapter, a consideration of the tools used to trace reference material of the kind discussed so far and other published information sources. Economics, commerce and management, together with their various specialised branches, are well documented and are served by a wide range of bibliographies, which differ greatly in detail and purpose, and a number of bibliographic guides. By a guide to the literature of our subject, we mean a work of reference which reveals to us, with examples, the appropriate sources of information within the field. These will include major bibliographies, encyclopedias, periodicals, government publications and other pertinent types of material, but the literature guide will usually also acquaint us with information sources other than published literature—that is the major organisations, including government departments, and libraries which work within the specialised area of activity. Thus this textbook may itself be regarded as a guide to economics literature; there are many other such guides, although they are virtually all broader or narrower in scope, dealing either with sociological studies as a whole or solely with commercial or management activities. This chapter sets out to describe some of the most important guides and also discusses some bibliographies of economics which appear in pamphlet form, leaving a consideration of the more substantial bibliographies used for retrospective searching for chapter five.

First of all, the guides to the literature should be considered and the librarian working with a specialised social science or commerce collection would be unwise to neglect general guides such as Roberts, A D: *Introduction to reference books;* Walford, A J: *Guide to reference material;* Winchell, C M: *Guide to reference books;* Collison, R L: *Bibliographies: subject and national;* Louise Malclès: *Les sources du travail bibliographique;* or *Index bibliographicus,* fourth edition, volume two (social sciences); for they often serve as very valuable indicators of publications of a reference character or can be used with profit in the role of bibliographies of bibliographies.

The American work *Winchell* and the new edition of *Walford* may be particularly helpful to the social science librarian in this respect.

SPECIALISED GUIDES AND LITERATURE REVIEWS

When we come to consider more specialised sources of guidance, it is natural that we should begin with a British work that has already been briefly cited in the preface and our introductory chapter. This is Lewis, P R: *The Literature of the social sciences: an introductory survey and guide,* 1960. Here we have an attempt to outline in a single volume the main sources for obtaining information on the literature of sociology, economics, statistics, politics, commerce, law and international affairs. While, as the compiler admits, the treatment is necessarily somewhat superficial in character, the work covers a very wide area with remarkable clarity and cohesion, and serves as a platform which can support more intensive and restricted biblio-graphical surveys. There is a helpful emphasis on the material that the British librarian is likely to encounter and, in each subject field, Lewis lists current and retrospective bibliographies, standard works of reference, textbooks, and periodicals, briefly discussing the value of the items enumerated; he also provides some consideration of the librarianship problems involved in the acquisition and organisation of material and indicates, for each special field, major libraries and societies. The book was compiled when its author was on the staff of the Board of Trade Library and the literature of economics is understandably well treated, with separate chapters dealing with econ-omic history. Naturally, however, in a work with this breadth of coverage, a discussion of any particular title must be limited. At times, too, the student who is new to economic and commercial literature may feel bewildered by the quantity of the material which Lewis mentions, although if this is a fault it is a very common one in guides to the literature of specialised fields. This guide is now becoming rather dated and a new edition of it would be most welcome; perhaps its most striking features of merit lie in the way in which the author emphasises the unity and interdependence of the social sciences and, as has already been stressed, in the manner in which his work reveals the great potential of bibliographical surveys of this nature.

The American equivalent of *Lewis* is the product of several hands and is a more substantial volume which the librarian in the United Kingdom must use as a major key to social science material from the other side of the Atlantic. It is not strictly a guide to information sources, but rather a detailed review of the literature. The work under consideration is White, Carl M and others: *Sources of information in the social sciences: a guide to the literature*, 1964. Here we have a book of nearly five hundred pages which begins by discussing the literature of the social sciences as a whole, and then considers individually seven important segments of the sociological field, one of these being economics and business administration. The work attempts essentially to guide professional librarians in using bibliographical resources; it is a ' chart ' to serve as a guide to ' seeing, within all the tiered rows of books, a highly organised system of communicating information '. The chapter on economic literature discusses the nature of various branches of economic activity, lists textbooks and then describes bibliographical material of various kinds and other guides to business and economics information. White and his collaborators draw upon the contributions of earlier and slighter American guides, notably the annotated *Sources of information in the social sciences, an annotated bibliography*, 1959, also by C M White and others. The 1964 volume is excellent in its detail, its extensive treatment of American texts and bibliographies and because, as Lewis points out in a review article which is mentioned at the end of this chapter, of the contributions made by subject experts.

There are some slight omissions and, for economists, the most unfortunate one is possibly the lack of a separate chapter on statistical sources. Yet it seems rather unfair to quibble about this point as statistical material of different kinds is discussed in the various chapters and this literature review is undoubtedly the most detailed work of its kind in the English language.

Occasionally, economists may use other guides such as Mukherjee, A K: *Annotated guide to reference material in the human sciences*, Asia Publishing House, 1962; or the *British library of political and economic science: guide to the collections*, 1948. The Indian work, however, will only rarely be of service in this country in libraries where Lewis and White are available, while the latter volume is now badly in need of revision. More serviceable possibly, despite its lack of bulk, is the Columbia University Library School's *Business and economics literature*, 1964, compiled by J *Bogardus;* or we might use another American tool, B Hoselitz: *Readers guide to the social sciences*, 1959. It is highly probable that we will have in the near future several more guides to the literature of pure and applied economics produced both in the USA and in Britain, and many of them may deal with a single important branch of economics rather than covering all social science literature. Indicative of such a trend, perhaps, is the soon to be published volume from Pergamon Press, written by a British public commercial librarian—Hopkins K: *How to find out: exporting and marketing.*

The above named text has strong links with commercial practice as well as with economics and, when we come to consider guides to the literature of business methods and commerce, there are several volumes which demand our attention. From this country, for instance, we have Davinson, D E: *Commercial information: a source handbook,* 1965, a volume which is valuable for its discussion of the way in which libraries can serve the businessman, and which is intended for management rather than for the library profession. Its main significance is seen in the way in which it stresses the value of and need for the active dissemination of business information and for the description of a wide range of organisations and services which entrepreneurs can profitably use.

Most guidebooks of this character, however, are American and the profusion of guides to the literature of administration and business management produced in that country is really simply a reflection of the extent to which business techniques and entrepreneurial activity have been developed there. American guides and bibliographies are, in a sense, of restricted value to the British businessman but there is a comparative dearth of United Kingdom equivalents and the intelligent librarian will use American guides both as a check on United States material and with a view to hunting for equivalent items and information sources in the British management literature. Some of the major and larger American guides to business and management literature include Coman, E T: *Sources of business information,* second edition, 1964; Manley, M: *Business information: how to find and use it,* 1955; Wasserman, P: *Information for administrators: a guide to publications and services for management in business and commerce,* 1956.

Coman, being the most recently revised of these works, is perhaps likely to be frequently consulted. Its first four chapters discuss the technique of tracing business information and describe important bibliographies. It then goes on to consider information sources in individual subject fields—management, finance, accountancy, statistics, marketing and foreign trade, for instance. Manley's guide is now somewhat limited, although we must commend the author for the way in which she explains to businessmen the tremendous scope and potential of commercial directories. Dr Wasserman's detailed work can be used not simply for the material which it lists on business and public administration, but for its wise discussion of the role of libraries, societies and chambers of commerce also. Its author, formerly on the staff of Cornell University and now dean of the Graduate Library School at the University of Maryland, is a renowned authority on management literature; he has also produced bibliographies on *Decision making* (1958) and the *Measurement and evaluation of organisational performance* (1959), and is now editor of a series of detailed and highly specialised information guides for management, a number of volumes already having appeared in this series.

If these are the three main guides to American management and commercial literature, it is still possible to obtain some aid in this direction from Harvard University Graduate School of Business Administration: *Business literature for students and businessmen*, 1955, although, it may be pointed out, the assistance given may need some adaptation if it is to be applied to the documents found in a British commercial or management library.

PAMPHLET BIBLIOGRAPHIES AND READING LISTS

It has been thought advisable to describe in this chapter, in addition to major guides to the literature, some of the bibliographies on economics which can be used for retrospective and, sometimes, for near-current searching, that have been published in pamphlet form. The reasons for this are twofold: firstly, the smaller bibliographies are sometimes constructed with a similar purpose to that of the guides, in that they attempt to indicate the chief information sources for their subject, as well as listing its major textbooks and journals; secondly, it is useful to distinguish these pamphlet bibliographies from the more substantial and exhaustive retrospective bibliographies of economics that are described in the next chapters.

There are a number of bibliographies in booklet form which deal with economics or one of its important branches. These endeavour, usually, to mention some of the more substantial bibliographical works in the field concerned, to list the major textbooks and journals for the subject area and, possibly, to indicate some organisations that can be

45

approached with subject queries pertaining to the topic dealt with in the bibliography. Despite their lack of bulk, these bibliographies can be useful in tracing details of textbooks on a particular theme for a reader or for discovering, in a stock-building programme, the principal books published in a specialised area of economic science.

Bibliographies or reading lists of this nature which deal with economics in its entirety include British Council: *Economics: a select booklist*, 1963; Hall, M and others: *A bibliography in economics for the Oxford honours school of philosophy, politics and economics*, second edition, 1959; Library Association: *Readers guide to economics*, 1957; National Book League: *Readers guide to economics*, compiled by R L Smyth, 1960. It is natural to compare these four British publications; each offers a classified list of textbooks and journals, but the British Council list is obviously more useful for comparatively recent works and the Library Association guide particularly is now in urgent need of revision. The National Book League publication is the only one which attempts to annotate the items selected and, although such annotation is brief, this is a most welcome feature in a pamphlet bibliography.

When we turn to comparatively slight bibliographies that are more specialised, we find that many publications compete for our attention. The student should attempt to see and examine one or two of the following: Bakewell, K G B: *Productivity in British industry*, 1963; Bromley, D W: *What to read on exporting*, second edition, 1965; Fanning, D: *Market research*, 1964; Millard, P: *Advertising*, 1962; Schurer, H: *British trade unionism*, 1955; Wild, J E: *The European Common Market*, third edition, 1962; Wimbledon public library reference department: *Which shall I buy? (some aids to wise spending)*, fourth edition, 1964. These are all in the Library Association special subject list series and they naturally vary in the number of works listed on their respective subjects. The common market bibliography, for example, lists some 750 items, but has very few annotations; brief, but useful, annotations appear in most of the other guides and some of them, either directly or indirectly, indicate to us the main organisations which offer help in that area of speciality. The Wimbledon guide, it should be noted, does not merely provide the consumer with an index to past copies of *Which* and the *Shopper's guide;* it also provides a key to articles on the selection of goods—including things as diverse as gravestones and book clubs—which have appeared elsewhere. If this proves, as it should, a useful tool in helping the reader to decide how to plan his personal spending, several of the other guides mentioned above will certainly prove almost invaluable as a key to the major texts on their subject and, in the case of *Wild's* book list, to important periodical and newspaper articles.

These Library Association lists are by no means the only works of this kind in our subject field; the commercial or economics librarian may well encounter others such as Rostas L: *Select bibliography on productivity* (Board of Trade), 1952; which is naturally now of limited value, as it covers books published during 1948-1952; Wild, J E: *Quality and reliability: a select bibliography,* 1966; or Randall, C R: *A select bibliography on computer applications in commerce and industry,* 1963. The latter pamphlet was produced by the Hertfordshire Technical Information Service (HERTIS), and is of use in libraries in assisting or preparing bibliographies for managers in addition to its relevance to applied economics and commerce.

The reference to managers leads the writer to mention, as the remaining examples of bibliographies in booklet form, some publications that are devoted to the organisation of literature on management techniques. We have already considered some *guides* to information sources on management literature and referred briefly to two specialised bibliographies by Dr Paul Wasserman; the Library Association list on advertising is, of course, dealing with a theme that is of great interest to management also. Yet there are many other bibliographies, which are heavily utilised by libraries, both for building up their stock of older management books and pamphlets and in assisting readers to trace appropriate literature. In this country, the organisation that has undoubtedly done most to produce guidance of this kind is the British Institute of Management. Some of its more specialised bibliographies will be mentioned in a later chapter, but it is most important to consider here the valuable British Institute of Management: *Basic library of management,* 1966. This is a broadly classified list of standard works, with author and subject indexes, which is regularly revised. The latest edition, supported by a 1967 supplement, gives nearly 250 important texts selected from the BIM library resources by its staff and the Institute's subject specialists. The authority of the list and the emphasis on British publications make this bibliography, despite the lack of annotations in this edition, an essential work for all management libraries.

Other important management booklists compiled in Britain include Business publications: *Hundred best books on business management,*

1962 and the National Book League's *Business management,* by G Whatmore, 1958. Or, again, we may find it helpful to consult the United States Information Service: *Books on labour and business management,* 1960; Institute of Personnel Management: *Personnel management: a bibliography,* 1962. These are not likely to be called upon as often as *A basic library of management* but, if used in conjunction with it and with other more detailed bibliographical tools for retrospective searching of management literature such as those described in the next chapter, they can be extremely useful.

It is inevitable that there should be a wealth of American publications of this sort, but we can be content here with noting three of these, one of them being highly specialised. First of all, the student should consider bibliographies dealing with various branches of management activity. The two publications in mind are Georgi, Charlotte (editor): *The Literature of executive management,* 1963; and Blum, A A: *An annotated bibliography of industrial relations,* 1960. The latter is a Cornell University publication which may be of help both to management and to certain workers in the sphere of applied economics, while Georgi's bibliography, which is well arranged and annotated and lists nearly 500 items in all, is published by the Special Libraries Association. The highly specialised bibliographical list referred to is the *Classified guide to the Frederick Winslow Taylor collection at the Stevens Institute of Technology, New Jersey,* compiled by E G Hayward, 1951. This is mentioned because the importance of the management pioneers needs to be stressed; writings by or about them are often demanded by students and the existence of bibliographies about them is often the best method of compiling a list of the most valuable literature.

One could enumerate further examples, both of guides to the literature and of bibliographies in pamphlet form, for economics, commerce, and management. Yet to do this would be tedious for the reader and probably of little value in that the items already discussed should illustrate quite adequately the potential of such material. The guides to the literature will reveal the different sources of information and their roles to us; they can also furnish us with many more examples of specialised bibliographies. Bibliographies and booklists, such as those mentioned here, endeavour to introduce the reader to the main textbooks and journals within their own restricted field and their value is increased by the provision of annotations. The greatest gap within these categories from the British librarian's viewpoint is the lack of a revised edition of *Lewis'* guide (for, despite the value of more specialised guides, an up-to-date survey of the social sciences as a whole would be invaluable) and the comparative absence of British guides to management information. The development of advanced management studies within this country is increasing the need for equivalents to the American works by *Coman* and *Wasserman* and it is likely that guides with an emphasis on United Kingdom literature and libraries will soon appear. Indeed, since the beginning of 1967, we have had one such guide; it is the excellent volume Bakewell, K G B: *How to find out: management and productivity,* 1966. This work is like many of the American equivalents in that it is directed chiefly at the subject specialist, yet it can be used with great profit by librarians also for a succinct but lucid description of bibliographical tools in the various major branches of applied economics and, more especially, management. Its chapters range, in Universal Decimal Classification order, over the literature of each segment of management activity, and it is perhaps especially valuable for the description given of British and overseas organisations. It should certainly be regularly consulted as an outstanding example of a management guide; the librarianship student must also be prepared to use it as an additional textbook for the information sources in this field.

Once the student has grasped the scope and usefulness of these guides and smaller bibliographies, he can be much more profitably employed in examining for himself the character and limitations of some of the more important items in these categories rather than attempting to learn, perhaps parrot fashion, yet more titles. He should strive to distinguish between reading lists and guides which attempt to provide a comprehensive coverage of the area with which they deal and those which are necessarily highly selective or more cursory in treatment. It has always been a strong contention of the present writer that reference work and advanced professional assistance to readers represents the very heart of librarianship, but that some potentially excellent librarians in this sphere have been deflected from their purpose by a mass of titles indicated in a textbook or, more likely, by the inevitable enumeration and brief description of reference books that is offered in the college classroom. Neither of these things can atone for a lack of regular first hand acquaintance with the works of reference themselves and if, for example, the student is concerned by the range of publications mentioned as being worthy of examination, he must be selective to a large extent. Economics and commerce and their ramifications are a large terrain that, despite the gaps which undoubtedly exist, is comparatively well documented and it has proved necessary in this book to mention many bibliographies and lists of various kinds, some being discussed along with guides to the literature in the present chapter while others are considered in those that follow.

SUGGESTED READING

1 Lewis, P R: ' Guide lines in the social sciences ', *Library Association record,* October 1964, *pp* 443-446.
2 A useful American survey of guides to the literature and other bibliographical material is that by E T Coman: ' Economics bibliography: current state and future trends ', *Library trends,* April 1967, *pp* 601-615.
3 One pamphlet guide well worthy of scrutiny, both as a recent example of such guides and for the information it contains is *Business bibliographies,* Manchester Public Libraries, 1967.

CHAPTER FIVE

RETROSPECTIVE BIBLIOGRAPHIES

EVERY SUBJECT FIELD has, or should have, detailed bibliographical surveys of its past literature. These systematic bibliographies are nearly always concerned with periodical articles, government publications and other items as well as with books and, in the broad field of economic science, major bibliographies of this kind will be heavily utilised in all libraries where older literature is still of some positive worth. In several aspects of commercial activity the value of retrospective searching may be but slight; however, in others it is certainly of some importance, while in economics and kindred social sciences substantial retrospective bibliographies are almost indispensable. If we are asked, for example, to compile a reading list on industrial relations, or the development of social security in twentieth century Britain, or of writings about the work and influence of a great economist, or to trace items on such themes, we will lean very heavily on bibliographies of this kind. They are useful to us as librarians in this respect, but they can often be profitably employed by the research worker directly, to see what has been written in a highly specialised area of study or to minimise the risk of expending his labour on a project which another has already more than adequately carried out.

BIBLIOGRAPHIES OF ECONOMICS

The bibliographies described here are necessarily far more thorough and comprehensive than the book lists considered in the previous chapter. They are often international in scope and may well cover thousands of items. In terming them retrospective, it is meant that, while they are used as the key to the economic literature of very recent or of earlier years, they are not sufficiently up-to-date to be employed for a survey of literature that is currently being published. It should be observed that not all the outstanding retrospective bibliographies of economics come within the scope of this chapter; those that are confined to pre-twentieth century books and documents are the subject of a separate chapter and, equally important, when we

51

later come to a discussion of current bibliographies we must remember that the back numbers of such publications can be among the most important tools used in the searching of the literature of former years. It may be noted too that several of the most specific retrospective bibliographies are not separately published but appear in textbooks or periodicals and the existence of these should never be neglected.

Sometimes the more valuable retrospective bibliographies are those which provide annotation or attempt to evaluate the worth of the items listed, although this is a hazardous task; it is interesting, from the point of view of economics bibliography, to read A D Roberts' quotation from the pen of John Maynard Keynes (A D Roberts : *Introduction to reference books, p* 66, third edition, 1956) on the value and difficulties of evaluation, or definitive selection of the items that are to appear in a large bibliography covering a fixed span of time. A certain amount of annotation from the pen of the bibliographers usually more than justifies its existence, yet very extensive bibliographies may be forced to disregard it.

In this chapter many bibliographies in foreign languages have been ignored and it has not been thought necessary to list completely general bibliographies for, although some of these would be of service when hunting for the economics literature of previous decades, it is assumed that most readers will have encountered them at an earlier stage of their studies. One of the most important of all the economist's bibliographical tools does, however, cover a wider field than economic matters. It is *The London bibliography of the social sciences.* This is a vast work, arranged alphabetically by subject, which is chiefly used as a key to the stock of the great British Library of Political and Economic Science. Its first five volumes deal with the holdings up to 1931 of several social science libraries, but volume six covers additions from 1931-1936 in the British Library of Political and Economic Science, the Goldsmiths' Library and the Edward Fry Library of International Law only. (The Fry Library is a specialised collection within the BLPES.) Volumes seven to eleven cover further additions to the British Library of Political and Economic Science down to 1955, and volumes twelve to fourteen, which are now almost completed, record accessions up to the end of 1962. Several volumes, for example volume eleven, give a list of the subject headings adopted as an aid to the user of this vast catalogue and many of the earlier volumes have detailed author indexes. In these earlier union catalogues, we also find the location of items being indicated by symbols and lists of the periodicals taken by the British Library of Political and Economic Science. The holdings of the latter are brought up-to-date by a card catalogue in the library, but other institutions which use the printed catalogue as a bibliography must supplement these volumes by means of the monthly list of accessions.

The value of this work for retrospective searching in economics and in many marginal or overlapping fields can hardly be overemphasised. It is the key to the stock of what is probably the largest library in the world devoted exclusively to the social sciences, and an institution which P R Lewis described as the nearest thing we in Britain have to ' a national reference library of the social sciences as a whole '. (See his article ' The present state of documentation services in the social sciences,' ASLIB *Proceedings*, February 1965.) Despite the fact that the bibliography does not provide annotations, its volumes offer us, in aggregate, an almost embarrassing display of riches. We can turn to them for details of a vast number of British and American books, for government publications of many countries, for bank reports and a good many other items. Although it is a subject catalogue it has entries under persons as subjects (Ricardo for instance) and works which themselves contain a bibliography are specially indicated. Some six or seven years ago, the then librarian, Geoffrey Woledge, suggested that ' it is all the more valuable because (social science) . . . literature is in general very inadequately signposted '. One can only say when its detail is reviewed and the increasing tendency to survey the social sciences as an essential unity is borne in mind that, despite the increase in the quantity of ' signposts ' in recent years, its utility to other libraries has in no way diminished.

Another bibliography which is found in many larger libraries and which, together with its companion volumes, stresses the interdependence of the social sciences that is remarked upon above is the *International bibliography of economics*, 1952-. This is published each year by Tavistock Publications under the auspices of Unesco and is prepared by the UNESCO International Committee for Social Sciences Documentation and the International Economic Association. The companion volumes mentioned are three bibliographies, also published annually, which cover politics, sociology, and social and cultural anthropology. These bibliographies, which overlap to a certain degree, are sometimes regarded as current, but this is a very dubious decision since there is a time lag of at least twelve to fourteen months after each year before the volume dealing with that year's publications on economics is issued. The arrangement is a classified one, with author and subject indexes in English and French. In coverage, the bibliography is truly international and it aims at listing the most important publications of countries, regardless of the form in which they have appeared. Many aspects of pure and applied economics, especially the latter, are dealt with; subject themes include prices, income distribution, international economics, finance and management. About eight thousand items appear in each annual issue of the economics bibliography and the list of periodicals consulted shows that articles are taken from some fifteen hundred journals; nevertheless, as already indicated, the bibliography is not restricted to books and articles. In searching the literature of the last decade or so, we may find it useful also for the details which it provides of items like overseas government publications on economics.

The UNESCO economics bibliography and its related annual volumes have, to a remarkable degree, succeeded in their aim of producing international bibliographies 'for basic (social science) disciplines where they were lacking'. They may well be used in conjunction with the less well known *Bibliography on income and wealth* 1937-, which is a voluntary co-operative effort undertaken by trained economists and is published by the International Association for Research in Income and Wealth. It is now published in Connecticut and the eight volumes that have appeared to date cover literature published during the period 1937-1960 and they are arranged in two parts. Part one deals with general material, a discussion of concepts and international wealth comparisons; the second section concerns estimates and analysis by regions. Both sections follow a broad classified arrangement and are supported by author and subject indexes. The literature recorded relates to some fifty countries.

This is obviously a rather more specialised bibliography than the *International bibliography of economics,* but while the latter covers only published material, the bibliography we are now considering includes some unpublished items as well. It is a good survey of literature relating to standards of living and per capita income in many lands and gives useful data on statistical themes and social accounting as well as economics. Relying heavily for its success on the enthusiasm of contributors, it cannot really be regarded as being as useful as the UNESCO initiated annual, but a striking and most commendable feature is seen in the quality of the annotations which are liberally provided.

We must now turn our attention to a bibliographical tool that is restricted to periodical literature and deals solely with economics, but which extends its coverage back to the late nineteenth century. This publication, which has only been available for a few years, is the valuable American Economic Association: *Index of economic journals*. It is at present in six volumes, each volume dealing with articles falling within the calendar years indexed. Volume one covers literature published from 1886-1924, while volumes two to six deal respectively with literature for the years 1925-1939; 1940-1949; 1950-1954; 1954-1959; and 1960-1963. Further volumes are to be issued. It is truly an index, for no abstracts are given and the arrangement follows a well thought out classification with a subject index. There is also a very full author sequence which arranges, in chronological sequence under each name, that person's periodical articles for the years concerned. It can thus be of tremendous value for tracing articles by a particular modern economist or on an especial economic theme or a great economist of the past.

Government periodicals and some highly specialised journals are excluded from this work, but it nevertheless succeeds in indexing some ninety journals and, in volume six, a further twenty six magazines have been added to this total. Although designed as an index of articles, the work does include also details of some comments and rejoinders from economic magazines, and some obituaries if these give useful critical or biographical information. Despite one or two rather surprising omissions with regard to the journals indexed, this is a remarkably good bibliographical survey of nearly eighty years' periodical literature and both librarians and modern students of economics (and the latter are invariably checking or searching for suitable articles in journals) should make extensive use of it in tracing important contributions to economics magazines published in the English language.

BIBLIOGRAPHIES ON ECONOMIC HISTORY

Applied economics is covered by the scope of the *Index of economic journals*, but one suspects that it may prove at least as valuable as a bibliography of economic theory and economic and social history. (In the latter context, it may be supported by collections of outstanding articles, such as E M Carus-Wilson: *Essays in economic history;* or the American *Index to economic history essays in festschriften, 1900-1950,* by H Schleiffer and R Crandall, 1953.) The historian will, however, find that there are other bibliographies—many of them treating economic history as but one of a series of historical themes—which he should employ. There are, for instance, good sections on economic history in several volumes of the Oxford University Press *Bibliography of British history*, the volumes concerned including Read, C (editor): *The Tudor period 1485-1603*, second edition, 1959; and Pargellis, S and Medley, D J (editors): *The eighteenth century, 1714-1789*, 1951. Also well worthy of consideration as a bibliography for the economic historian is the 1961 edition of *Guide to historical literature*. This American work (still sometimes called by the name of its original compiler, Dutcher) is classified with an index of authors and subjects and R L Collison, not without reason, has referred to it as ' a model bibliography '. It lists many books and information sources on the economic history and conditions of several nations and contains annotations.

A more specialised bibliography of a historical character, which is still of some occasional use despite its age, is Hall, H A: *A select bibliography of English medieval economic history*, 1914. This was published as a result of a co-operative effort on the part of students at the London School of Economics. It contains an introduction, a list of sources, and works on medieval economic history published up to 1910. Its value now really lies in the indication of sources and the manuscript material which it reveals to us.

MORE SPECIALISED BIBLIOGRAPHIES

Other bibliographies of economic history are included in the list of bibliographies that have appeared in the form of periodical articles which is given later in this chapter while, in chapter ten, we find an indication of some bibliographies of individuals who are important in the historical development of economic thought. However, it is necessary for us to return to bibliographies that cover economics as a whole, rather than concentrating on its historical aspects and we cannot afford to entirely neglect bibliographies which are published in countries other than Britain or the USA. Two outstanding examples of such are the Osaka University of Commerce: *Bibliography of economic science* which appeared in four volumes over the years 1934-39 and is particularly strong with regard to financial economics, and the Institute for World Economics: *Subject catalogue*. The latter publication and its associated volumes, recently made available (see the advertisement of the catalogues: *Library Association record*, July

1965, *p* ii), are obviously magnificent tools and of tremendous potential for retrospective scanning of the literature but, while the *Osaka* volumes will not be found in many libraries, the catalogues of the great resources of the Institute for World Economics in Germany will be even more rare on account of the very great expense involved in their acquisition.

Returning to separately published bibliographies emanating from English speaking countries, it is necessary to consider at least one or two examples of works which are restricted to a particular theme or an important branch of pure or applied economics. The reader is therefore encouraged to examine some of the following:

American Behavioral Scientist: *Guide to recent publications in the social and behavioral sciences,* 1965;

Denman, D R and others: *A bibliography of rural land economy, 1900-1957;*

Hazlewood, A: *The economics of underdeveloped areas,* second edition, 1959;

Masui, M: *Bibliography of finance,* 1935;

Revzan, D: *A comprehensive classified marketing bibliography,* three volumes, 1949-1951 (and subsequent supplements);

Wales, H G and Ferber, R: *A basic bibliography on marketing research,* 1963;

Wish, J R: *Economic development in Latin America,* 1965.

An apology may be in order for the herding together of such diverse bibliographies as the above; they are simply brought together as examples of substantial restrospective bibliographies of a more specialised character, from which the student should select and evaluate one or two titles. Selection, of course, is predetermined to a large extent by the availability of items. *Hazlewood's* bibliography follows a broad classified arrangement and is annotated. Some 600 items have been included, but the compiler has endeavoured to assist users in selecting items by marking some of the more important entries with an asterisk. A sequel, entitled *The economics of development: an annotated list of books and articles published 1958-1962,* appeared in 1964. It is interesting to contrast Hazlewood's bibliographies with that of UNESCO on *Assistance to underdeveloped countries,* 1957, if the latter is available. The ABS volume lists, with short comments, over 6,000 items, several of which relate to economics, while the two marketing bibliographies listed also call for comment and comparison. Revzan's work shows items published to the end of 1949 and includes books, research monographs, relevant government reports and articles from technical and trade journals; its supplements bring it up to the early 1960's. Both this and the work by Wales and Ferber are American and the latter was compiled for the American Marketing Association. There are good annotations also in the *Latin America* bibliography which covers over four hundred documents and in the vast, if dated, *Masui* bibliography which describes, in the tongue of the original, documents in three languages.

In choosing one or two examples of specialised bibliographies to study, the reader may well encounter the *International economics selections bibliography* (formerly *Economics library selections*) and once the work of the Johns Hopkins University, Baltimore, but now issued from the university of Pittsburgh. Series one of this publication will be described with the current bibliographies in chapter six, but the second series consists of a number of volumes, each devoted to a particular topic, that can be extremely helpful in surveying and selecting items from the writings of the past. Series two contains basic bibliographies of such themes as *International economics; statistics and econometrics; business fluctuations; economic theory and the history of economic thought; and the economics of development and growth.* Rather different from these specialised lists on heterogeneous subjects within the broad scope of economics, but also a part of the second series, is the *Selected bibliography of economic reference works and professional journals,* which lists and annotates entries for bibliographies and reference material of various kinds. This series two of *International economics selections bibliography* really belongs to the 1950s but, despite the emphasis on American literature, and this is quite understandable, its range of bibliographies is very helpful, for much of the material listed consists of standard texts and basic reference sources. Pittsburgh have produced a cumulative index to the items included 1954-62 when the publication was under the Hopkins aegis.

BIBLIOGRAPHIES IN TEXTBOOKS AND PERIODICAL ARTICLES

Before leaving economics bibliographies to take a brief look at some retrospective bibliographies pertaining to the literature of management and business administration, it behoves us to recall the possibility of finding some shorter, and yet extremely valuable, bibliographies which are appended to monographs or which appear as articles or features in some of the scholarly journals on economics.

Many textbooks on economic theory in particular are well supported by this kind of bibliography, and among journals, the *Economic history review*, to take what is perhaps the most prominent British example, has published over the years many contributions which are solely or mainly bibliographical in character. Many of these bibliographies and bibliographical articles are comparatively slight and are akin, perhaps, to the reading lists or pamphlet bibliographies described in our previous chapter, rather than to the more commodious and exhaustive publications we have just considered. Nevertheless some of the bibliographies that are not separately published can prove helpful in searching for particular books or articles on a specialised theme or in drawing up a short reading list on that theme. Some examples are called for, therefore, and those selected are Ashton, T S: 'Industrial revolution', *Economic history review*, 5, 1934-1935, *pp* 225-230; Bowyer, T H: 'Basic books on economic theory and basic books on descriptive and applied economics', *British book news*, March-April 1960, *pp* 225-230; 'Critical guide for a general bibliography of the history of economics, 1768-1963', *Journal of world history*, 1964, part one, *pp* 182-209; 'Tools of modern management: a selection of books on operational research, decision theory and computer techniques . . .', *Manchester review*, Summer-Autumn 1964, *pp* 155-162.

The above, it must be realised, represent only a few of the worthwhile bibliographical articles in economic and kindred journals which may be utilised, while to attempt to give a few representative examples of textbooks with good bibliographies seems invidious indeed, although among well established works the *Economic analysis of the American* by K E Boulding, third edition 1955, or M W Thomas (editor): *A survey of English economic history*, 1957, may be quoted in this respect.

MANAGEMENT BIBLIOGRAPHIES

In the management realm we also have some retrospective bibliographies of value; these must be considered, in addition to the literature guides and reading lists indicated in the last chapter, when a search for pertinent writings on a branch of business activity is carried out. Again it is almost inevitable to record that the major examples are published in the United States. The guides mentioned will provide us with the names of many bibliographies and sources of bibliographical data but, among the chief retrospective bibliographies on business published in recent years and, indeed, too recent to be mentioned in those guides is Stewart, C F and Simmons, G B: *A bibliography of international business,* 1964. Here, the publications of various countries on a wide range of economic and business operations are listed, many of the items included being periodical articles. The bibliography falls into four subject sections: comparative business systems; government and international operations; the firm in international operations; and individual nations. The object of this final section is to bring together entries from the first three parts under a particular country and some thirty five nations or groups of countries have been dealt with in this way in the geographical sector of the bibliography. The value of the work is considerable for a vast number of items have been included, but the lack of annotation is a drawback and a more serious one is the absence of an index of authors.

Stewart and Simmons' bibliography will nevertheless be heavily used in management libraries to support British reading lists and those on special subjects compiled by *Wasserman.* Occasionally, it will also be advantageous to use more specialised management bibliographies of a substantial character, good recent examples being Batchelor, J H: *Operations research: an annotated bibliography,* four volumes, 1959-1964; and Cutlip, S M: *Public relations bibliography,* second edition, 1965, which is also annotated. These bibliographies, emanating from the universities of St Louis and Wisconsin respectively, are extremely full; in fact they really strive to be comprehensive, at least with regard to American literature for their own field, although *Batchelor's* work selects the end of 1961 as its terminus for the inclusion of literature.

It is vital that the person who aspires to work in a library in this sphere should understand the ways in which these important and substantial bibliographies can be used. The specialist reader himself is often ignorant of at least some works of this kind, works that could save his energies by systematically setting out the major past writings on each branch of his studies enabling him to pick out the items that are of greatest value in his work or research programme. The onus of becoming acquainted personally with at least some of these major tools and of mastering their potential therefore rests on the shoulders of the librarian. The initial labour needed to accomplish this is well rewarded for, with use and experience, he will become skilled in knowing which of these tools to turn to when dealing with a particular enquiry for which some retrospective bibliographies are demanded and, as with all other kinds of reference sources, there is a great deal of satisfaction in having accumulated this knowledge and placing it at the reader's disposal.

The bibliographies described at the beginning of our chapter are especially valuable; in the social science library, we shall use tools such as the *London bibliography,* the *International bibliography of economics* and the *Index of economic journals* again and again to trace important books, pamphlets, articles, government reports, or other documents. All serious students of our subject must examine and be able to describe these and a selection of the other publications briefly discussed as well as appreciating, if a point made earlier can be reiterated, that the back numbers of current bibliographies—and these current awareness services are described in a later chapter— are often among the best tools for detailed retrospective literature searches.

CHAPTER SIX

BIBLIOGRAPHIES OF OLDER BOOKS AND DOCUMENTS : SOURCE
MATERIAL FOR THE ECONOMIC AND SOCIAL HISTORIAN

THE PREVIOUS CHAPTER has discussed some of the major bibliographies which the librarian uses to trace economic or commercial
literature that has, usually, been published in the comparatively recent
past. However, while much of this material will have appeared during the last ten or twenty years, many of these bibliographies also go
back to earlier decades in their coverage; we have seen, for example,
that the *Index of economic journals* reveals the content of economics
periodicals down to 1963 but that its earliest volume records articles
published in the period 1886-1924. In this present chapter, we shall
consider retrospective bibliographies which are concerned mainly
with the literature of the nineteenth or earlier centuries rather than
with that of recent times. Some of these works will be wider in their
connotation than the sphere of economics, others like G Ottley's
Bibliography of British railway history, 1965, from the economic
historian's viewpoint, deal with a comparatively restricted area in the
province of his studies, although they may encompass publications
from the twentieth century as well as from earlier years.

Such bibliographies are likely to be used but rarely in a busy
library where current economic affairs or commercial activity is the
main concern; they are, nevertheless, invaluable to the serious student
or research worker who is investigating closely certain aspects of
economic and social history or the history of economic thought. A
well equipped academic library ought certainly to provide a good
selection of the bibliographies of this kind and the large public library system or a special library which serves a research institution
is sure to possess many of them also. Furthermore some of the best
developed academic and special libraries in particular will house some
of the documents listed and described in the bibliographies—
documents which include early government publications, tracts,
pamphlets, extant letters and similar items in addition to books. It is
often only by gaining access to such material, that is the contemporary
accounts and opinions of the period he is studying, that the economic

or business historian is able to enter into the spirit of a former age and produce a book or thesis which is written with vigour and conviction.

Sometimes for this record of the economic material of bygone centuries, we turn to retrospective bibliographies of an entirely general character. To a certain extent, for instance, we could profitably consult *The English catalogue of books*, published annually 1801-   ; Pollard, A W and Redgrave, G R: *Short title catalogue of books (1475-1640)*, 1926; Wing, D; *Short title catalogue of books (1641-1700)*, 1945-1952; or works which have a similar deserved reputation and which deal, to a limited extent at least, with commercial and economic as well as with other themes. Also best regarded as a general source, as far as the literature of economics is concerned, but more specialised than the above is Morgan, W T and Morgan, C S: *Bibliography of British history (1700-1715)*, five volumes, 1934-1942; which is certainly a work of great scholarship, but which, again, contains comparatively few economics books and pamphlets in the items described and listed.

MORE SPECIALISED BIBLIOGRAPHIES OF OLDER MATERIALS

Very often, therefore, the librarian will prefer to consult, when available, sources which specialise in revealing the older extant documents in the broad field of economics. One such work, restricted as indicated in its title to the principles of economics, but very useful for late nineteenth and early twentieth century material is Batson, H E: *Select bibliography of modern economic theory*, 1930. This volume consists of two distinct sections. The first is a subject bibliography for the period 1870-1929 with items arranged in appropriate categories; the second is an author bibliography for the same period, which tries to be exhaustive as far as the writings of the selected authors are concerned. English, German and French authors are included. The work has been well indexed and includes many references to pertinent periodical articles.

The title of the above bibliography is obviously a misnomer nowadays, yet the period which Batson covers is modern when compared with that over which most of the bibliographies to be described in this chapter range. But, before considering bibliographies of old books, pamphlets and manuscripts relating to economics, it is worthwhile to note some guides which introduce the research worker in economic and commercial history to his primary sources. Among such

63

guides we have Williams, Judith B: *Guide to the printed materials for English social and economic history (1750-1850)*, two volumes, 1926; Davenport, Frances G: *A classified list of printed original materials for English manorial and agrarian history during the Middle Ages*, 1894; Reeves, D D: *Resources for the study of economic history: a guide to pre-twentieth century printed material in collections located in certain American and British libraries*, 1961; Clark, G N: *Guide to English commercial studies 1696-1782*, 1938. All of these except the last named are American bibliographical guides; *Reeves'* volume, in fact, emanates from the Baker library at Harvard university and is a key to the historical collections of several American and a few great British libraries. While all these volumes are potentially useful tools to the social historian, that of *Williams*, which like *Davenport's* guide has been reprinted in comparatively recent times, is by far the most valuable and detailed. It is, indeed, one of the most important bibliographical guides in all of our studies and must be examined carefully by the student. In her first volume, Dr Williams deals with general source material—encyclopedias, catalogues, biographies, bibliographies and so forth—while volume two deals with subject themes which include economic theory, economic conditions, industry, and social movements. Much rare source material is listed and, while the annotations provided are brief, they reveal the compiler's erudition and her ready appreciation of the value of this material in historical research concerning the industrial revolution.

When we come to consider bibliographies of economics for the nineteenth and earlier centuries, there are many valuable works of reference to review. We are fortunate, for instance, in having a reprint of the valuable nineteenth century bibliography: McCulloch, J R: *The literature of political economy: a classified catalogue . . . with historical, critical and biographical notes*, 1845. It may be noted that McCulloch was himself an economist of some standing; he corresponded with Ricardo and produced a biography of him. His bibliography consists of twenty chapters each dealing selectively with the literature of a distinct theme. Within each chapter, items chosen are listed in order of their date to illustrate historical development. Author and title indexes are given. An outstanding characteristic of this work, reproduced in 1938 by the London School of Economics in the same series as that in which Batson's volume appears, is the very long annotations which McCulloch often supplies. These may be invaluable to the research student; if, for instance, some of these early documents listed are unavailable, McCulloch's comments will serve as an abstract and convey their essential theme and emphasis.

For a much more comprehensive listing of economic documents from the beginning of the eighteenth century to mid-way through the nineteenth, we must turn to other bibliographical sources. The next three bibliographies to be described may be conveniently regarded as a trilogy since, although they differ in the periods covered, they all adopt a chronological arrangement, and list, under each year, the items published during that year. From the United States, we have the most valuable *Catalogue of the Kress library of business and economics*, four volumes. This is a record of the holdings of one of the specialised libraries serving Harvard university and its catalogues have appeared over the years 1940-1965. The first volume of the catalogue lists items published up to the year 1776 and there is a supplementary volume dealing with the same period. These cover, says Carl M White, ' several hundred tracts and pamphlets as well as books which appeared long before Adam Smith's *Wealth of nations* '. The next catalogue brings the listing of items down to the year 1817 (the date of Ricardo's principal work) and here the growth in the quantity of the literature has led to the omission of many government publications, the equivalent of which are found in the earlier volumes. The final volume, which appeared in 1965, lists items published after 1817, selecting as its terminal milestone J S Mill's *Principles of political economy*, 1848. The arrangement is primarily chronological; for each year the catalogue lists the publications of that year that are represented in the Kress collections and certain other Harvard libraries. Each annual sequence is sub-arranged alphabetically by author and there is an index of authors and titles in every volume. Some 7,000 books and documents are mentioned in each of the main volumes.

Many of the items shown in the Kress catalogues may not be available to the British economic historian, although our larger scholarly libraries will certainly house several of them. Yet, in any case, these catalogues may help the historian in that they reveal to him the range of publications and the kind of documents that appeared in each of these years—years that, with the acceleration of the industrial revolution and the continuous development of economic thought, are crucial ones in economic and social history.

There is also an important retrospective bibliography of a very similar type compiled by a British economist, which has been deservedly praised by librarians and which overlaps chronologically in its coverage with the first volume of the *Kress catalogue*. This is Higgs, H: *A bibliography of economics (1751-1775)*, 1935. Henry Higgs has already been mentioned in this book as the editor of the *Dictionary of political economy*. His bibliography was produced for those engaged in exhaustive research into the economic history of the period immediately preceding Adam Smith's great masterpiece and because 'much valuable material remains unused in great libraries . . . inaccessible unless the name of the author is known or the title of the anonymous work'. He believed that chronological grouping of the literature would save the time of the historian engaged in original work with the contemporaneous documents. Thus he brings together his references to the literature of each year, sub-arranging it according to the following classification: 1 general economics; 2 agriculture; 3 shipping and navigation; 4 manufactures; 5 commerce; 6 colonies; 7 finance; 8 transport; 9 social conditions; 10 topographical items of economic interest; 11 miscellaneous.

The bibliography is equipped with author and title indexes and lists 6,741 items. Unfortunately, locations are not given, although we are told that the Goldsmiths' library at London university has nearly 1750 of the documents listed, but, as in the case of the Kress catalogue, the research worker must benefit from having the nature of the literature of the period exposed to him in this way and Higgs' descriptive annotations of many items are very helpful.

This valuable work has been supported in recent years by the companion volume Hanson, L W: *Contemporary printed sources for British and Irish economic history (1701-1750)*, 1963. There is an interesting link between this bibliography and the two just described in that Higgs informs us that it was his intention to continue his work 'backward and forward'; his death prevented this, but Hanson, then a member of the British Museum staff and later a Keeper of the Printed Books at the Bodleian library, discovered from the introduction to one of the volumes of the *Kress library catalogue* that the galley proofs of Higgs' volume for the earlier period had been prepared. Hanson obtained these and pursued the exacting task of examining individual items and checking and amending details. His own bibliography, which includes nearly as many items as Higgs', endeavours to list every new English work on economic affairs published during the period covered, with the exception of newspapers. The arrangement again is founded upon chronological progression, although the broad classification of documents adopted within each year differs slightly from that used by Higgs. Only first editions are given full entries and collation details other than size are excluded from entries. A general index has been provided and also an index of titles. The annotations given are most helpful and, unlike Higgs' work, this bibliography indicates locations for the books, pamphlets, bills etc, listed under each year. Over sixty libraries have been cited, but only one location per item is given—this representing the library where Hanson had examined it.

The *Kress library catalogue* and the works of Hanson and Higgs are thus very similar in intent and arrangement and, between them, they provide us with a scholarly, reliable and almost invaluable record of economic and business writings published from 1701-1848. In the opinion of the present author, the late Laurence Hanson's work is among the very best examples of a bibliography restricted to any single subject field that has been produced by a British individual within the last decade. We have no other comprehensive record of the economic documents published during the first half of the eighteenth century; documents which provide the raw material for the reconstruction of the events and thought of that time.

It has already been noted that in many libraries concerned with the modern economic scene and present day business literature, such retrospective bibliographies will not be required very often. There are, however, other libraries where tools of the calibre of the three just described will be heavily utilised by the social and economic historian and by others involved in post-graduate research and study. Such libraries may also utilise older and highly specialised bibliographies, if available, such as Watt, R: *Bibliotheca economica*, two volumes, 1824; Wagner, H R: *Irish economics (1700-1783)*, 1907. Some of these may relate to a particular collection of the books or pamphlets of bygone centuries and a good example of a bibliography that is so restricted is Shaw, William A (editor): *Bibliography of the collection of books and tracts on commerce, currency and poor laws (1557-1763) formed by Joseph Massie.*

Shaw's catalogue of the collection of this eighteenth century economist appeared in 1937 and librarians and economic historians may well find it both interesting and useful, even though its editor confesses that the work of compiling it gave rise to several bibliographical problems. There are 353 undated tracts listed and the remainder follow in chronological order, an author index being supplied. Shaw also furnishes us with the title pages of Massie's own books and pamphlets and the details of his extant letters on commercial themes.

Finally, in surveying bibliographies of the contemporary record of economic events of former ages, we should not neglect those which appear in languages other than English; the language barrier will be an obstacle it is true, but we can nevertheless sometimes extract helpful items of information from works like Grandin, A: *Bibliographie générale des sciences juridiques, politiques, économiques et sociales de 1800 à 1925*, three volumes, 1926; and Maunier, R: *Manuel bibliographique des sciences sociales et économiques*, 1920. The first of these has supplements in various forms which bring its coverage up to the nineteen sixties but, it must be confessed, it is much stronger on French legal literature than it is on economics.

COLLECTIONS OF SOURCE MATERIAL

It is sometimes possible too, to examine actual collections of these older documents, as distinct from their bibliographies and bibliographical guides. Good examples include: Bland, A E and others: *English economic history: select documents*, 1914; Tawney, R H and Power, E: *Tudor economic documents*, three volumes, 1924; Salter, F R (editor): *Some early tracts on poor relief*, 1926; McCulloch, J R: *Early English tracts on commerce*, 1856 (reprinted 1954). The first of these is a collection of source documents for the economic historian down to the year 1846. The work by Professor Tawney and Miss Power, on the other hand, is obviously restricted to one chronological period, but gives examples of pertinent early documents relating to agriculture, industry, commerce and social conditions. McCulloch, whose important bibliography, *The literature of political economy*, has already been described, gives in his more specialised work cited above the text of eight tracts, all of which are from the seventeenth century except the last—*Considerations on the East India trade*, 1701. Some of these documents and tracts are extremely rare and those in McCulloch's volume are, as their editor claims, ' an epitome of the commercial knowledge of the seventeenth century both in its theory and practice '. (In the field of economic and social history, a comparatively recent volume, M W Flinn's *Readings in economic history* (1964), has attempted to popularise the study of such documents.)

THE VALUE OF CONSERVING BUSINESS DOCUMENTS

If the modern librarian can appreciate the value of older material on economics—the contemporary books, government publications, broadsides, tracts and the like of previous centuries—and of bibliographies and guides to information sources with regard to such material, then he must surely be led to realise also the acute need for the conservation of pamphlets, business letters and important administrative records of today, for these will become in turn the source materials for future generations of economic historians. The problem of selectively preserving such documents is, fortunately, now being examined in this country, by both appropriate bodies and interested archivists, librarians and businessmen. This problem can be a most rewarding study in its own right; it is discussed as the theme for the latter half of this chapter because the measures taken to preserve present day documents of an economic or business character are necessarily best studied, in a textbook of this kind, in conjunction with an examination of important extant economics documents from former centuries and their bibliographies.

In the United States, the study of economic and business history through the preservation of important older documents has thrived for many years, being fostered by the universities and organisations such as the Business Historical Society. There are a number of guides designed to assist the student in his perusal of such documents, such as the Harvard university-produced Larson, H M: *Guide to business history: materials for the study of American business history and suggestions for their use,* 1948; and, also from Harvard, the slighter and less ambitious Daniells, L M: *Studies in enterprise: a selected bibliography of American and Canadian company histories and biographies of businessmen,* 1957. Miss Daniells' bibliography covers almost entirely literature of comparatively recent times, but Larson's guide, a vast and excellent work with nearly five thousand entries and many annotations, deals with a wide range of basic source items and describes bibliographical material for the study of each industry as well as general background bibliographies. It covers much important nineteenth, as well as twentieth, century source material.

One British historian, A W Coats of Nottingham university, has drawn our attention (in ASLIB *Proceedings,* January 1961) to the wide variety of purposes for which economic and business records have been used in the USA. These include the checking of the principles put forward by economic theory; the tracing of the reasons for the success (or failure) of a particular business venture; to hunt for valuable statistical data on wages, prices, and profits; to investigate the development of economic growth in a capitalist society; or to study, with regard to motivation research and the psychology of the businessman, the essence of past entrepreneurial activity. It is clear that such study can be carried out most profitably if vital documents from the past have been retained and its future success must depend upon present measures for the retention of such documents, so that data which is extremely difficult to glean from other sources may be obtained. It is sad to record that, in Britain, such records have not been so extensively retained or documented; nor have they been put to nearly such a wide variety of uses for business records remain a relatively unknown tool to many historians.

Yet one can point to some important British books, dealing either with some phase of economic history or with a certain industry or firm, which have leaned to some extent upon records of business activity preserved for such purposes from the documents of the nineteenth or early twentieth century. Books on the history of a particular industry (for instance T S Ashton's *Iron and steel in the industrial revolution*) or of a particular firm (for instance T C Barker's *Pilkington Brothers and the glass industry*, F E Hyde's *Blue funnel* or C Wilson's excellent account of the development of *Unilever*) may be cited in this respect. Perhaps the most striking example of all, however, when we consider the use of business archives as source material, is George Unwin's *Samuel Oldknow and the Arkwrights* (1924). This led to a distinct readjustment of the twentieth century economic historian's ideas concerning the role of the cotton industry during a most important period of economic history—and it was based chiefly upon old accounts, letters and other administrative documents found in a disused portion of a cotton mill! The reader is invited to consult W H Chaloner's account (*Journal of documentation*, June 1948).

Assuming that the potential value of such documents is recognised, how does one determine what is to be kept for the future, or which of the items preserved from the past is likely to prove most fruitful to the modern research worker? The relative value of minute or accounts books must be weighed against pamphlets, newspaper cuttings, and diaries or other personal records in manuscript form. Ideally, most emphasis should be placed, in the field of business archives, on papers which relate to a firm's policy, rather than an endeavour being made to retain those that concern the minutiae of its day-to-day routine. A report made by an expert to a firm concerning some important branch of its work, or a personal diary which notes trends in business activity or the firm's achievements and setbacks—these are examples of the items which would be of tremendous use as raw material for future workers in the sphere of economic and business history. But with much of the material that is accumulating today, it must be confessed that it is difficult to sort the wheat from the chaff; what is more, the relevance of a particular kind of item from the past may fluctuate according to the period to which it belongs. Chaloner, in the article already cited, suggests that from the second half of the nineteenth century onwards, account books and ledgers become less important while annual reports, company minutes, chairman's speeches and newspapers reports increase in value. What can be said with confidence with regard to this complex question of selective conservation is, firstly, that all the very old extant records of this kind (that is, those produced before 1850) are especially valuable on account of their rarity; secondly, that, if the material of today is sifted with a view to deciding which items should be preserved for posterity, it is certain that we *must* retain several items which may appear ephemeral or even worthless to many librarians.

There are, of course, many severe problems relating to the effective storage of the type of documents mentioned above. Businessmen are not easily persuaded to devote time to the sorting and housing of records relating to their past activities; they understandably believe that their primary task is to develop new ideas and promote present and future efficiency and expertise. They may thus argue that to keep old business documents is space consuming or that the weeding out of such documents demands time—and wasted time is wasted money. The point is, of course, that the businessman may not appreciate the value of the past records of his firm. They may be useful not only as source material for the economic historian, and this will be especially true if we concur with Miss Larson's dictum that ' the sine qua non of business history is the original record of the businessman or firm ', but also to the entrepreneur himself. In the latter capacity, they may be helpful in revealing past procedures, in checking for taxation purposes certain old accounts, for satisfying government enquiries (such as an investigation by the Monopolies Commission), or for the production of a book or brochure to celebrate a firm's centenary. Thus it may just be possible to convince an executive that there is a personal motive for his firm in prolonging the life of some business papers. As one modern booklet on this subject points out

(Business Archives Council: *Management and control of business records*, 1966), 'experience shows that the classes of records which are most helpful for economic and historical research and which ought to be preserved for posterity are among those of greatest value to the organisation itself'. And, if preserving records costs money, it can be argued that the destruction of such material may be increasing the cost and merely transferring the payment to a later date while, if space is the major difficulty in the conservation of important minute books, diaries and ledgers, then such material should be removed from the company's premises and donated to appropriate societies, record offices or libraries.

There is, it is true, much evidence in this country of growing interest in business history in academic institutions and libraries and there are many excellent collections of the business papers or economic manuscripts of bygone years. The success of the magazine *Business history* published by the Liverpool University Press, or at a more specialised level, Leicester University's *Journal of transport history*, reflects this interest and, among the outstanding collections, those of the Guildhall Library, the British Library of Political and Economic Science, and the universities of Glasgow and Manchester may be quoted, while the British Transport Commission has the largest collection of the records of private businesses in England within its own specialised field. Yet a great increase in the systematic conservation of company records is still required, for many archive repositories have only a small proportion of what they should contain. The modern business executive needs to be shown that, if he encourages archivists and libraries in this work, the firm he serves may reap positive future benefits from the collection as well as the individual scholar.

The preservation of government records was the theme of the 1954 white paper known as the Grigg report (Cmd 9163: *Report of the Committee on Departmental Records*, chairman Sir James Grigg). This recommended that departments should review their records five years after they have passed out of regular use and again after twenty five years. It recognised the enormity of the problem, estimating that documents in the hands of government departments which would eventually be placed in the Public Record Office would require 120 miles of shelving unless carefully weeded out, but the report also underlined the value of judicious selection for preservation, stating that, 'the making of adequate arrangements for the preservation of its records is an inescapable duty of the government of a civilised state '. It is impossible to legislate for private enterprise along the lines of such a report, of course, but the work of the British Records Association and, more particularly in our subject field, of the Business Archives Council is helping enormously. The latter organisation, in addition to the booklet already quoted, provides much useful data about its activities in its magazine *Business archives* and in its annual reports; one of the most useful facets of its work lies in the way in which it is seeking to publish information showing the availability and whereabouts of business records to interested economic and social historians. The *National register of archives* is also extremely helpful in the latter respect, for it enables the economic historian to locate and gain access to family papers and other records that are in private hands.

Meanwhile there is still a great deal that can be done by record offices and by academic and public libraries; industrial librarians too could seek to collect and sift the business papers of their own firm. The public librarian should endeavour to persuade large firms in his own locality, especially any that do not have a librarian or archivist, of the value to themselves and to others of the preservation of business documents. If it is at all possible, he should offer a part of his own premises as a safe repository for the most valuable documents relating to each company. He may need to advise also on what should be kept—for limited and highly selective conservation will become more and more essential—and can examine the possibility of extracting information from the records, in certain cases, and reproducing it in a form that facilitates more compact storage. Indeed there is need for more investigation of the value of condensing the bulk of economics and business documents by skilful abstracting, difficult though the latter task undoubtedly is.

In these activities, it is essential that record offices and libraries should co-operate rather than compete with each other and that there should be adequate organisation of the documents held with enquirers easily able to determine what is available and where it is located. If a fully organised pattern for the selective retention of economic and business records for posterity is to be developed in this country, one can imagine a large number of libraries of different kinds and record offices with extensive collections of this material, while many firms will choose to retain certain items on their own premises. But, if these efforts are well co-ordinated, and if there is

73

an appropriate specialised body (presumably the Business Archives Council) at the centre of the national scheme of co-operation in this work, maintaining a national register of what is available and where it is housed, then the prospect of the future industrial historian gaining access to vital primary sources will be bright. The central body could act as a clearing house for enquiries and could spread the gospel of the conservation of important records to business men nationally, while archivists and librarians reinforce this message at a local level.

The thoughts expressed in the last few sentences are merely a sketch of what could be achieved; it must be confessed, with regard to the present situation, that many important ledgers and diaries have already been destroyed and that many businessmen still need a great deal of persuasion before they will recognise this kind of work as a practical activity. Yet while such conservation is, as R L Collison once described it, an 'act of faith', in that one is preparing an intellectual harvest for future generations of historians and business men to reap, there can be no doubt that the industrial archives of the past and the bibliographies of them have served the modern historian well. In the light of this experience, there is surely a solid case for the production of further guides and bibliographies for this kind of source material and for the development of a thorough and orderly procedure for the co-operative retention of the documents themselves. This case rests not only on the academic needs of the historians and other research workers of tomorrow, most valuable though their work may be to the community; it rests also, in many instances, on the likely future requirements of the very organisations who have produced business papers and other records containing information which is possibly not accessible elsewhere.

SUGGESTED READINGS

1 Business Archives Council: *The management and control of business records,* 16pp, 1966.
2 Historical Association: *Business history,* 1960. (A 36-page pamphlet prepared by T C Barker, R H Campbell, P Mathias and B S Yamey, this is intended for the historian, but the student may well find its discussion of primary source material of interest.)
Some of the following periodical articles should also be consulted:
3 Allen, C G: 'Manuscript collections in the British Library of

Political and Economic Science ', *Journal of the Society of Archivists*, October 1960, *pp* 52-60.

4 Barker, T C: 'Business records for the future ', ASLIB *Proceedings*, October 1964, *pp* 302-307.
5 Chaloner, W C: 'Business records as a source of economic history ', *Journal of documentation*, June 1948, *pp* 5-13.
6 Coats, A W: 'Value of business archives to the economic historian ', ASLIB *Proceedings*, January 1961, *pp* 9-14.
7 Lightwood, M: 'Corporation documents: sources of business history ', *Special libraries*, May-June 1966, *pp* 336-337.
8 Plant, M: 'Business history and its sources ', *Journal of documentation*, June 1950, *pp* 100-106.
9 Saville, J: 'Research facilities and the social historian ', *Library Association record*, September 1963, *pp* 319-323.
10 Thompson, C H: 'Training for business records work ', ASLIB *Proceedings*, August 1961, *pp* 205-212.
11 The collection of papers in ASLIB *Proceedings* June-July 1957 is based on an ASLIB conference on business records held earlier that year. The papers are: 'The records requirements of industry ' by H R Mathys; 'Business records and the archivist ' by R C Jarvis; 'The work of the Business Archives Council ' by R S Sayers; 'Business records and the historian ' by J Simmons.
12 A recent and valuable contribution is *Source materials for business and economic history*, published 1967 by Harvard University's Baker Library, 154 *pp*.

The reader is reminded that the above cover only the theme of the latter half of this chapter; they are no substitute for the examination of the major guides and bibliographies which are the key to the important older documents that constitute, for the economic historian, original sources of information.

CHAPTER SEVEN

CURRENT BIBLIOGRAPHIES AND PERIODICAL LITERATURE

IT IS NOW necessary to turn our attention to bibliographies and bulletins which are designed to make economists and allied workers aware of current material, or recently published items, that are of great significance to their studies or professional activities. Much of this material will naturally appear in journals, and the reason for dealing with retrospective bibliographies first in this book is that, while several of them deal with periodical literature to a marked degree, most current bibliographies are almost exclusively concerned with such literature; it is indeed the article, the news item, or the government white paper which, rather than books, is usually destined to be the vehicle of the most up-to-date commercial and economic intelligence. The current awareness services, therefore, form a natural prelude to the consideration of the range of journals that would be housed in an economics and commercial library and, in this chapter, it is intended to discuss a selection of such services before appraising the various classes of periodicals that come within our purview and the tools needed to locate or select them.

The files of the bibliographic services considered here must, of course, be added to the tools for the searching of older literature already examined, but the economist is likely to be equally interested in ascertaining the nature of very recent literature and, indeed, in many branches of applied economics and certainly in commercial activity, current bibliographies will be much more heavily utilised than retrospective ones. As A L Smyth puts it, 'most commercial information does not get into book form, mainly because it dates quickly. . .' (*Commercial information: a guide to the (Manchester) Commercial library*, 1964, p 3). If such information is of very great importance, and this is often so, it is vital that it should be quickly passed on to the appropriate library users. The current bibliographies we are to consider play a vital part in this programme of locating and selecting and disseminating recently published data.

It would be wrong, nevertheless, to believe that all the current bibliographies must, *ipso facto*, deal with journals or government reports that have been rushed from the press. For economics literature, as distinct from commercial intelligence, recent texts may well be utilised to glean current, or near-current information. The librarian of a social science collection would naturally, therefore, scan the pages of the weekly *British national bibliography* and may well arrange to receive lists of recent accessions from the great libraries in his province of knowledge; the latter assist him in determining which new books are of most significance to his readers. He should also, as far as economics is concerned, make use of an important American quarterly publication which, despite a certain inevitable time lag in the listing of new books, must be considered an important current bibliographical service. This was formerly a product of the Johns Hopkins University, but is now prepared by the staff of the University of Pittsburgh. It is their *International economics selections bibliography series 1: New books in economics*, 1954—and its companion series, covering basic retrospective bibliographies on certain selected themes has already been described. The object of series 1 is to list and describe, every quarter, a selection of books that are considered important from all segments of economics. The emphasis must be on English language publications, but some books published in certain foreign languages, French and German for instance, are included and recent issues have increased the international appeal of the bibliography. There are short but extremely useful annotations and works included are graded by a system of letters to indicate whether they are suitable for the college library, the university library or an institution of some other kind. There are, in fact, five of these categories, four dealing with variant needs of academic libraries and the final category covering highly specialised and advanced volumes. Over three hundred books are selected for each issue and the gap between date of publication and evaluation in *New books in economics* is sometimes commendably short, although it does vary considerably from one work to another. Arrangement of entries is by subject and author indexes are provided.

An article which discusses the reasons for the temporary cessation of these bibliographical series in 1962, is mentioned at the end of the chapter. It is fortunate that Pittsburgh have been able to revive the two series of *Economics library selections*, as it was known until comparatively recently, after a year's gap, and to maintain the quality of the earlier issues. The recently published cumulative bibliography of all the titles listed in the days when the series were under the control of Johns Hopkins is a valuable work and worthy of acquisition by any economics library of stature that does not already possess, as retrospective bibliographies, the publications issued in the two series during the period 1954-1962; it truly represents 'an almost complete list of economic books published' in English during this time and, it may be remarked, some earlier ones. The Pittsburgh staff are also intent on producing new volumes for the second series.

For the social sciences as a whole, one of the most valuable current bibliographies we have, despite the fact that the language problem seems to have discouraged some libraries from subscribing to it, is the German *Bibliographie der sozialwissenschaften,* Gottingen, 1905-1943, 1950-, which is published three times a year and includes, annually, over five thousand items. It has the merit, as do other publications which consider the social sciences as an essential unity, of enabling the economist or other specialist worker to review new material in his own province and on the periphery of his subject. The arrangement is a classified one and the object, to echo the words of Carl White, is to succeed in 'surveying German and foreign language publications, books and articles . . .'. This it accomplishes well.

When we turn to bibliographical surveys that are confined to economics once again, and consider those current services that cater mainly or entirely for those who wish to scan, and perhaps evaluate, contributions to journals, we find several publications competing for our attention. One should certainly not despise, in this context, general tools such as the Library Association's *British humanities index* or H H Wilson *Social sciences and humanities index* (formerly *International index to periodicals*), for these can certainly be helpful; we need, nevertheless, the specialised tools that are able to consider economics literature both in greater depth and breadth. Some of these services, the *Economic abstracts* (1952-1960) of the New York Graduate School of Arts and Sciences for example, have been ill-fated. Nevertheless we have a number of useful bibliographies of this kind, some of them dealing with books and articles, while others concentrate solely on the latter. From France, among other current bibliographies, there is *Documentation économique,* 1934-1938, 1947-, which is published by the Paris University Press and appears five times per annum. It covers both books and periodical articles, the latter being culled from nearly two hundred journals of various countries. The arrangement is a subject one and annotations are given in French. The value of this current bibliography is somewhat restricted by the fact that there is often a period of some ten months or so elapsing before a newly published article has its abstract in this service.

More often encountered in British libraries is another continental publication, but this emanates from the Hague and is arranged by the Universal Decimal Classification. It is *Economic abstracts*, 1953-, which must not be confused with the American publication of the same name that is mentioned above. This work is well described by its sub-title: ' a semi-monthly review of abstracts on economics . . .' and the themes covered include finance, trade and industry, labour, and management. It is prepared by the library of the Dutch Economic Information Service with the assistance of the Netherlands School of Economics and the library of the Ministry of Social Affairs. About three hundred and fifty journals are abstracted, and there may be as many as 120-140 abstracts of articles in each issue. Subject indexes are provided and there is an annual index of both authors and subjects. The language of the abstracts depends upon that of the original article but the service is very thorough for the languages dealt with, these being French, English, German and Dutch. This may indeed be regarded as the best abstracting service we have which is co-extensive with the broad subject area of pure and applied economics.

Despite the value of the summaries of articles provided here, and the potential of *Economic abstracts* for both current and retrospective scanning, many librarians who appreciate the services which they could offer their readers with the aid of promptly published abstracts which concentrate on articles in English, must necessarily have wished for a British or American service of the same calibre. It is with the last phrase in mind that one is inclined to pronounce the *Journal of economic abstracts*, 1963-, which is published quarterly from Harvard University under the auspices of the American Economic Association, a disappointment. This is not because of the length or quality of the abstracts; they exceed in fact comparable services in this respect. The deficiencies that at present exist lie in the sphere of indexing and arrangement, plus the fact that only some thirty or forty journals are abstracted and the delay before the appearance of any particular abstract is often considerable. The lack of cumulative author and subject indexes makes searching through back numbers extremely tedious and, in the early issues of this abstracting service, articles were arranged in alphabetical order by the name of the journal from which they were taken. This has now been abandoned, fortunately, in favour of a subject grouping of abstracts. The faults noted detract from the value of the back numbers of the service, but the current issue can be used with profit for scanning abstracts in English embracing a range of recently published economics periodical literature from several countries, and many of the abstracts, which are usually prepared by the author of the original article, are quite excellently done. Perhaps it is best to regard this tool as purely a current awareness service but, as it is now being distributed as a regular publication to members of the American Economic Association, it is to be hoped that abstracting can be extended (through the co-operation of more journals) and speeded up, so that American economists and others can reap the full benefits of the Association's labours with a bibliographic service of this kind.

MORE SPECIALISED CURRENT AWARENESS SERVICES ON
ECONOMIC LITERATURE

Some abstracting services are needed too in more specialised areas. It is fortunate indeed that the International Labour Organisation has undertaken to produce, since January 1965, an extensive programme for the retrieval of books and articles on labour economics; a programme which involves the preparation of a weekly current bibliography and the building up of a vast file of references to older books and articles and a thesaurus, so that these books and articles may be scanned by means of a system of post co-ordinate indexing. The weekly current awareness bulletin records, in each issue, about a hundred articles and books with an A-Z subject index. It is called *International labour documentation* and, although items are recorded in their original language, each is provided with a short abstract in English. By the end of 1966, some twelve thousand items from its issues had been put into the post co-ordinate indexing system and accurately defined to facilitate retrospective scanning.

The international scope of the work that is being carried out at the International Labour Office, the rapid growth rate of the collection of literature references, the quality of the abstracts, and the fact that the weekly abstracting service and its cumulative subject indexes are produced by computer, all combine to make this a highly important specialising service in economics bibliography. The present system has been employed since the early part of 1965 and it will soon be supported by further bibliographical aids such as the *Cumulative subject guide to ILO publications 1919-1964,* which is at present in preparation. The progress report on the organisation's documentation and retrieval programme (August 1966) should be read, if available; it considers the role of weekly current awareness services and post co-ordinate indexing, with many useful comments on the employment of flexowriters and other equipment and, incidentally, on the value of English as a comparatively ' international ' language.

Few current bibliographies can hope to be nearly as comprehensive as the ILO weekly bulletins. But, turning to other specialised branches of our subject, it would certainly be helpful if we possessed for many departments of applied economics good abstracting services for serials giving recent trends or news items. Although not an abstracting or indexing service in any real sense of the term, the British publication *Incomes data* is certainly of value for current news and, as it is also concerned with labour economics, it is fitting that it should be mentioned after the work of the International Labour Organisation. It is published by Incomes Data Services, and consists of reports which are issued twice each month. The object of these is to give an intelligence service on wages and incomes in Britain. Each issue contains a review of important wage claims and similar developments over the last two or three weeks and statements made concerning these matters in Parliament, reports of actual negotiations, agreements and settlements, and finally a section called ' intelligence ', which analyses important publications and speeches relating to incomes and wage increases. The bulletins have been supported by panoramic surveys designed to summarise the main trends and developments over longer periods and, although at present the publication is insular in its coverage, material on continental wages and labour relations is being collected for the possible future expansion of the publication. It is also intended to initiate, in 1968, an enquiry service for the bulletin's subscribers. The virtual necessity for an incomes policy in this country and the ever increasing value of reliable and rapid information on wage settlements and possible increases make this report bulletin, initiated in 1966, of great potential worth; it will be interesting to see if it enjoys the growth and support that it un-doubtedly deserves.

Most branches of economic activity are not, of course, as well documented as labour economics and kindred matters. There are

81

few good specialising abstracting and indexing services, especially if we exclude management and concentrate on economic science as such. In our own country it would be very useful to have for at least two or three major segments of the province of current economics a service which is on a par with that offered by the British serial *Market research abstracts,* 1963-, which appears every six months and contains, in each issue, about seventy long abstracts. There is again a time lag in the preparation of abstracts but, if support for this publication continues to increase, the Market Research Society who are responsible for its production may be able to combat this particular problem to a large degree. Useful also in the field of marketing are the abstracts provided in the American magazine *Journal of marketing* which is an American Marketing Association publication. A number of these abstracts can be found in each issue and, in this country, their value lies in their severely pragmatic approach to marketing; in contrast to them, *Market research abstracts* is concerned with the theoretical aspects as well as, to a certain extent, practical branches of marketing.

Marketing has ties with commerce as well as with applied economics, and a consideration of abstracts on this theme leads us on to contemplate the range of indexing and abstracting services, especially the former, that exist to provide details of commercial news items and periodical articles of service to management. Most of these are published in the United States, but the number of British publications of this kind is steadily multiplying. It may be recollected, too, that the information provided by these services on commerce and business matters may be supported occasionally by references to articles which affect commercial and management activity and which have been provided in a service concerned with abstracting and indexing for economics. Both the *International bibliography of economics* and *Economic abstracts* may, at times, prove serviceable in this way although, as has already been stressed, attempts to claim the former as a current bibliography are of somewhat dubious validity.

COMMERCIAL AND MANAGEMENT BIBLIOGRAPHICAL SERVICES

Turning to the current bibliographies that are concerned with commerce and business exclusively, we should again recall that the accessions lists of libraries can be among the best of these. When, however, we examine pertinent British abstracting and indexing services in this province, we may begin with the Business Surveys'

Research index, which has appeared fortnightly since August 1965. This consists of two sections. The first of these indexes a wide range of commercial news items from trade journals and other sources, while the second provides a key to recent information on particular companies, by extracting details of relevant reports and articles from well over a hundred journals and newspapers. It is anticipated by the publisher that this service may expand, but already it indexes about one hundred thousand items per annum and is beginning to prove of great worth to commercial librarians. Its coverage of the abundance of business and management information in *The financial times,* for instance, is certainly to be commended for this can prove difficult to retrieve from other sources.

For details of very recent news items or periodical articles in the management sphere we have, of course, a service which has persisted in various forms for some years. This is the British Institute of Management's *Management abstracts,* which is now published quarterly. This provides abstracts on articles in business journals under such headings as marketing, production, financial management, and human relations in industry and also contains book reviews. It can be criticised in that there is some delay in the appearance of abstracts, or because the coverage of material is not as wide as many librarians would wish; nevertheless this publication is an important one in management bibliography as the abstracts are good and touch upon all aspects of entrepreneurial activity.

More specialised but also very useful are the various publications which comprise the *Anbar documentation service.* This consists of a monthly abstracting service, a bibliography published three times per annum, an index to these, and other services including translations and the provision of punched cards which operate on the ' peek-a-boo ' principle. The abstracts are excellent and cover numerous journals including those of fourteen overseas countries. *Anbar abstracts* and the *Anbar bibliography* follow a classified arrangement, but the key to this is provided quarterly in *Anbar index.* The original service was abstracts of articles and, in the case of the bibliography, of documents in the subject areas of office organisation and equipment, work study, and similar techniques for the improvement of office efficiency; indeed the editor of the services, H Cemach, is well known as an expert in these matters. But for libraries where a number of readers are likely to be helped by details of books and articles of this kind, the quality and rapidity of appearance of the abstracts more than atones for some evident specialisation. *Anbar abstracts* is a most useful selective guide to recent periodical literature on management, and the services of Anbar as a whole are well described by D E Davinson as ' probably the most significant contribution to reference and information service in the field of office methods and procedures '. The subject coverage has now been widened.

When we embark on an examination of current bibliographies which pervade the whole area of management and business activity, however, we must begin to consider those that are published in the USA. As in the case of guides and retrospective bibliographies, there are many of these and one can only hope to evaluate some of the better known and most generally useful publications. Among these we must certainly place the *Business periodicals index,* which is one of the many H W Wilson publications, and which has been published monthly (excluding July) in this form since the *Industrial arts index* was divided into two separate entities some ten years ago. It is a service which covers the contents of approximately one hundred and seventy magazines and lists the articles which appear in them under appropriate subject headings. It is unfortunate that few British magazines are indexed, but the publication is nevertheless of considerable aid to the librarian for current and (if its back numbers are available) retrospective searching when articles on management, commerce and, possibly, some branches of applied economics are sought. It should be mentioned that *Business periodicals index* cumulates every three months and six months, and finally into annual volumes.

Equally helpful, indeed possibly more so since it indexes certain books and government publications as well as periodical articles, and similar in its arrangement and provision for cumulation, is the *Public affairs information service bulletin,* 1915- . This was initiated by the Special Libraries Association as a co-operative indexing project between libraries and also has a strong leaning towards United States publications. Yet it must be stressed that it indexes selectively about one thousand publications in the English language and, although no abstracts are given, there are sometimes short annotations of new books or pamphlets that have been listed. As a weekly service it is prompt in including material, while the value of past annual cumulations for the searching of older literature, if demanded, may be gauged from the span of years which these cumulations enfold.

The subject material indexed by this publication ranges over many branches of business, economics, politics and current affairs but we

84

are told that the emphasis is on 'factual and statistical information'. Some of the items indexed undoubtedly prove ephemeral, but this is a risk which any abstracting and indexing service must take and, in fact, because it reports almost all new items of importance that are published, in the English language, within its wide field, this must necessarily be regarded as an essential bibliography for both the social science and the commercial and business library.

From Canada we also have a publication of a similar kind, although much less ambitious, which may, from time to time, prove of use in British commercial libraries. It is the monthly *Management index*, which covers books and articles, the latter being listed on a selective basis from some two hundred periodicals, and is published by the Keith Business Library, Ottawa. This library also publishes bibliographies of books published during a particular year in America, Canada or Britain, on an especial business theme, such as advertising. These may prove helpful in assisting the librarian if detailed retrospective searching needs to be pursued. Some American libraries, an example being Cleveland Public Library, have produced current bibliographical works of this nature; indeed in the USA we also have some more specialised indexing services within the commercial and business field, the *Accountant's index*, for instance. One such specialised service, which may be briefly described, because it concerns a topic which has connections with applied economics and marketing as well as with commercial activity, is the *Index of supermarket articles*.

Published in Chicago by Supermarket Institute Incorporated, this is a classified annual list of selected articles relating to the grocery and supermarket trades. Although the American emphasis is very great, this is a publication which can prove very useful in some British special libraries in helping to unearth articles from which trends and ideas in marketing on the other side of the Atlantic can be gleaned—and these may well soon be put into practice in Britain, as past experience in the world of retailing abundantly proves.

PERIODICALS

It would be possible to note the titles of other abstracting services like the Russian *Ekonomika promyshlennosti;* but however enough examples have been given to illustrate to the reader the range of bibliographies and current awareness services that serve economics, and we can add to them by using the accessions lists and bulletins of recent additions issued by important libraries. The published bibliographies illustrate well the way in which economics overlaps with commerce and business methods, for some of them can be used both for tracing articles on applied economics and commerce, while one or two cover, at least to some degree, all branches of our subject field. Yet there is still a need for more abstracting bulletins, for information retrieval in the social sciences is likely to assume much greater importance within the next decade. The current bibliographies are concerned mainly or even exclusively with periodical literature, and it is now necessary for us to begin a consideration of other kinds of reference material by appraising some of the major journals which would be covered by these abstracting and indexing services. Once again, it is necessary to distinguish between publications of different kinds but, when listing and briefly describing or evaluating periodicals, it seems best to employ five categories—scholarly and research journals on economics and economic history; magazines on some aspects of applied economics; economic journals of a more popular nature; trade journals reporting current news on some commercial activity; and periodicals of interest to executives and other businessmen.

These categories, although they contain numerous examples, do not provide an exhaustive survey of all the journals which economists and allied workers are likely to use regularly; journals published by government departments and magazines which are purely statistical in character have been excluded and are discussed in the two chapters which follow. The reason for such (not altogether satisfactory) division is that, while we have many bibliographies covering socio-economic and commercial activity and their wide ramifications, the journals truly are legion. Because of this a full survey of the range of economics periodicals and the tools used to trace and exploit them would include examples of important journal titles that are given in chapters eight and nine in addition to some from the selection that follows here.

The first category is a very important one, for we have several periodicals of a scholarly or semi-scholarly character which are employed in economics especially, perhaps, by those pursuing research into some abstruse aspect of economic principles or of economic and social history. Such economists will not use periodical literature as heavily as do workers in the technological fields; nor will they turn to their journals for news items as the businessman will do with commercial magazines and newspapers. These journals are none the less very valuable and embody several important and original articles; some of the information or theories put forward in them never appears in book form. A very important key to these articles is the retrospective bibliography, *Index of economic journals,* although several other retrospective bibliographies will naturally be used in tracing them also. Current bibliographies, such as *Economic abstracts* or, possibly, *Journal of economic abstracts* will be employed when searching for their very recent contents. These research journals may also be of value for their shorter articles or for the critical comments on some problem given by specialists; again, they may be employed for bibliographical purposes on account of the reviews or notices of new books which many of them provide. A selection of these journals with concise notes on each title is given below. The year in which they commenced publication can, in most instances, be ascertained from reading lists, such as the British Council booklist on *Economics.*

Scholarly and research journals on economics: *Economic journal*: Published quarterly by the Royal Economic Society. Several long articles in each issue—these are usually very advanced. Good bibliographical information, comprising long book reviews, lists of books received and lists of contents of some other current economic periodicals of primary worth. It was, for many years, edited by Keynes.

Economica: Published quarterly by the London School of Economics. Long articles usually on highly specific aspects of theoretical economics. Good book reviews and a list of books received.

Review of economic studies: Quarterly; Economics Study Society, Cambridge. Advanced articles. No reviews, but details are given of the contents of recent issues of other scholarly periodicals on economics. Other British journals of this nature include *Manchester school (of economic and social studies), Oxford economic papers* and the *Scottish journal of political economy,* although these are less valuable than the above for reviews and notices. One might also cite here *Economics,* which is designed to aid the teaching of the subject in further education colleges and secondary schools and is published three times per year by the Economics Association. There are a few long book reviews in each copy.

North American publications of a scholarly nature are: *American economic review*: Published quarterly by the American Economic Association. Long and excellent, although specialised, articles. A list of books received is given in each issue and there may be as many as fifty book reviews. A special issue incorporates the papers of the AEA's annual meeting.

Quarterly journal of economics: Harvard University. Contains scholarly articles on economic principles plus notes and discussions. A long list of recently published books is given, but there are no reviews.

Canadian journal of economics and political science: Quarterly. Some good reviews support the scholarly articles.

From European countries we have magazines such as *Revue économique; Revue des sciences économiques; Economie appliquée;* and *Economia internazionale,* while to return to the journals of our own nation we have, on the historical side of economics, such periodicals as

Economic history review: Published by the Economic History Society, two or three copies appearing each year. Each issue has six or seven articles plus rather short but good book reviews. A primary feature over the years has been the bibliographical and other kindred articles appearing under the heading ' Studies in bibliography '.

Business history: Published every six months by the Liverpool University Press. Specialised articles plus long book reviews and notices of books received.

Their most important equivalents in the USA are probably *Journal of economic history*: Published quarterly for the Economic History Association by the New York University Graduate School of Business Administration. This usually contains some half a dozen articles plus long book reviews and a list of books received.

Business history review: Quarterly, from Harvard University. Excellent articles and reviews. More specialised journals of a scholarly character include magazines such as the *Journal of agricultural economics,* which is published three times per annum in this country, the American *Economic geography,* a quarterly with excellent reviews, and another American quarterly publication, *Econometrica.* The latter reflects the increasing application of mathematics to the problems of economic theory.

Our second category also contains some journals which may be described as semi-scholarly in character; but most of these pay much more attention to applied economics than to theoretical principles, although it must be stressed that the academic journals do often deal with the application of economic principles in addition to theory and history.

88

Magazines on some aspect of applied economics:

Economic review: Produced quarterly by the National Institute of Economic and Social Research, it gives both articles and statistics, surveying the current economic scene and Britain's future prospects. The February issue gives an especially detailed picture of the country's economic situation.

Times review of industry: Published monthly. Has good factual articles and some statistics. Publication is ceasing in 1967.

Banker: Also monthly. Articles are advanced and of a scholarly character. There is an international review of the banking scene and some banking statistics. In the specialised sphere that is the concern of the latter journal we also have the *Bank of England quarterly bulletin,* the *Bankers' magazine,* the *Journal of the Institute of Bankers,* and the reviews of the commercial banks; all of these have banking as their central theme, but often give articles ranging over a number of problems in applied economics. Also noteworthy are publications such as *Export,* which is the magazine of the Institute of Export; the *British export gazette,* the German *Export market* (text in English) and the Institute of Marketing and Sales Management's *Marketing.* The Basil Blackwell publications *Journal of industrial economics* (three per annum), and *Journal of common market studies* deal with rather different economic situations and problems; the latter has some useful book reviews. There are too, of course, many United States journals that are concerned mainly with the practical side of economics. An example is the *Industrial and labor relations review,* published quarterly from Cornell University.

Periodicals of a more popular character: These need only be considered briefly but they include several journals which give investment advice such as the *Investors chronicle,* very general magazines of the nature of *New society* and, inevitably, *The economist,* which is important as a source of contemporary news and economic opinion and which also provides a host of useful facts about British companies. Businessmen and students alike are fortunate in having a weekly British periodical which reviews the home and foreign economic scene in such a readable manner.

Commercial magazines and trade journals: The potential of these magazines is considerable and many titles within this category will be housed in large commercial libraries. *The accountant, Advertisers weekly* and *Taxation* are good examples of three magazines of a largely commercial character, while among the journals of a strictly trade variety, the *Meat trades journal* and the *Fruit, flower and vegetable trades review* may be cited. The object of magazines of this latter kind is essentially to report current news and developments in the trade or profession concerned. Articles are short and demand for many back numbers of these periodicals in many libraries is almost non-existent as, unlike the periodicals noted in the previously identified categories, almost the entire emphasis here is on current commercial intelligence. Nevertheless, the back numbers of trade journals can be utilised; indeed they form, for the industrial historian, a potential primary source of information.

Management journals: There are many such periodicals and they are comparatively well documented in guides to management literature and elsewhere. A few outstanding titles are: *Business management*: an outstanding British monthly. Includes some brief book reviews.

The director: Monthly. Produced by the (British) Institute of Directors.

Journal of management studies: Published three times a year by Basil Blackwell Ltd. Some book reviews.

Management today: This monthly is published by the British Institute of Management in association with the Haymarket Press and *The financial times*. It replaces the former institution's magazine *Manager* and aims to be ' a well-presented and authoritative journal which can reach beyond even the rapidly growing number of BIM's membership '. Some book reviews are provided.

Management journals from other countries include *Management international review*, which is published six times per annum in Germany with its text in English, German and French, and such important American magazines as *Fortune, Harvard business review, Administrative management,* and *Advanced management journal*. Some of these, such as the last named quarterly, offer reviews of books in addition to their numerous articles. There are, too, a host of periodicals in the management sphere which deal only with a single branch of management techniques—office management or personnel management, for instance. Many of the commercial journals will also be of great value to management.

Our five categories, especially the first one, have ranged over a number of magazines; magazines which extend from scholarly economics and management journals with long authoritative articles, down to trade journals with commercial news items. The range of journals taken must of course vary with the nature of libraries. The periodicals in our first and second categories fall within the province of the social science or economics library; some of the more popular economics periodicals will also be found in such an institution. The commercial library (public or special) will house trade journals, and certain special libraries will subscribe to several magazines on applied economics or management. It is probably only in a large, departmentalised, public library system, however, that good examples of journals from all five categories will be found.

WORKS USED IN TRACING DETAILS OF PERIODICALS: LOCATION LISTS

When we add to these the statistical and other periodicals issued by government departments or international bodies, the task of selecting and organising these journals may seem formidable indeed. Yet it has been noted that we have a wide and, in many ways, excellent range of current and retrospective bibliographies which indicate the subject matter of the journals and there are also a number of tools which assist the librarian in selecting the journals which are most likely to be of benefit to his readers, or to borrow back numbers of magazines which his own library does not contain. In selection, which is considered again in a later chapter, we are aided by directories and guides such as Toase, M: *Guide to current British periodicals*, 1962, or the American *Standard periodicals directory*, 1964-1965, which covers some twenty thousand United States and Canadian periodical publications. There is, too, the splendid *Ulrich's international periodicals directory*, and this, in its current eleventh edition, lists important journals pertaining to the arts, humanities, business and social science, in its second volume. These works and others like them indicate the publisher, price and frequency of the journals concerned; they sometimes provide other useful data also, such as the name of an abstracting or indexing service that covers a particular journal that is being described. At a more specialised level, we have the UNESCO *World list of social science periodicals*, third edition, 1966, which, unfortunately, does not give locations in important British libraries for the items that it lists.

Selection is still a problem despite such aids, and no library can hope to always satisfy users from the periodical holdings of its own collections. It is, therefore, also necessary to use tools of a different kind—union catalogues and location lists—to trace the whereabouts of a copy of a magazine which is not in stock, for the purpose of borrowing it. General tools of this kind, such as the *British union catalogue of periodicals,* are heavily used in arranging the inter-library loan of journals; it might be added that there is scope for their use in the selection of magazines also—for the indication of the number of libraries in an area that subscribe to a particular title may well influence a librarian in his decision regarding a periodical that is a marginal purchase. We really need union catalogues of a more specialised kind as well as the invaluable BUCOP and, in this latter respect, the special librarian in particular in our subject field may profitably employ the ASLIB Economics Group: *Union list of periodicals,* second edition, 1959. It is unfortunate that we do not have more tools of this nature, for other examples of this kind which come to mind all belong to countries overseas. A list of this kind may, however, be profitably supported by union catalogues of periodicals which, while fairly general in their subject appeal, are limited to the holdings of libraries of various kinds within one particular geographical region of the British Isles.

SUGGESTED READINGS

1 Jordan, R T: ' Economics library selections ', *Library journal,* April 15th 1963, *pp* 1625-1629. (An account of the early history of *International economics selections bibliography,* which illustrates both the value of the current awareness services in our province and some of the difficulties they have faced in striving to be effective and self-supporting.)

2 Thompson, G K: *From boiler room to data bank: some problems facing documentalists in sociology,* 11*pp.* (A paper presented at the sixth world congress 1966, of the International Sociological Association which discusses some of the work being done in the International Labour Organisation Library with particular reference to the current awareness service.)

3 The present writer has contributed a short review and appraisal of *Journal of economic abstracts* and the valuable retrospective service *Index of economic journals* in *The library world,* March 1965, *p* 227, entitled ' Two American bibliographical services for economists '.

CHAPTER EIGHT

GOVERNMENT PUBLICATIONS AND THE ECONOMIST

THE STUDENT OF librarianship in Britain now has a good text for his study of the published output of the government. This is *An introduction to British government publications,* 1965, and its author, J G Ollé, provides a sensible discussion of the reasons why it is usual to consider these diverse items as a single category of reference material. Government published documents cover many subject areas, but in the social sciences, Ollé tells us, they ' make a unique and valuable contribution to the literature '. It is obvious, therefore, that many of these publications must be of direct value to the economist and several others are of marginal significance to him. Some of these documents are in statistical form and are left over for consideration in the next chapter; some are published as serials or journals and, as has already been remarked, our study of periodicals must in its totality extend over three chapters.

FORMAT AND NATURE OF GOVERNMENT PUBLICATIONS

Government publications are often issued in the form of pamphlets or even single sheets, but to believe that all non-periodical items emanating from governments take such a form is a fallacy; there are certain publications which form substantial volumes. But, for economists, the value of such publications, whether they appear in book form or not, is likely to lie in their authority, the wide range of information they provide, and their tremendous current appeal—for many important government documents are printed at very short notice and issued within a few days of the decision to publish. We shall be mainly concerned here with the government publications of our own country but, despite the quantity of these, it must be remembered that economists and businessmen may also be well served by the documents issued by overseas governments and by those of international organisations.

In our broad field of interest it is wisest to begin by considering bibliographies of government publications, then by discussing British parliamentary publications and the non-parliamentary publications of appropriate departments, and deal finally with the economics literature issued by international bodies. When contemplating bibliographies of British government documents we shall virtually be concerned with the keys to the output of HMSO, for, although not all of our government publications are issued through the Stationery Office, all the parliamentary publications and those non-parliamentary documents that are relevant within our province of investigation come from this source. The daily lists and monthly and annual goverment publications catalogues issued by the Stationery Office, and the catalogue cards which can be purchased for its publications, are obviously major bibliographical sources for librarians. HMSO also publish a number of sectional lists which are regularly revised and usually indicate the publishing activities of a particular department. The most important of these for our purposes are *Sectional list 21 Ministry of Labour* and the *Sectional list 51 Board of Trade*. These comprise catalogues of recent items issued by the department and some older material that is still of consequence; they may also show that some parliamentary papers have been prepared by the staff of the department concerned. These lists can thus be used to focus our attention on past publications dealing with a specific area of economic activity, while we use the daily, monthly and annual lists and catalogues to survey a complete range of HMSO material (although the monthly and annual catalogues exclude statutory instruments) on our subject.

The monthly HMSO catalogue includes entries for certain overseas publications which are sold in this country by the Stationery Office. These are the publications of the United Nations and its agencies, and European communities and the Organisation for Economic Cooperation and Development. They are excluded from the annual catalogue, but appear in a separately published supplement to it entitled *International organisations*. We may also trace United Nations material through the monthly *Documents index* prepared by its Dag Hammarskjold Library, and through the UN annual catalogues, while the specialised agencies and the other organisations mentioned above also issue catalogues of their publications. Some larger British libraries may acquire, too, the monthly catalogue of United States government publications and select some items from it for purchase.

Overseas government publications can, of course, be traced from alternative sources—the *Bulletin of the Public Affairs Information Service,* or other published bibliographies, for example, or perhaps both British and foreign publications will be chosen from reports of them in the daily press, and from accessions lists of some important libraries and, as far as we are concerned these will be libraries with strong social science or commercial interests. However, in spite of criticism over the years regarding the quality of their indexing, the regularly published HMSO lists and catalogues must remain our primary source for tracing British government publications of recent years. In passing, it may be mentioned too that the monthly catalogue contains a regular inset—HMSO *Monthly selection;* this gives a useful description of some selected items from the catalogue, but these are usually chosen for their general appeal and economic and business material is considered too specialised to figure often in the annotated inset.

Some of the more recent HMSO sectional lists have dealt with subject themes rather than with the publications of a single department; this is to be welcomed and it is unfortunate that there are no subject sectional lists for our sphere of interest. There is, however, the most valuable *Commerce, industry and* HMSO: *a selection of government publications for the businessman,* which is revised fairly often, the latest edition being that of 1966. This is not a sectional list, but is a special catalogue intended to 'be of great help to exporters seeking commercial intelligence and background information, and to everyone involved in the management and organisation of commerce and industry'. The present writer can think of no other single publication which demonstrates so readily the tremendous information potential of British government publications, and of those international organisations for which HMSO is the sales agent in this country, for economists, statisticians and businessmen, whatever their special interest may be, although it does not always clearly show the department from which the British publications emanate.

When, however, extensive retrospective searching through the government publications issued over a considerable period of time is needed, we must turn to other bibliographies and aids, although the publication just described and the sectional lists do indicate some older material, yet, for departmental publications, we shall require past annual catalogues of HMSO. These are available back to 1922 and searching is made easier by the cumulative indexes, each of which covers a five year span.

Many of the documents needed by economists and economic historians are, however, likely to be parliamentary publications, especially command papers, rather than the non-parliamentary items issued by the departments. For these there is the valuable *General index to the bills, reports and papers . . . 1900-1949*, 1960, which covers command papers and House of Commons papers and bills. There are also a number of earlier indexes and indexes to sessional papers which can be employed but the most noteworthy of the remaining bibliographical tools are undoubtedly what Ollé calls the 'Ford-Hansard bibliographies'.

The firm of *Hansard* originally produced a catalogue of the parliamentary publications issued during the period 1696-1834 and Professor Ford of Southampton University and his wife revived interest in this bibliography by having it reprinted in 1953. To it they have added their own volumes produced over the period 1951-1961 and covering the years 1833-1899; 1900-1916; 1917-1939; and, finally, 1940-1954. The first of the *Ford* volumes is a select list, but the others are described as 'breviates'. They do not simply list the material of the period, they provide an abstract or condensed account of each document, the object being 'to increase the appreciation and use of the original documents'. While these breviates can be no substitute for the publications themselves, it may be remarked that their use is considerable, both in identifying early parliamentary papers and in enabling us to appraise them; they can be profitably used in association with some of the bibliographies of older material already noted. Very often also, if an early publication is not quickly accessible, the appropriate *Ford* volume can be given to the reader while it is brought; a reader interested, for instance, in the report of the Royal Commission on the Poor Laws, a command paper published in 1909, might receive considerable help in obtaining a preliminary birds eye view of the document in this way.

EXAMPLES OF RELEVANT GOVERNMENT PUBLICATIONS

It is usual to make a distinction, based partly upon tradition but serving also certain administrative purposes, between parliamentary and non-parliamentary publications. The non-parliamentary, or departmental, works are of most interest in our study of British government publications for the businessman, yet the value of acts, House of Commons or House of Lords papers and bills, and command papers must not be underrated. The published official reports too, recording debates in the two houses (originally published by the firm of Hansard and still often popularly known by that name) will sometimes throw light upon economic matters. To give a simple example, if asked to trace the vicissitudes of the value of the pound over a period of time, the indexes to the reports of the House of Commons debates will reveal several occasions when information on this subject was provided for Parliament. Some of the general acts deal with major economic matters; we may cite as examples *The companies act, 1948; The restrictive trade practices act, 1956; The local employment acts, 1960 and 1964; The European Free Trade Association act, 1965.*

Some of the above are supported by other acts of parliament on the same or similar themes and they are not, as one might suppose, always comparatively slight publications. The companies act referred to, for instance, is very substantial and extends over more than a single volume of the *Statutes revised.* The bills and papers of the houses are likewise often helpful in that they may constitute proposals for new legislation on economic or business themes, or involve annual reports by a department concerning the execution of existing acts. The Board of Trade annual report on the administration of the local employment acts is issued as a House of Commons paper.

But, of all the parliamentary publications, command papers will probably be far more often of service to economists and entrepreneurs than either the general acts, the reports of parliamentary debates or the many papers and bills emanating from the House of Lords and House of Commons. These command papers are reports, sometimes by a royal commission, which are presented to parliament and which concern matters upon which members urgently require authoritative and, possibly, detailed information. Several of these are devoted to economic topics, and their worth is tremendous to the student of applied economics. Some illustration of their relevance can be provided by an indication of a few titles of command papers that have appeared over a number of years: *Report of the Royal Commission on the Industrial Population (cmd 6153, 1940); Report on resale price maintenance (cmd 7696, 1949); Social insurance and allied services (cmd 6404, 1942)* (this is the famous Beveridge report); *Committee on the working of the monetary system (cmnd 827, 1959)* (sometimes called the Radcliffe report); *Taxation of capital gains (cmnd 2645,*

4

1965); The Scottish economy (cmnd 2864, 1966); Prices and income standstill (cmnd 3073, 1966); Prices and income policy after June 30th, 1967 (cmnd 3235, 1967); Preliminary estimates of national income and balance of payments, 1961-1966 (cmnd 3244, 1967).

It must be emphasised that the nine examples selected are but a few of the command papers that the economist may use; although such papers do cater for a wide number of subjects—the Grigg report referred to on page 72 is a command paper—a large number of them must necessarily cover topics of major concern to economists or themes which are of indirect interest to the economist's studies. No serious worker in the field can afford to neglect them.

Statutory instruments may be of help also, but in the consideration of non-parliamentary papers here, we can afford to ignore these and proceed to a direct consideration of the output of the various departments which issue a whole host of publications on themes like exporting, labour problems and various facets of national and regional economic planning. The chief of these departments or ministries as far as our investigations are concerned are almost certainly the Board of Trade, the Ministry of Labour and the Central Statistical Office, but the publications of the latter must obviously be reserved until the next chapter whereas, while the other two departments contribute their fair share or more to Britain's series of economic statistics, many of the works which they issue are not primarily statistical in character and may be dealt with here.

The Board of Trade is concerned with a wide range of commercial and economic activities. It is involved in home industry, for instance, with regard to such matters as the administration of acts of parliament relating to company bankruptcies and monopoly abuses, and it also advertises details of investment grants and produces reports of the working of the local employment acts. It has many duties relating to the publicising of trade fairs and exhibitions and must report news on international markets and overseas trade regulations. Board of Trade publications include:

The Board of Trade journal: is a weekly magazine that contains a wide variety of information, including statistical data, pertaining to the activities of this very important department. It must certainly be closely scanned for its worth to those engaged in applied economics and commerce is almost incalculable, one can understand, and indeed support, the statement made in *Commerce, Industry and* HMSO to the effect that 'nowhere else is so much vital commercial information

98

to be found packed into a single periodical '. The department's economists and statisticians collect a vast amount of current information for the pages of this periodical, but it is interesting for librarians to note that the departmental library staff also make a contribution, notably through their provision of book reviews and in the compilation of the annual index. The reviews are of a high quality and prove very helpful for selecting new material in appropriate branches of the subject field.

The export service bulletin: is more specialised in its appeal, but is also of considerable value. Published daily, it provides information on opportunities for British firms to sell overseas. They may, for instance, wish to know that there is a request for surgical gloves and other hospital equipment in Costa Rica, or that a firm in Greece is inviting tenders for the supply of measuring instruments, and it is the task of this publication to attempt to bring such information to the notice of appropriate British companies.

Hints to businessmen visiting . . . : is another helpful and frequently revised Board of Trade publication; this is not a journal but a series of pamphlets designed to assist the businessman with interests in various countries. Each pamphlet deals with a particular country and gives much information of a general character—on population, climate, etc.—as well as economic data relating to banking, currency, import regulations and many other matters. Pamphlets in the series are amended or reissued as the need arises.

There are also a number of publications emanating from this department which are not issued so regularly. Striking examples include the *European Free Trade Association compendium for the use of exporters,* second edition, 1965; the splendid 1965 booklet *How to export: a guide for the newcomer,* which was issued in association with the Central Office of Information; and the reissue, early in 1967, of handbooks on services for British exporters and the work of the Export Credits Guarantee Department. But there are many other interesting and valuable Board of Trade publications apart from those on export matters; the reader is invited to scan the relevant HMSO sectional list and other recent government catalogues and bibliographies for details of them.

The Ministry of Labour sectional list should also be consulted for an appreciation of the scope of its publications. This department deals with a large number of matters relating to wages and hours of work in various industries, employment levels, industrial training, and the plight of the disabled worker. Its best known publication is the *Ministry of Labour gazette.* This appears monthly and contains many news items, certain statistics relating to labour and some specialised articles. It is a most valuable medium for keeping a finger on the pulse of Britain's current labour problems and working conditions and must be housed in every library of any status in our subject area.

The Ministry's other publications of a non-statistical nature include such works as the *Industrial relations handbook,* 1961; the *Directory of employers associations, trade unions . . . etc,* 1960 (with subsequent amendment); the *Guide to the 1964 Industrial training act;* pamphlets on manpower studies and, of course, a series of booklets on careers, some of which are about prospects in business and commercial fields.

If the Board of Trade and the Ministry of Labour are among the pre-eminent departments for economists, there are several others with a large output of published information which can only be hinted at here. The Central Office of Information issues some documents of great appeal to economists and businessmen, such as the frequently revised reference pamphlet on *The British system of taxation,* or its annual survey entitled *Britain: an official handbook.* The *Customs and excise tariff* and its amendments are of great value in giving details of duties chargeable on goods imported into the United Kingdom and can, in addition to their value in current commercial intelligence, be of significance to the student investigating the history of tariffs levied by this country. The Customs and Excise Department also produce an *Export list,* and various other items of a commercial character. The Export Credits Guarantee Department has a booklet advertising its services and this supports the Board of Trade pamphlet on exporting mentioned above. In addition, the Ministry of Agriculture, Fisheries and Food, the Foreign Office and the Treasury are all departments which make some valuable contributions to literature regarding various aspects of the economy. The number of such publications has been swelled in recent years by the creation of new organisations so that we have, for example, the regional surveys of the Department of Economic Affairs, such as *The challenge of the changing North,* 1966; the reports of the National Board for Prices and Incomes; and the wide range of economic pamphlets that have emanated from the National Economic Development Office. The latter include *The growth of the economy,* 1964, *Management recruitment and development,* 1965, *Investment appraisal,* 1965, *Conditions favourable to faster growth*, 1963, and *Productivity: a handbook of advisory services*, 1967. With economic planning now a firmly established norm in Britain, it seems inevitable that the output of the DEA and the NEDO will soon begin to rival that of the two departments which have been singled out as issuing publications of especial significance for a description of the current economic scene and for commercial intelligence.

Nor should we forget, to return once again to the longer established departments, the Inland Revenue and its publications on tax rates within and without the Commonwealth, plus its booklets explaining taxation matters. But economists really cannot be content with the government publications of their own country alone, although only the larger British libraries will have a good selection of those from overseas nations and the country chiefly concerned will be the USA. With over twenty thousand items being mentioned each year in the United States Government catalogues, it is important that an effort be made to acquire some of the significant documents issued by, for instance, the Departments of Labor and Commerce, such as the latter's monthly *Marketing guide*. If, as previously suggested, the monthly catalogues are taken in British social science libraries, they will illustrate the range and potential of American government publications on economics and some outstanding ones could be bought for the benefit of the purposive reader.

PUBLICATIONS OF INTERNATIONAL BODIES

Even more important to us are the documents and papers on descriptive and applied economics which pour forth from the international organisations. The United Nations has regional economic commissions and is also served by various agencies—UNESCO, The Food and Agriculture Organisation, The International Bank, the International Monetary Fund, the International Labour Organisation and others of lesser interest to us—while the General Agreement on Tariffs and Trade is a partial step towards achieving a UN agency for international trading. These bodies are supported, as voluminous authors on international economic conditions, by the Organisation for Economic Co-operation and Development and the European communities (and we must specially note the European Economic Community or 'common market'), while the European Free Trade Association publishes fewer but very useful documents. The best way to indicate the scope and purpose of the UN and other organisations' economics publications is to provide a few examples of their non-statistical items here and to urge the student to see as many of these as possible and to trace other items from published bibliographies and lists—outstanding among which, to return to a theme touched upon earlier, are the *United Nations documents index*, the annual *Reference catalogue of United Nations publications* and the lists of agencies such as the *Current list of* UNESCO *publications*.

The United Nations itself issues a very wide range of items of concern to us, from economic bulletins relating to the current scene in various continents or countries, to the bibliographically valuable accessions lists of its great libraries; the latter can, naturally, be of great import as tools in other libraries and documentation centres. A fair proportion of this output is promoted by the United Nations Economic and Social Council, a body which is pledged to working towards the fulfilment of UN aims on living standards, full employment and other economic goals, while many items are issued by the various regional economic commissions. Regular publications of the United Nations include the annual *Economic survey of Europe;* the twice yearly *Economic bulletin for Europe, Economic bulletin for Africa* and *Economic bulletin for Latin America;* and the quarterly *Economic bulletin for Asia and the Far East.* At a broader level, we have the annual analysis of developments in virtually each economy that is found in the *World economic survey.* In addition to serial publications of this kind, there are a number of specialised reports and studies and accounts of conference proceedings that are published. The last named include details of conferences on economic growth, population, international trade, statistical studies and many other matters while, as substantial examples of reports and studies, *Helping economic development in Asia and the Far East* 1964, and *Development prospects of basic chemical and allied industries in Asia and the Far East* 1965 may be cited. It should be noted that UN publications may have their text in English, French, Spanish or Russian or it may be available in several of these languages. The official catalogues provide a useful guide for us in this matter.

Turning to the specialised UN agencies, we find again a wide range of material on the international economic scene as well as some publications of a bibliographical nature. The work of UNESCO in social science documentation (through the preparation of four annual bibliographies dealing with important disciplines, the compilation of an authoritative social science dictionary in English and the publication of bibliographies on special themes like the under-developed countries) has already been briefly indicated. There are also several UNESCO reports on economic themes such as the 1963 volume on the *Role of savings and wealth in Southern Asia and the West,* edited by R D Lambert and B F Hoselitz, or the report by R Vining entitled *Economics in the USA: a review and interpretation of research,* that was reprinted in 1964.

Even excluding statistical works, there are many examples of economic reports from the other agencies. The Food and Agriculture Organisation issues special reports like the 1960 one on *The world demand for paper to 1975,* and many studies on agriculture and commodity policies, while from the International Monetary Fund we have a monograph series, an annual report on *Exchange restrictions* and its annual report on its own activities—the latter supplying, as a by product, a good deal of data on economic conditions in member countries. From the International Labour Organisation, which existed for many years before the creation of the UN and became in 1946 its first specialising agency, we have many studies and reports, including the *Symposium on family living standards,* 1961, and *Employment and economic growth 1964,* not to mention the valuable articles on employment, wages and industrial relations that appear in its monthly journal the *International labour review.*

One could multiply examples from the UN *agencies,* but other international organisations which are not affiliated to the United Nations must not be neglected; many of these focus attention in their reports upon crucial matters relating to the structure of a nation's economy or its growth and development problems. There are many of these organisations. The International Bureau of Fiscal Documentation disseminates, for example, information on taxation matters through its various publications and the International Customs Tariff Bureau produces a record of current tariffs of nations in its *International customs journal,* while there are a very large number of reports and journals issued by the European Economic Community and the Organisation for Economic Co-operation and Development. Of these, the former are likely to be of increasing importance to the British economist in view of the nation's interest in the common market. They include serial publications like the monthly EEC *Bulletin,* the quarterly *Economic situation in the community,* and the *Community business survey,* the latter publication appearing three times per annum. One tends to find more details of EFTA publications than of the ECC in official catalogues, since the United Kingdom has, for some time, been a member of the EFTA trading group. It issues an annual report and several documents on specific themes such as the one on *Regional development policies in EFTA, 1965,* or the 1964 survey of the *Structure and growth of the Portuguese economy.*

The OECD was initiated in 1961, succeeding the Organisation for European Economic Co-operation, and widening the concepts and territories of its predecessor to embrace the USA and Canada in a scheme of international economic alliance. It has contributed a good deal towards economics documentation; publications include a host of reports issued over the years on such varied topics as fuels, price stability, productivity measurement and consumer food buying habits. The organisation regularly produces accounts of economic conditions in particular countries, a comparatively recent example being the October, 1966 survey of the Netherlands. It also covers a number of special themes, including among its publications items such as *What it takes to be a good manager,* 1962, *Training methods for older workers,* 1965, and the *Guide to legislation on restrictive business practices in Europe and North America,* which is in loose-leaf form and is constantly updated. There is also the bi-monthly OECD *Observer,* which is an extremely readable periodical on broad economic trends and current activity in applied economics throughout the OECD area. The above publications are supported by volumes of trade and other statistics which will be mentioned in the next chaper.

This survey has not found it possible, in most cases, to do more than mention some outstanding titles issued by an organisation or department; these should be seen and examined, whenever possible, if their potential is to be grasped. It must be evident, nevertheless, even from what has been said above, that a well stocked British social science library must provide a vast range of our government publications for economists and should support these by the acquisition of a few outstanding items emanating from overseas governments and a good selection of the reports, surveys, periodicals and other publications emanating from the UN and its agencies, EEC, OECD and other bodies. The value of these documents *in toto* lies in their provision of up-to-date and very necessary information which cannot be gained from textbooks or non-governmental economics journals; the authoritative presentation of data which is virtually guaranteed in the works of these organisations, the variety of subject themes over which the documents range and, with regard to the publications of the international organisations, the way in which the comparison of the economic growth and problems of different nations is facilitated and information provided on current situations in various economies. Libraries will certainly vary in the number of these items which they acquire, but perhaps the titles mentioned as examples in this chapter will serve both to convince economists and allied workers and the librarian-cum-information officer that the potential usefulness of these documents (and, of course, the bibliographies of them) is very great indeed.

SUGGESTED READINGS

Some of the most fundamental work involves the examination of Stationery Office lists, especially *Commerce, industry and HMSO*, other lists and catalogues and, if the reader's knowledge of British government publications is very scanty, Ollé's book. The following should also be consulted:

1 Birtles, H: *British government services for exporters*, ASLIB *Proceedings*, July 1962, *pp* 186-190.
2 Burkett, J and Morgan, T (editors): *Special materials in the library*, 1963. (Contains papers about government publications by K A Mallaber and P R Lewis on *pp* 1-14 and 15-26 respectively.)
3 Staveley, R and Piggott, M (editors): *Government information and the research worker*, second edition, 1965, 267 *pp*. (Many chapters are very helpful, especially those on the Board of Trade and Ministry of Labour.)
4 A concise list of some basic documents relating to Britain and the European Economic Community is given in the *Library Association record*'s inset *Liaison*, July 1967, *p* 56.

4*

CHAPTER NINE

SOURCES OF INFORMATION ON ECONOMIC STATISTICS

IN CONSIDERING THE publications of the British government and of
international organisations, we have so far deliberately ignored those
which are solely, or primarily, statistical in nature. A full survey of
publications must include these, just as a complete view of periodicals
used by economists must necessarily comprehend, in addition to
examples given in chapter six, titles such as the *Board of Trade
journal,* the *Ministry of Labour gazette* and the statistical journals
of the present chapter. Yet there is such a wide range of economic
statistics, national and international, and they can be used for such
a variety of tasks, that it is worthwhile to devote a chapter exclusively
to a brief discussion of the leading statistical publications and series.

The economic historian will be interested in statistical compendia
which take us back over many years or even centuries, while other
economists and businessmen will need statistics which throw light
upon comparatively recent trends in wages, employment, investment,
population expansion, manufactures, marketing, trading figures,
tariffs and so forth; the exact emphasis must, of necessity, depend
upon the work which the expert concerned is doing, and the needs
of a market research worker would naturally differ from the use made
of statistics by a person working upon, say, regional unemployment
figures. Yet all those engaged in the study of economic events and
problems will find the serial nature of statistics invaluable for measuring economic growth or long term trends and for making comparisons
over a number of years. Most of the statistical series mentioned in
this chapter are concerned with modern developments and most, but
certainly not all, of them emanate from government departments or
other official bodies, their compilation being an important part of the
duties of such organisations.

BIBLIOGRAPHIES OF STATISTICAL SERIES

It is again wise for us to begin by considering the bibliographies
which we need to trace these statistical series, thus controlling and

making readily available in libraries the information which they house. The HMSO lists and catalogues will again be of use and many of the more specialised bibliographies and guides which concern sources of British economic statistics are also prepared and published by our government. They include the Interdepartmental Committee on Social and Economic Research: *Guides to official sources,* a series of compact booklets which indicate the scope of the government produced statistical information that is available and where it is to be found. Examples from the series include no 1 on *Labour statistics,* no 4 *Agriculture and food statistics* and no 6 on *The census of production reports.* A great deal of helpful information is given in these volumes concerning the compilation of the statistical tables concerned and similar to them in scope is the Central Statistical Office pamphlet *National income statistics: sources and methods.*

The above booklets have been published over a number of years, although none of them can be justifiably described as dated. More recent than most of the guides to official sources, however, are HM Treasury: *Government statistical services,* second edition, 1962, and the splendid Central Statistical Office: *List of principal statistical series available,* 1965.

The latter shows that its concern is with economic, financial and regional statistics and, within this sphere, it indicates reference sources for a wide range of statistical information, annotating its entries. It will refer us, to employ some simple examples, to statistical tables relating to agricultural workers employed in various regions, those showing accounts of insurance companies, statistics relating to wholesale prices within the United Kingdom, or those giving details of Britain's current position in relation to the International Monetary Fund. Since its publication, we have needed the Treasury volume more rarely in our efforts to help the economic statistician.

Another work, more general in character, which might be consulted is Kendall, M G: *Sources and nature of the statistics of the United Kingdom,* which is in two volumes, these being published in 1952 and 1957 respectively. They are still of occasional use, although they are now in urgent need of revision and it is to be hoped that the publisher, the Royal Statistical Society, will endeavour to have these volumes brought up-to-date. If, of course, we wanted a much fuller survey of books and articles on statistical problems and methodology rather than references to statistical series, we would turn to another work by the above author, the detailed listing and description that is found in Kendall, M G and Doig, A G: *Bibliography of statistical literature*, volume 1 (1950-1958), 1962; volume 2 (1940-1949), 1965; but it is unlikely that an economist in his professional role would need the bibliography of statistical publications as much as actual economic statistics. Professor Kendall's more substantial work is, nevertheless, a scholarly tool of great potential value to statisticians although unfortunately, as P R Lewis pointed out in discussing how librarians can help specialists in the preparation of bibliographical material, the arrangement and indexing leave a good deal to be desired.

Returning to sources which we would consult to locate series of economic statistics, it might be mentioned that there is a slight, but helpful guide which has many references to published statistical information. This is Fenelon, K G: *Economic intelligence sources*, 1963. At a more specialised level, one could cite the *Guide to sources of statistics in common market countries* which was compiled by the ICI Fibres Division Library in conjunction with the ASLIB Economics Group. It appears in ASLIB *Proceedings*, June 1962, *pp* 163-175. In addition, the librarian could consult the HMSO lists and catalogues for details of pertinent material published by the British government, and some public or special commercial libraries, as we shall find later, compile an index of their own to the statistical data that is available within directories, annuals and government publications in their collections. We can also make use of the very detailed American compilation *Statistics sources*, edited by P. *Wasserman* and others, second edition, 1965. This covers a wide range of topics and, while there is some understandable emphasis on United States literature, the work is truly international in scope and directs the enquirer's attention to the chief vehicles for the dissemination of statistical information of all countries. The official catalogues of overseas governments can be used, together with those of the United Nations and other international bodies, in conjunction with *Wasserman's* guide to provide for the bibliographical control of international statistical information, while the British works previously described offer, between them, a comprehensive picture of our own statistical series.

HISTORICAL STATISTICS

When we examine the statistical publications themselves, as distinct from bibliographies and guides to them, we shall naturally be chiefly

108

concerned with those that impart up-to-date or comparatively recent information. Yet historical facts in statistical form certainly cannot be completely ignored, for the industrial and social historian will need works of the calibre of Mitchell, B R and Deane, P: *Abstract of British historical statistics,* 1962, and Schumpeter, E B: *English overseas trade statistics 1697-1808.* Mrs Schumpeter's work, reprinted in 1960 by Oxford University Press, is important, if relatively specialised; the other work quoted is in some respects even more interesting. It covers many economic themes—production, trade, labour, finance—and its population statistics include estimates taken before Britain's first census in 1801. Most of the statistics given are for the nineteenth century only, but a few refer us back to the early part of the thirteenth century and these are valuable indeed.

ANNUALS, PERIODICALS AND OTHER STATISTICAL COMPENDIA
However, it is the current or near-current series of economic statistics that are most frequently demanded and which, on this account must merit our closest scrutiny. A selection from the wealth of publications housing them must be examined by all students of economics bibliography, with a view to observing the range of data offered and the way in which many series facilitate economic comparisons over several years. Our description begins by surveying the output of the British government and, as the bulk of statistical information is found in journals and annuals issued by appropriate departments, we can ignore parliamentary papers within this province and consider, in turn, the output of the various departments involved.

The Ministry of Agriculture's statistical publications include the two annuals, *Agricultural statistics,* and *Domestic food consumption and expenditure.* The latter is particularly of interest as a publication which can be used by market research workers and other economists with an interest in the changing patterns of spending on food in different regions or in different stratas of society. Ministry of Agriculture statistics also appear in white papers and in the statistical periodicals of a rather general character that are issued by other government departments.

More important in our survey is a review of the wide range of statistical publications that are issued by the Board of Trade. These include:

Report on overseas trade: A monthly journal, providing figures of imports and exports and designed to give a broad pattern of the

nation's trading, employing the UN standard international trade classification, that will in many ways be complementary to the information
provided by

Overseas trade accounts of the United Kingdom: Formerly published as a House of Commons paper with a slightly different title
and format, this monthly magazine has been issued by the Board
of Trade since January 1965. It is now prepared by computer and
reproduced by photolithographic methods. Its object is to provide
a thorough analysis by country and products, with tables which, to
encourage comparison, cite the equivalent figures for earlier years.

Another serial, similar in subject appeal to the above pair, but
published annually by this department, is the *Statistical abstract of
the Commonwealth and Sterling Area*. On the home scene, the
board's statistical publications include *Company assets* . . . , an annual
which classifies by size many large British public companies, but of
greater significance in our studies are the detailed

Census of distribution reports: The latest series of booklet reports
is of the 1961 retailing census, and consists mainly of marketing data
in various areas, shown as a series of statistical tables.

Census of production reports: These are based on the thorough
quinquennial production census conducted by the Board of Trade,
and each pamphlet volume in the series consists of a minute analysis
of a particular industry. There are usually, in each production census,
well over a hundred volumes in all, and the last such count took
place in 1963. The time lag involved in the publishing of these reports,
due to the work involved in their preparation, is often more than
two years. An outline census is, however, conducted annually and
is also reported on, albeit briefly.

On the subject of production, we need to add to our information
by consulting the board's *Business monitor production series*: This
consists of a number of periodical bulletins, each of which is published either quarterly or monthly, to give recent facts about the output of particular products within the United Kingdom. There is, for
example, a monthly bulletin on ' electric lamps ' and a quarterly on
' pens and pencils '. Some sixty bulletins of this kind have been issued
regularly since the series was initiated a few years ago.

Finally, with regard to this important department, we may note the
Board of Trade journal, a weekly which contains, in addition to
other information which has already been commented upon, regular
statistical series giving a wide range of facts on production, overseas

trade and many other matters. It shows every quarter, for instance, figures relating to the completion of new industrial buildings, but each issue carries statistics of some value to the economist.

The voluminous and varied statistical information published by the Board of Trade is only equalled, or possibly excelled, by that of a department devoted entirely to statistical compilation. The Central Statistical Office is the department concerned and its output includes:

Economic trends: This is a valuable monthly periodical, which contains some articles in each issue, usually closely relating to the contemporary economic scene, but which is primarily statistical. The statistics given cover a wide range of themes including prices, employment, finance, and the balance of payments. It is a magazine which, like the *Board of Trade journal* and *Ministry of Labour gazette*, must be held in all developed social science or commercial libraries. It is interesting to note, in passing, that the government pamphlet, *New contributions to economic statistics* (now in its third series, 1964) consists of articles taken from past issues of this statistical journal.

From the same department and equally well known are two other items, *The monthly digest of statistics*, which gives a wide range of tables, many of them dealing with matters vital to the United Kingdom economy and contains, in its January issue, a supplement giving explanatory notes and definitions. Its companion volume is the *Annual abstract of statistics*, which gives some series that are not in the monthly publication and confirms and cumulates the ones which are. It appears during the final weeks of each year and has a wide subject range with a full index; for many years now it has appeared under its present title, but its predecessor, the *Statistical abstract of the United Kingdom* stretches far back into the nineteenth century. These two publications, the *Monthly digest* and the *Annual abstract*, are rather broad in coverage when contrasted with many of the items mentioned in this chapter. They manage to convey a good deal of information, nevertheless, many of their tables being based, as are many statistical series, upon the concept of index numbers. The index of retail prices, still popularly referred to as the ' cost of living index ', appears in them as well as in the *Ministry of Labour gazette* and elsewhere.

For economic planning in various regions, businessmen can now find a great deal of helpful information from another annual volume, entitled the *Abstract of regional statistics*. This has only been published since 1965. The Central Statistical Office also publishes digests of statistics for Scotland, Wales and Northern Ireland. Other publications of the department include a yearbook on *Balance of payments* and a detailed monthly journal entitled *Financial statistics*. The latter was initiated in 1962 as a result of the recommendation in the 1959 command paper commonly known as the Radcliffe Report, to the effect that the publication of more official statistics on banking and money matters was required. This mostly contains tables relating to central and local government finance, stock exchange dealings, interest rates and many other similar matters. Then lastly, as far as the CSO is concerned, we must note *The national 'bluebook' of income and expenditure*, a vital annual source volume to many professional economists, delving into public revenue and expenditure and offering statistics for what, for many years, have been termed macroeconomic problems. More up-to-date figures or, failing these, estimates for some of the themes with which this publication deals may be found in *Economic trends, Monthly digest of statistics*, or *Financial statistics*.

Another organisation finding a place in HMSO catalogues and one which must be mentioned with regard to economic statistics, is the Commonwealth Economic Committee, which issues a valuable series of annual volumes on commodities—*Meat, Fruit* and *Industrial fibres* being examples. The statistical information provided in volumes like these covers many aspects of production, consumption and international trading in these products all over the world, although there is a special emphasis on trade as it affects Commonwealth countries. Details of legislation in various countries which is likely to influence the future pattern of trading in the product concerned are also given.

Very different in character is the work of the department of Customs and Excise, which has already received a brief mention in the previous chapter. We have noted already the Board of Trade's *Overseas trade accounts of the United Kingdom* as an important monthly service which gives summary statistics of the United Kingdom's overseas trading and comparative figures for the previous year. Far more detailed is the vast body of trade statistics laboriously compiled by various specialists and issued by the Customs and Excise annually in five volumes. Full summaries of import and export details appear in volume 1, while the other heavy tomes give a wealth of statistical information of trade with individual countries, items re-exported and other matters. Volume five is perhaps especially interesting and useful on account of its provision and analysis of the foreign trade handled at each United Kingdom port. The title of this detailed statistical guide to trade with other nations is the *Annual statement of the trade of the United Kingdom*. It appears of necessity very slowly, often as much as three years after the end of the twelve month period to which it relates. But some of its information, and much of that in volume five may be cited as an example, is not available elsewhere. Thus where current data is not strictly required and a minute breakdown of the statistics is important, this work may be indispensable in commercial libraries. Other useful publications issued by the same department include the *Statistical classification for imported goods and for re-exported goods*, and, of course, the *Customs and excise tariff* and the *Export list* which were mentioned in chapter eight. These are not statistical publications, but help in the interpretation of trade statistics, while the Board of Trade's *Overseas trade accounts of the United Kingdom* is arranged in accordance with their ' classification ' of commodities.

Moving on in our glance at the statistical output of the various government departments, we come to the publications of the Ministry of Labour. Its monthly gazette regularly provides many useful current statistics, but the department also issues some serials which are purely statistical in scope. These include a quarterly bulletin which has appeared since 1962, entitled *Statistics on incomes, prices, employment and production*, which is proving of great assistance in measuring the effects of economic policies and facilitating national and regional planning; and the annual *Family expenditure survey*. The latter, with its clear demonstration of the amount of consumer spending within different income groups, and by type and size of household, is an excellent sourcebook for many workers within the fields of advertising and market research. (An article on the increased scope of the *Family expenditure survey* appears in *Ministry of Labour gazette*, January 1967, pp 4-6.) It shows the amount spent (usually given as a weekly figure) by different households and is based on an annual questionnaire given to some five thousand families. The marketing specialist will find this, together with the Ministry of Agriculture's *Domestic food consumption . . .* and the Board of Trade's *Census of distribution*, indispensable. Also from the Ministry of Labour comes the valuable analysis of wages in British manufacturing industries that is found in *Time rates of wages and hours of work;* this is another annual that is updated by the recently available information that is disseminated through the monthly gazette.

The Registrar General's work is important to economists also, and

113

librarians must house General Register Office publications on account of their population statistics. Anticipated fluctuations in population trends can have an insidious, sometimes even a dramatic, effect upon the demand for certain products and services. There has been a decennial census since 1801 (apart from 1941 on account of the war) and it gives us a very full picture of changes in the geographical distribution of the population or the structure of industries, for instance. The older census returns can be very useful to the historian, but the current ones are more heavily used. It was decided a few years ago that an interim check on population developments should be made between each census, involving a ten per cent sample of households; such a check was made for the first time in 1966. In addition we have an annual estimate of population and, among the other statistical publications, we may single out the quarterly and weekly returns relating to births, marriages, deaths and infectious diseases. These give much useful, although comparatively broad, data on vital statistics and include interesting forecasts of future population trends; these more frequently issued returns (and there are separate ones for Scotland) are useful in view of the understandable time lag involved in making available the very detailed figures collected at the official population census. A useful by-product of the ten year census, incidentally, is the issuing of an index of place names in England and Wales—a tool which can give valuable support, in reference libraries, to gazetteer information.

Publications of other departments which are of interest to us need only be mentioned very briefly. They include the Treasury's *Financial accounts of the United Kingdom*, this appearing as an annual, as does the Ministry of Power *Statistical digest*. But these and other departments issue, from time to time, statistics of some consequence in the study of problems in applied economics and commerce. One can spend, however, too much time on publications of marginal import; the economic statistics shade off gradually into series which are rarely of value to businessmen or professional economists, and we have already provided sufficient examples of the main government statistical series. The wise student of librarianship will make fuller notes on a number of these, the choice depending partly on availability—although *Annual abstract, Monthly digest, Economic trends, Overseas trade accounts,* and *Statistics on incomes, prices, employment and production* are statistical titles which most well developed reference collections may be expected to possess. If other items, such

114

as the massive *Annual statement of trade,* are available they should, of course, be consulted also.

Some important statistical information on the British economy is, despite the very wide range of pertinent government publications, to be gleaned from other sources. These sources are comparatively few—the quantity and authority of the government produced statistics virtually ensures that—but they exist. Examples that may be cited include the *Motor industry of Great Britain,* an annual published by the Society of Motor Manufacturers and Traders which gives helpful statistics on car production, and the Co-operative Union's *Co-operative statistics,* which also appears annually. There are a number of yearbooks and trade directories which give information of this kind, many of them limited, like the titles mentioned immediately above, to some particular branch of industrial or commercial activity. Experience in reference and information work enables librarians to put the statistical tables which are hidden away in such volumes to good use and some obtain statistics from trade associations.

For our purposes one of the most helpful tools from a non-governmental source is *The British economy: key statistics 1900-1964,* which was published in 1965 for the London and Cambridge Economic Service, this comprising a group of economists and statisticians from the London School of Economics and the Department of Applied Economics at the University of Cambridge. This work can be extremely useful for comparatively recent information, but the long run growth and changes revealed in its tables mean that it can be of great help to the economic historian too; in the latter respect, it may be consulted in conjunction with the work previously cited by *Mitchell and Deane* and with past volumes of the *Annual abstract of statistics* and its predecessor. Many of the statistical tables given have been based on the series appearing quarterly in the *London and Cambridge economic bulletin* which was issued as an inset in the *Times review of industry.*

OVERSEAS AND INTERNATIONAL STATISTICAL PUBLICATIONS

We should collect in our libraries some statistical material relating to economies other than that of the United Kingdom—such as the German *Statistisches jahrbuch,* or the annual *Statistical abstract of the United States.* For older figures on the latter country, there is *Historical statistics of the United States: colonial times to 1957,* which appeared in 1960 and its supplement for the years 1958-1962, published 1965. It was produced by the Bureau of the Census and has many economic statistics. But it is when we turn again to the publications stemming from the international organisations that we really see what a mass of statistical material is available on the world economic situation, on international liquidity, on trade between nations, on the thorough analysis of statistics relating to individual economies and similar matters. These publications give comparative information for a number of countries over a period of time, and are usually set out in a form which encourages year by year comparison. While the statistics can be used for many purposes, it is clear that they must provide us with an exhaustive pattern of changes in world trade, and the means for contrasting economic growth and problems in many lands in what is virtually an internationally understood language.

The statistical publications issued by the United Nations and its various specialised agencies, established by inter-governmental agreement, may be considered first of all. In the last chapter, one of the six principal policy shaping bodies of the UN, the Economic and Social Council, was mentioned, and it was observed that there are also four regional economic commissions. Many of the works to be considered here, however, spring from the United Nations Statistical Office. Its *Statistical yearbook* provides, in subject order, a wealth of information on economic and non-economic themes, the former including figures of national income, prices and wages, the volume of world trade and economic aid given to developing countries. There are detailed indexes and explanatory notes given in English and French. The population figures in this volume, which is not confined to UN member countries and covers some two hundred and fifty nations in all, are supported by the detailed world population survey given in the UN *Demographic yearbook,* while trends in the pattern of world trading are shown in another more specialised annual, the *Yearbook of international trade statistics.* We shall often need an equally detailed but more up-to-date analysis than that provided in these annuals and for this we may turn to the quarterly *Commodity trade statistics,* or, more likely, to the invaluable *Monthly bulletin of statistics,* which provides data on over sixty subjects and from many nations and territories. It includes some special tables illustrating important economic developments and, like the *Statistical yearbook,* it takes great pains to present its information in a form which aids international economic comparisons. The newcomer to the subject field must take great care not to confuse its title with the *Monthly digest* issued by the (British) Central Statistical Office.

The word about presentation of information serves as a reminder that the UN also produces a *Standard international trade classification,* which is used as the basis for arranging several of the statistical tables issued by the UN or other international bodies such as the OECD. In addition, one could swell the number of titles mentioned here by enumerating the various statistical documents of a rather specialised character which are published by the various economic commissions, an example being the Economic Commission for Europe's *Quarterly bulletin of (European) coal statistics.* There are, too, examples of statistics which are collected by the United Nations and issued by commercial bodies, a primary one being the four volumes called *World trade annual,* published by Walker and Company, New York, and covering trade relating to some thirteen hundred commodities and twenty three countries.

To mention every publication of the UN specialised agencies which yields economic statistics would indeed be tedious, but one must draw attention to the data provided in the International Labour Office's *Bulletin of labour statistics,* which appears quarterly, and its *Yearbook of labour statistics.* The International Monetary Fund issues a publication entitled *International financial statistics,* which has justifiably been described as 'the standard source of statistics on all aspects of domestic and international finance'. It is a monthly which is supported by a supplement of the same frequency, *Direction of Trade,* and the IMF also produces a *Balance of payments yearbook.* The World Health Organisation, the International Bank and the Food and Agriculture Organisation also produce statistical publications such as the latter's *Production yearbook,* or its *Monthly bulletin of agricultural economics and statistics.* Finally, the international treaty known as the General Agreement on Tariffs and Trade (GATT) has resulted in the release of much statistical data, most of this appearing in GATT's annual volume *International trade.*

There are also a host of statistical publications which report and contrast economic progress in European countries, apart from those appearing under the auspices of the UN or its agencies. The European Economic Community has, together with the other two European communities, a statistical office which issues a number of important serial publications, among them being the annual *Basic statistics of the community,* the monthly *General statistical bulletin, Foreign trade: monthly statistics* and the quarterly *Foreign trade: analytical tables.* The Statistical Office has devised a special classification to enable statistics to be presented in these publications according to a systematic and regular pattern. There are many similar publications which cover affairs in the ' outer seven ' countries and which are issued by the European Free Trade Association. Both the EEC and EFTA publications are described briefly but well in the bibliography *Commerce, industry and HMSO.*

The other international organisation which really contributes extensively to series of international economic statistics is the Organisation for Economic Co-operation and Development. Its most general monthly statistical bulletin is entitled *Main economic indicators* and is of very great value in commercial and economic libraries. It is reinforced by the very detailed *Foreign trade statistical bulletins.* The latter are in three series—series A shows the trade of OECD member countries by origin and destination; series B, known as 'Analytical abstracts ', breaks down statistics by area and by commodity categories; series C is also based on a commodity analysis. This last series appears twice per annum, whereas the bulletins in the other two series are published quarterly.

USING STATISTICAL MATERIAL

In dealing with so great a range of statistical publications—national and international—in such a rapid fashion, one must inevitably receive an impression of a welter of titles with little attempt to describe, let alone to evaluate, the most important statistical series. But the librarian has at least three other problems with which to grapple. One of these relates to the elephantine nature and complex arrangement of many of the statistical volumes; another concerns the task of deciding which of these his own library must acquire and to what extent statistical information can be obtained through library co-operation; the third arises from the fact that the statistical needs of a particular library's clientèle may vary greatly. The student of economics librarianship must recognise that, with regard to the last mentioned difficulty, the approach of statisticians, academic economists, sociologists, investment analysts and market research workers—to single out some potential users of statistics in an economics or social science library—and the emphasis these people place on different publications, will not be the same. The conference referred to below and organised by the Library Association and the

Royal Statistical Society indicates that librarians wish to face up sensibly to these problems (and indeed the joint working party set up by the two organisations has initiated a research project concerning the tracing of economic statistics), but the student will almost certainly appreciate that it is difficult to do justice to the scope and potential of these documents in a single chapter; the reader must examine many of the important ones for himself in libraries and find further information about them in the profusion of published catalogues and guides. The author has already directed his reader to *Commerce, industry and HMSO* for an account of publications of the international organisations and this and other booklets and official catalogues will yield descriptions of many of the British statistical bulletins and yearbooks also. But while the twin operations—scanning the publications and reading about them in bibliographies—should both be pursued, the latter is a poor substitute for the former activity.

Which of these statistical compendia are likely to be subjected to the heaviest usage in British social science and commercial libraries? This question will not admit of a glib answer but certainly, with regard to the output of our own government, a library needing current economic statistics will lean heavily on the series in the outstanding publications of the Central Statistical Office, the Ministry of Labour and the Board of Trade; while, at an international level, for details of production and consumption in many lands and trade figures, we must rely on a selection from the vast and increasing output of the United Nations organisation and its agencies, and the European Economic Community, EFTA and the OECD. But, if a fully developed reference library has a good stock of such publications, many collections must make do with a more modest provision of statistical yearbooks and magazines. In either case, there is still the need for the librarian to be enthusiastic and determined enough to gradually come to know, through experience (and perhaps by judicious indexing of publications by his library) what information the major statistical publications contain and how this data can be put to work in aiding enquirers. It is desirable that the foundation for this knowledge should be laid early and gradually consolidated through work in appropriate libraries. Certainly it is better to be able to describe some of these publications intelligently, if briefly, than to be able to recollect all the titles without appreciating their function; their examination should be conducted with this in mind.

Finally the value and authority of these statistics must once more be reiterated; together with the publications covered in the previous chapter, they mirror the interests of the government department or international body that produces them and some of the statistics on production or employment or prices changes may well prove of tremendous value as the raw material for future economic planning. To quote from the debate following the 1965 conference on librarian-statistician relations, C G Allen of the London School of Economics argued that ' one of the things most needed . . . is an intimate knowledge of what is in various (statistical) publications and what answers we might get out of them '. The person who works, or hopes to work in a library providing an economic information service will find that the labour involved in striving gradually to obtain this intimate knowledge will be well worthwhile.

SUGGESTED READINGS

The Stationery Office lists and those of the international organisations should be re-examined in conjunction with:

1 'A new statistical service on British industry' (Board of Trade Business Monitor) *Library Association record*, March 1962, *pp* 91-98.

2 Howcroft, B: ' Some sources of market research information on consumer products ', in Smyth, A L (editor): *Library Association North Western Group occasional paper* no 4, 1967, *pp* 9-15.

3 Lewis, P R: ' Bibliographical co-operation between statisticians and librarians ', in Mallaber, K A (editor): *Conference on librarian-statistician relations* . . ., 1966, *pp* 57-63.

4 Ross, I G: ' Statistical and other information services ', ASLIB *Proceedings*, June 1962, *pp* 152-162. (This is a useful article and is prefaced by one on the European communities by R Pryce.)

5 A useful work of reference, with several interesting comments and recommendations is the bulky parliamentary paper *Government statistical services*. This was published in December 1966, (House of Commons Paper 246, 1966-67 session).

6 There are two important forthcoming volumes prepared by Joan M Harvey. One is to be issued by CBD Research Ltd and is entitled *Statistics—Europe : sources for market research*. The other, dealing with a wider theme is called *Sources of statistics* and will be published by Clive Bingley Ltd.

CHAPTER TEN

OTHER INFORMATION SOURCES: SOME GAPS IN ECONOMICS DOCUMENTATION

THIS IS THE last of the chapters in this book that is primarily bibliographical in character, and its objects are to deal with some remaining categories of material—these being dissertations, atlases and, more especially, biographical and critical works about economists —and to review the bibliography of the subject with a critical eye and a view to ascertaining how it might be improved. The information sources reviewed here are, it will be noted, a mixed assortment but, although they can all be of value in assisting enquirers and must certainly not be overlooked, none of these three categories of material is really as important as those we have previously examined.

DISSERTATIONS: RECORDS OF RESEARCH IN PROGRESS

Theses completed or in course of preparation can certainly serve as an important guide to research that is being carried out and records of such work will be of great use in scholarly social science libraries. Such institutions will naturally seek to acquire the lists of dissertations or theses registered at the various British universities and there is also the annual ASLIB publication *Index to theses accepted for higher degrees in Great Britain and Ireland*. Resources in this respect are not as extensive in Britain as they are in the USA where, in addition to Traweeks' *Survey of university business and economic research reports,* there is the monthly *Dissertation abstracts*. The latter publication is a record of theses on microfilm, abstracts of theses being submitted by over a hundred and sixty organisations. Each monthly issue has author and subject indexes to the abstracts. Since July 1966, the publication has appeared in two distinct parts, and series A covering the humanities and social sciences gives generous attention to abstracts of theses relating to economics and business administration themes. The other American publication mentioned above is briefly discussed in Davinson's *Commercial information* and the same writer draws attention to the work of the OECD in this sphere. It is one to which, at the international level, UNESCO has also made a contribution.

In Britain we have, apart from the ASLIB index and those published by individual universities, the government's Warren Spring Research Laboratory which records advanced work in progress in the human sciences; yet it is a great pity that the National Institute of Economic and Social Research publication *Register of research in the social sciences* petered out in 1956/57. In its comparatively short life span, this work recorded a great deal of advanced labour relating to economics and kindred fields, and there has been no British annual register of social science research during the last decade to take over its role. The need for an annual record like the now defunct NIESR register is indirectly emphasised in the 1961 report on *Research in the humanities and the social sciences*, which is a record of a survey carried out by the British Academy over the preceding three years. This report stressed that if ' research in the humanities (including the social sciences) decays from neglect or indifference, their whole place in our educational and cultural system will suffer very serious damage '. Attention is drawn to the small amount of government spending in these fields in comparison with other European countries, and it is pointed out that adequate funds for research would only be a small fraction of those needed to promote scientific advancement.

We are not principally concerned here, however, with the fostering of research in social science fields, but rather with the problem of the documentation of the work that is being done; in this respect, it must suffice to say that we need a good annual record of research in progress to support and complement the ASLIB index of theses. The adequate registering of dissertations and research projects in economic and sociological subjects, and the use of such registers in learned libraries, would obviate a good deal of the partial duplication of effort that is still evident in higher research. Such registers can also be of more positive value in that they reveal to the prospective research scholar the kind of project which might be acceptable, or they may stimulate thought, perhaps helping him to mould rather nebulous ideas for a thesis into a more definite shape.

GEOGRAPHICAL WORKS OF REFERENCE

We may turn now to an entirely different published source of information, but one which will also be of great assistance in our field, particularly in providing commercial data. Maps and atlases, as used in libraries within our province, cover many topics, but they certainly have close affinities with commercial intelligence as well as with the

122

social sciences. The maps employed may vary from those of the Ordnance Survey to diagrams of town centres; some commercial libraries may also house maps of a more specialised character, such as the area marketing maps that are published by Geographia Ltd. We are chiefly concerned here with the specialising map or atlas providing commercial or economic information—the main areas in the world where a particular commodity is produced, the major trade routes, the chief suppliers of raw materials, the distribution of a country's industrial population and so forth. Many of the best maps of this kind are, in fact, housed in atlases, and many of the larger atlases that are general in scope offer good facts of this kind. *The times atlas of the world* must be cited in this respect and, for our own country, one could use some of the maps provided in the Clarendon Press *Atlas of Britain and Northern Ireland,* 1963, or in *The readers digest complete atlas of the British Isles,* 1965.

Nevertheless, atlases which are restricted to commercial and economic matters are bound to be required to complement the details given in the more general works. Prepared by the staff of the Economist Intelligence Unit is *The Oxford economic atlas,* third edition, 1965. Part I of this atlas consists of a number of maps showing the production of goods and the pattern of trade throughout the world, plus maps giving details of world communications and demography. Part II, a statistical index arranged alphabetically by country, is a key to the national economic statistics supplied by the maps. The atlas is supported by the volumes of the *Oxford regional economic atlas,* which is appearing in a series of volumes, those for the *USSR and Eastern Europe,* 1956, and the *Middle East and Africa,* 1960, being already available. From the United States, we also have several important specialised atlases of this kind, among them being Kish, G and others: *Economic atlas of the Soviet Union,* 1960, and Rand McNally *Commercial atlas and marketing guide,* the latter being revised annually. Such atlases will be of great value in yielding commercial data and economic information on various regions relating to the areas where certain products are chiefly produced and other similar matters; sometimes indeed they may support the yearbooks and bulletins described in the last chapter by providing us with valuable trading figures and regional economic statistics, as well as trade routes, and they certainly indicate in a striking manner a country's economic character and its dependence on other nations. If, in fact, our library is serving economists and students of economics as well as providing commercial information, these atlases and many more of their kind will be used for a wider variety of purposes; in an academic library, for example, where economic geography features in the university or college curriculum, the employment of both the general and the more specialised atlases may well be heavy indeed. The librarianship student should need no reminding that any collection of maps and atlases (and this is certainly true of those with a commercial or economic emphasis) will need to be supported by gazetteers like the *Columbia Lippincott gazetteer of the world*. Provided that adequate support of this kind is forthcoming, a good collection of atlases and maps will form a most useful part of the material designed to provide an economic information service in libraries.

SOURCES OF BIOGRAPHICAL INFORMATION

The demand for geographical information in our province, which will range from that of the enquirer wanting regional maps of Britain designed to promote market research, to that of the economist studying the pattern of world trade, will be matched by an almost equally varied demand for information of a biographical kind. The academic library, and in many towns the public library, will be called upon to provide critical and biographical works on the lives and influence of the great economists or, in the case of students pursuing management courses, on the pioneers of scientific management. The latter are virtually excluded from the survey of biographical tools that is given here, although it may be mentioned that Heyel's *Encyclopaedia of management* and works such as Urwick, L F: *The golden book of management*, or Urwick, L F and Brech, E F L: *The making of scientific management*, which deals with the management pioneers in the first of its three volumes, will be extremely useful. The articles in *Heyel* will provide a suitable introduction to the more detailed accounts that are to be found in the specialised texts. For economics as such we can extract a good deal of preliminary information from scholarly biographical works of a general character. The great *Dictionary of national biography* has articles on the classical economists, although the bibliographical references that follow them are understandably dated. For an economist like Keynes, we might consult the *Twentieth Century DNB (1941-1950)*, edited by L G W Legg and E T Williams, and published in 1959, for this has a good article on him by his successor as editor of the *Economic journal*, E A G

Robinson. The main DNB volumes can be supported, with regard to references on nineteenth century economists, by *Who was who* and Boase's *Modern English biography;* the latter work, for instance, contains a good account of the achievement of John Stuart Mill. For brief information on contemporary names of significance in economic studies, on the other hand, we might consult general works like *Who's who, The international who's who, Current biography* or the H W Wilson *Biography index.*

The above might be supported by slighter biographical works of a general kind. There are many good volumes of this character and every reference library of reasonable stature will contain a fair share of them. Moreover, much information of a biographical nature seems to be almost ubiquitous as far as reference sources are concerned; thus works which are not primarily biographical may supply facts which help to piece together appropriate details of an economist's life and achievement—a chapter in a composite volume, the occasional periodical article, the obituary in a newspaper or journal—all of these may supply pertinent facts. The sequence of consultation, when the general sources are approached, must necessarily depend upon the approximate dates of the economist and the amount of information that is wanted about him. *Who's who, Chambers's biographical dictionary,* or Hyamson's *Dictionary of universal biography* may suffice for many queries, but there will be several where, if non-specialising biographical dictionaries can be employed at all, we must turn to the *Dictionary of national biography,* or to works published overseas dealing with great lives of the past in a similar detailed and authoritative manner. Yet the other general tools may still be indirectly of some assistance, if their bibliographical references serve to point the way towards more specialised and fruitful sources.

Encyclopedias can yield much information of a biographical and critical kind about great men in the social sciences. The general encyclopedias are far from unprofitable in this respect, but the *Encyclopaedia of the social sciences* and the *Dictionary of political economy* will be preferred to them for most queries. The latter title indeed is excellent as an information source on eighteenth and nineteenth century economists and economic movements. The smaller, more modern encyclopedias and dictionaries may be used too, either for a simpler article or for one on a twentieth century personality in economics. The *Dictionnaire des sciences économiques* and the *Everyman's dictionary of economics* are examples. Again, further possible references may be supplied from bibliographies appended to articles in the dictionaries or encyclopedias we consulted. Occasionally, there will be available biographical dictionaries of a more specialised nature; in the commercial field, the American publications *Who's who in marketing* and *Who's who in insurance* might be mentioned, but their use is rather limited in British libraries because of their understandable emphasis on the current American scene and, in any case, comparatively few British collections may house them.

Yet, if there is a dearth of specialising biographical dictionaries, there are a spate of studies which concern groups of economists and similar thinkers, and many accounts of the lives of individuals who are of the first rank in the progress of economic thought. Among the collective accounts we should note Gide, C and Rist, C: *History of economic doctrines*, second edition, 1948; Gray, A: *Development of economic doctrine*, 1931; Gray, A: *The socialist tradition: Moses to Lenin*, 1946; Heilbroner, R L and Streeten, P: *The great economists*, 1955; Kinloch, T F: *Six English economists*, fourth edition, 1950; Roll, E: *History of economic thought*, third edition, 1954; Schumpeter, J A: *The history of economic analysis*, 1954; Schumpeter, J A: *Ten great economists: Marx to Keynes*, 1952.

Of these, the book that is chiefly the work of *Heilbroner* has already been recommended as an admirable and most readable guide, which ranges over a number of illustrious names and is persistently interesting and informative. *Kinloch*, although slighter, is useful for the information given on the economists with whom it deals; the wording of its title, however, conceals the fact that the six great men include a Scot—Adam Smith! The volumes by Schumpeter, himself an American economist of great note, Roll and Gide and Rist are more scholarly in style and outlook, while Gray, if sometimes controversial, gives a detailed and often stimulating account of the evolution of economic systems and ideas.

BIOGRAPHIES AND OTHER WORKS ON INDIVIDUAL ECONOMISTS

The serious student of economics or of the history of economic thought needs more detailed studies of individuals than the type of work mentioned above. He may have been recommended by his lecturer to consult a particular work on the life and influence of a particular economist, or he may ask the librarian to trace works of this sort for him. The latter task very possibly means the consultation of bibliographies and reading lists, as well as the library catalogue;

it can even involve, as is noted in the last chapter of this book where the preparation of a reading list on an economist is considered as an example of a typical enquiry, some thought being given to the arrangement and presentation of the list of recommended books and articles, so that the task of the reader is made easier. The student librarian is recommended to draw up and examine a list of critical, biographical and bibliographical writings relating to an economist of his own choice, in order to appreciate how to approach a query of this kind. Below, the seven economists singled out for special attention in the introductory chapter of this book are, for the sake of example, listed again in chronological sequence with brief notes on some major writings (other than periodical articles) relating to their life and influence. It is a possible and a valuable exercise to select one of these and to expand and bring up-to-date the list of writings given under his name.

ADAM SMITH: Alexander Gray has produced a useful pamphlet for the Historical Association on Smith, but a standard work is Fay, C R: *Adam Smith and the Scotland of his day,* 1956, while a good biographical study, together with a bibliography, can be found in Pike, E R: *Adam Smith: founder of the science of economics,* 1965. For purely bibliographical purposes, it may be necessary to consult the work of the American publisher Burt Franklin—*Adam Smith: critical writings and scholarship 1876-1950,* 1950.

THOMAS ROBERT MALTHUS: There is a good modern edition of the famous and highly controversial population essay in the Dent *Everyman* series. This was published in two volumes in 1960. Glass, D V: *Introduction to Malthus,* 1953, includes a list of books, pamphlets and articles on population published during the period 1793 to 1880, while Smith, K: *The Malthusian controversy,* 1951, also carries a helpful bibliography.

DAVID RICARDO: We have a detailed and scholarly work which is a definitive edition of Ricardo's writings. It is Sraffa, P (editor): *The works and correspondence of David Ricardo,* and it was published for the Royal Economic Society in ten volumes over the years 1951-1955. It is a very valuable tool indeed; one which, as the American economist George J Stigler puts it, ' seems to breathe precision ' (*Essays in the history of economics,* 1965, *p* 303). There is also, in relation to this economist, Blaug, M: *Ricardian economics: an historical study,* 1958, which has a bibliography, and St Clair, O: *A key to Ricardo,* 1957, plus the work Shoup, C S: *Ricardo on taxa-*

tion, 1960. Neither of the above books, unfortunately, is supported by bibliographical references, but that of the American, Shoup, may be regarded as being of special interest, for it directs attention to an area of Ricardo's writings that has often been neglected. As a purely bibliographical guide, we have the Burt Franklin publication *David Ricardo and Ricardian theory*, 1949.

JOHN STUART MILL: There is a detailed biographical account of nearly six hundred pages which the serious student of Mill's work in economics and in other subject areas should examine. It is Packe, M St J: *The life of John Stuart Mill*, 1954, and it contains a very good bibliography. Two other items on Mill may be mentioned, for they can be used with profit: Cranston, M: *John Stuart Mill*, 1958, is a bibliographical supplement to *British book news*, while a good modern version of the text of Mill's economics masterpiece is Robson, J M (editor): *Principles of political economy*, two volumes 1965, which has a bibliography.

KARL MARX: This controversial and enigmatic figure is well documented; there is even a dictionary devoted to Marx and his influence which the specialist may consult! Some outstanding works to be considered by any economics bibliography student who singles out Marx as an economist about whom he will examine critical and biographical writings are Berlin, I: *Karl Marx; his life and environment* (with a bibliography), third edition, 1963; Cole, G D H: *The meaning of Marxism* (with a bibliography), 1948; Cornu, A: *Karl Marx and Frederich Engels: leur vie et leur oeuvre*, three volumes 1955-1962 (with bibliographies); Kettle, A: *Karl Marx; founder of modern communism*, 1963; Lewis, J: *Life and teaching of Karl Marx*, 1965; Vigor, P H: *Guide to Marxism and its effects on social development*, 1966. Of these, Cole's book is, like all his volumes, eminently readable, while Kettle offers a sound biographical account (although the present writer would consider his sub-title a more apt description of Lenin than of Marx). If available, the bibliographical guide Cornforth, M: *A reader's guide to the Marxist classics*, 1952, should also be consulted. It lists and annotates major writings by Marx and his followers.

ALFRED MARSHALL: Schumpeter gives a good account of Marshall in his *Ten great economists*, but there is also Pigou, A C (editor): *Memorials of Alfred Marshall*, 1925, which includes a bibliography of Marshall by Lord Keynes and several biographical articles. A useful summary of Marshall's teaching appears in Davenport, H J: *The economics of Alfred Marshall*, 1935. Pre-eminent here, of course, must be the modern version of Marshall's principal work which is a variorum edition, showing changes made by the author before a passage reached its final form and material from earlier editions of the *Principles of economics* which did not appear in its eighth edition. This is Guillebaud, C W (editor): *Alfred Marshall's ' Principles of economics '* ninth, variorum, edition, two volumes, 1961. It has been prepared with great care and scholarship by the nephew of the famous economist and was published by Macmillan on behalf of the Royal Economic Society. A feature is the inclusion of some of Marshall's extant manuscript material pertaining to this economics classic.

JOHN MAYNARD KEYNES: Keynes, with the possible exception of Marx, must be the most written about economist considered here, especially if one discounts the books which give most attention to the achievements of a writer like Mill in subjects other than economics. This is partly because he is an economist who is comparatively near to our own time, but partly also on account of the tremendous impact which he has made both upon practical affairs and on the rethinking of economic principles. The librarian may also find it noteworthy that, despite his many activities, Keynes himself found bibliography a worthwhile study and considered the compilation of systematic bibliographies to be an important and necessary task; his brother, Geoffrey Keynes is renowned as a bibliographer. The standard biography of Keynes is Harrod, R: *The life of J M Keynes,* 1951, while, among the many expositions of his work, and particularly the ideas expressed in his 1936 book, the *General theory of employment, interest and money,* we may cite Dillard, D: *The economics of John Maynard Keynes,* 1948; Hansen, A: *A guide to Keynes,* 1953; Harris, S E (editor): *The new economics,* 1948 (with a bibliography); Harris, S E: *John Maynard Keynes: economist and policymaker,* 1955; Lekachman, R (editor): *Keynes' general theory,* 1964; Lekachman, R: *The age of Keynes,* 1967. The above all view Keynesian economics in a favourable light and there are many other appreciative studies, several of them coming from writers in the United States. *Index of economic journals* will reveal many periodical articles which likewise emphasise the importance of Keynesian economics. There is, however, a minority school of thought, which maintains that Keynes' ideas are often either false or lacking in originality. Three works which belong to this category are Hazlitt, H: *The*

129

failure of the new economics, 1959; Hazlitt, H (editor): *The critics of Keynesian economics*, 1960; Hutt, W H: *Keynesianism: retrospect and prospect*, 1963.

Although ample space has now been devoted to biographical works, there are naturally many others, as indeed there are many more great economists. Sometimes, too, the best bibliographies of an economist are to be found in a catalogue of a special collection devoted to the writer concerned; an example in this connection is the University of London Goldsmiths' Library catalogue, published in 1959, of an exhibition dealing with the works of Robert Owen and material about him.

THE VALUE OF THE VARIOUS INFORMATION SOURCES

In reviewing these biographies and bibliographies pertaining to individual economists, we have virtually completed a survey of the published information sources which economists are likely to use, with the exception of some specialised material—trade catalogues and telegraphic codes for example—that is utilised in commercial information work. The emphasis placed on each category of material—bibliographies, periodicals, government publications, directories, theses and so forth, varies from library to library; the academic institution dealing with pure and applied economics and related social sciences, together with historical research, and serving scholars and specialists has a library which is at one end of the scale in this respect; while the public or special library providing a service relating to current economic and commercial intelligence is at the other. But in most libraries within this province of knowledge, all the categories of material are used to some degree. The bibliographical apparatus is needed more and more to organise material effectively for use, for, as Carl M White puts it, ' publications continue to multiply, and acreage for their housing and use expands '. He rightly goes on to point out that it is therefore necessary to marshall the material so that it can be used to the best possible effect in the time available. This problem of being able to extract pertinent information quickly from an expanding store of recorded knowledge is, in a very real sense, an economic one. Librarians seek to solve it by effective classification and cataloguing of items, and by the utilisation of the various categories of bibliographical material. In controlling the literature, to quote White again, ' each type of source . . . has its job to do '. Together with the information services provided by specialist organisations, these published sources dovetail to facilitate ready access to facts and principles concerning economics, management and various commercial activities.

GAPS IN ECONOMICS BIBLIOGRAPHY

It is perhaps natural at this point to review very briefly the present state of bibliographical services for economics and allied subjects, with a view to detecting weakness and gaps in coverage. Among guides to the literature, a revision of Lewis' *The literature of the social sciences* would be welcome, and, with regard to encyclopedias, a revision of *Seligman* would ensure a far more thorough introduction to economic topics than that afforded by the one volume dictionaries published in recent years. In examining retrospective bibliographies of pre-twentieth century items also, we find a certain hiatus between the completion of listing of items in the *Kress Library catalogues* to 1848 and the coverage of items in *Batson's* bibliography or the *Index of economic journals*, although several items from the latter part of the nineteenth century are recorded in the extensive *London bibliography of the social sciences*. The most serious needs at present, however, are surely for adequate guides to research in progress, and the further development of abstracting and current awareness services. It behoves us to consider these two points in more detail.

Research in the social sciences is receiving more and more attention and is being actively pursued by both organisations and individuals; a first class register of work in progress would certainly eliminate much effort which subsequently turns out to be a repetition of ground covered by another. *The report of the Committee on Social Studies* (cmnd 2660: 1965), usually known as the Heyworth committee, recommended the establishment in this country of a government council for social science research, and it seems possible either that this council, now formed, or an organisation like the Ministry of Technology's Warren Spring Laboratory could profitably undertake the compilation of an annual register of advanced social science research of various kinds taking place in the United Kingdom.

It may also be argued that a better standard of abstracting and a much wider range of abstracts is needed within the sphere of economics and indeed for much other social science literature. The increasing emphasis on the retrieval of current and near-current information that is becoming clearly evident in the social sciences underlines the urgency of this task. On the commercial and management side of the subject, there are many good indexes but few abstracting services of real quality, for Anbar *Abstracts*, though excellent, is rather specialised and *Management abstracts* has not the breadth of coverage that one might suppose. The situation with regard to economics in the strict sense of the word is even worse; some important libraries do not subscribe to *Economic abstracts* and, in any case, that publication does not always give the very full emphasis on British and American literature that, in this country, we would desire. Apart from specialised services like *Market research abstracts*, many of the best current awareness services are still to be found in the bulletins of additions issued by major economics and commercial libraries. The International Labour Organisation have shown what can be done by the success of their *International labour documentation;* what is now most needed is a similar service with a wider subject appeal, initiated and financed by a suitable organisation.

It is possible that the need might be met through a change in the character and scope of *Journal of economic abstracts,* or that a British organisation like the Royal Economic Society might take upon itself the burden of launching an abstracting service for economics articles, or one covering both economics and one or two other social science disciplines; the chief drawback is, no doubt, a lack of funds. The history of social science abstracting services has not been a happy one, but it is evident that nowadays, more than ever before, there is a real need for such services, and that if they cover the most appropriate journals and are well presented their reception will be good.

The student of economics librarianship and bibliography, however, may be better equipped to consider the societies and other bodies which might best promote the increase of the librarian's control over social science and commercial literature, after he has read about the major organisations in the field and their activities, in a later chapter of this book and elsewhere. It is certain that, while there is still room for improvement, the documentation of the social sciences has made great strides in recent years. The work done by the United Nations agencies, and especially by UNESCO, to promote such documentation cannot be overemphasised; nor, within this more specialised province, can we ignore the contributions of organisations such as the American Economic Association or the UN Dag Hammarskjöld Library (which is discussed in a later chapter, page 207), and those of a host of individual enthusiasts. If the rate of activity of the past few years and the interest manifested by individuals and organisations can at

least be maintained, optimism is possible over the future bibliographical control of commercial and economics literature.

SUGGESTED READING

Staveley, R (editor): *Guide to unpublished research material,* 1957,
141 *pp* (Section II, the social sciences includes ' Towards the bibliographical control of unpublished material ' by B Kyle; ' Statistical material and sources ' by L T Wilkins; ' Sources in market
research ' by T Cauter; ' The advertising agency and the interchange of information ' by B D Copland; ' Market research in
industrial fields ' by R D Godwin.)

CHAPTER ELEVEN

ECONOMICS AND COMMERCIAL LIBRARIES:
THEIR STOCK AND FUNCTIONS

A VERY VARIED group of collections indeed may be comprehended by the expression 'commercial and economics libraries'. Many of the larger public libraries have separate commercial departments, or a technical and commercial library combined, to serve individual businessmen and local firms, and to answer a wide range of enquiries most of which relate to trade and industry. These libraries will also have textbooks and other material on economics for the trained or student economist, works on modern management problems and techniques, and a number of bibliographies and guides to serve as a key to this literature; these textbooks and bibliographies are not, however, usually shelved in the commercial department. The smaller public library will merge economics, management and commercial items with the remainder of the stock in accordance with the scheme of subject classification that is in use, although there may be at least two sequences of the material—one for reference stock and the other for items which may be borrowed.

A university or college library must put far more emphasis on economics than on commercial documents, and will collect economics textbooks, scholarly journals, and material for the research worker rather than acquiring, for example, commercial directories or trade journals. The special library in this field may serve a government department, a society or an industrial firm and its stock and obligations will be closely defined in accordance with the organisation served; it may well have more concern with commercial intelligence and literature than with economics, but this need not be so. Indeed the emphasis in a library like that of the National Institute for Economic and Social Research would be very different from that of one providing a commercial information service for a large company.

Perhaps the most important distinction to make here is that academic, public and some special libraries will all be concerned to a certain extent in the provision of literature on economics and the other social sciences, while the larger public library and many special libraries will be called upon to provide a wide range of material and services of a commercial nature. The work of both the economics and the commercial library is discussed in this chapter, although there is a certain amount of emphasis on the problems of the latter. This emphasis is partly due to the fact that there are not many economics libraries in the strictest sense of the term, although many very extensive collections give a great deal of attention, or even pride of place, to economic science. As Lewis points out in his book, ' Comparatively few libraries are concerned exclusively with economics, but it is a subject which finds an important place in almost every social science collection.' Nevertheless all the libraries considered here have much in common; they are fundamentally designed to serve (possibly among other readers) professional economists pursuing various specialities, research workers, students, or businessmen and their firms, and though the exact nature of their service may differ, there can be no doubt that in many ways their work overlaps. Thus they can benefit greatly from an understanding of each others' aims and effort and by co-operating whenever possible in the provision of information and documents.

THE PUBLIC COMMERCIAL LIBRARY

We have noted already that in most cases economics textbooks do not find their way into the stock of such a department. They do in Liverpool, where the scope of the library has been extended to embrace both commerce and the social sciences, but this must be regarded as an exception to the general pattern of the provision of public commercial library services. Nevertheless, while a public commercial library is chiefly designed to help the businessman and local industry, there can be no doubt that economists will also find much of the material that they need there—in journals, directories and other works of reference, or in the other specialised material that is available.

The range of information work in a large public commercial department, concerning queries of the ' quick reference ' type is surprisingly extensive. The staff may deal with enquiries involving, for example, the tracing of a list of importers in Australia, the discovery of which British manufacturer uses a certain brand name for paint, the finding of recent periodical publications on supermarket trends, the location of a British merchant vessel, the decoding of a telegraphic address, or the search for financial and other details pertaining to a newly established firm. A few of the questions received will not be specifically for commercial and economic information but will be of a more general character—finding the address of a particular individual, or the provision of a town guide for a businessman or other traveller. Many queries are received by telephone and these days, in some of the more progressive commercial libraries, by telex.

It follows that the staff of such a library should be well trained in reference techniques and be aware of the reader's needs. They will need to know their library's book stock and other information resources thoroughly, for in work of this kind one must usually go quickly to the most appropriate item rather than progress systematically through a chain of reference sources from general to specific. Indeed if a rigid pattern of reference technique could be imposed upon commercial library practice, which it certainly cannot, it would be more likely to follow a specific to general approach; that is, one would consult specialised material first and then broaden the search if necessary. The staff of the public commercial library must, therefore, be given ample opportunity to examine specialised categories of material, apart from those considered in the earlier chapters of this book, and any indexes to them that may be compiled. The junior or trainee librarian who works in such a department should seek to blend the use of his own initiative in reference work with the ability to recognise when the experience of a senior colleague needs to be called in. All the staff will, of course, need to co-operate with colleagues in other departments, and the librarian must liaise with his counterparts in various academic and special libraries in the vicinity as well as with certain other local institutions—the chamber of commerce, the commercial banks and so forth. This latter point is considered more fully in the next chapter.

The usual practice in public libraries has been to combine technical and commercial information services within one department. The emphases of the respective services scarcely justify this for, although there are obvious affinities between items like patents and trade marks, it is obvious that a commercial library will provide an intensive service with regard to some materials—directories and statistical bulletins for instance—which the technical library finds of minor interest; the reverse is, of course, also true. It is financial reasons which dictate the integration of these departments, although those cities which have been large or bold enough to keep them apart have reaped obvious benefits. If, as A L Smyth suggests, ' the time now seems appropriate for expanding existing (public) commercial libraries and starting new ones ', we may find more separate commercial departments in the future.

A very brief word about the siting of a public commercial library may also be of value. It is often to be found in the central building along with other departments, yet in some cities (such as Birmingham) it has proved advantageous to locate it elsewhere, the object being to bring it to the heart of the local business community where the staff of banks, shipping and insurance offices, accountants and many other commercial workers can most readily utilise the services offered. The industrial and commercial geography of a town sometimes justify this practice, but the upkeep of a second library building in the town centre where land sites are heavily demanded tends to be costly and there are, naturally, great administrative advantages in having all the central departments of the library in one building. Often too, where the technical and commercial departments are telescoped into one, it is imperative that the department should be in the main building. To be dogmatic on this matter of siting would be foolish indeed; it is sufficient to reiterate that sometimes the pull of a business centre has dictated policy here, but usually there is either no one centre that is appropriate or else its attractions are insufficient to offset the financial and administrative benefits of having a single central public library.

CATEGORIES OF MATERIAL USED IN THE PROVISION OF COMMERCIAL INTELLIGENCE

As we turn to the stock of the commercial library, we find a very varied range of publications called upon; we are still concerned at this point with the public commercial service, but it should be recognised that many of the categories of material that are to be mentioned and described will be found in special libraries also. The student should note at the outset that there is a strong emphasis upon periodicals, pamphlets (including government produced documents in pamphlet form), on company reports, and on many other kinds of non-book material. Publications of a more substantial kind must not be neglected, however, and the larger government publications, volumes of trade statistics and directories will be heavily employed too.

The well developed public commercial library will indeed provide an extensive range of directories of various kinds. There may be a

137

full stock of British town and telephone directories, many British trade directories, and a good selection of trade and telephone directories dealing with overseas countries. (Manchester Public Libraries estimated that they had 3,750 directories in stock in 1964.) They will be very heavily used by businessmen, exporters and importers, and a host of general readers; many of these people will visit the library for their information, but several will have facts extracted from the appropriate volumes by the staff and given to them over the telephone. Many other reference volumes, such as *Croner's reference book for employers, Keesings* or *Whitaker's almanack* will give yeoman service in this department also, as may dictionaries of commercial terms and bi-lingual dictionaries. But many of the encyclopedias, bibliographies, and scholarly journals are more useful in assisting economists and students of economics, than in contributing to an information service for the businessman; several of them, therefore will be found in the general public reference library rather than in the commercial department.

The range of enquiries answered from directories indicates the value of these works in commercial intelligence. Other heavily used categories are government publications, as far as they concern applied economics and business methods, and including the statistical publications of the British government and of foreign governments and international organisations, and periodicals. The latter will mainly involve the more popular journals dealing with economic news or investment information, periodicals reporting commercial developments in a particular trade, and possibly some management journals. We will thus find titles such as *The economist, Investors chronicle* and the like rubbing shoulders with the trade journals. In addition many commercial libraries will contain issues of house journals—the magazines issued by firms to promote publicity and goodwill for the organisation concerned and to spread news of its activities. Neither trade nor house journals should be overlooked as information sources by staff or users of commercial libraries; the potential of the former in particular can be considerable.

The magazines held must be supported by newspapers. These will include financial and investment papers, such as the *Wall Street journal* or our own *The financial times,* the business insets of the general daily press, shipping papers like *Lloyds list* and the *Journal of commerce,* and possibly papers giving news of economic and commercial developments in other nations, the *Europe daily bulletin* being

138

an excellent example of the latter. *The financial times* is a daily storehouse of news and information on a wide range of matters relating to the current economic scene; it is extremely unfortunate that, for cost reasons, no official annual index to it is produced, although *Research index* or other published bibliographical tools can sometimes assist in tracking down information in its past numbers.

In addition to the items so far described, the commercial librarian must use publications and information sources that have been ignored or only briefly mentioned in earlier chapters of this book. Timetables, for instance, are frequently used in the public commercial library to check details of train or other journeys for both the businessman and the general reader; many such libraries collect too the official guides to large British towns, filing these in A-Z order in boxes and using them to assist readers who want information about a particular town before they visit it. Another most valuable source of information, but one that is entirely commercial in character, is the telegraphic code. This is a work of reference that is still heavily used, despite the popularity of telex, to send coded messages from one firm to another. Examples of well known telegraphic codes include the *ABC telegraphic code* and *Bentley's second phrase code*. The assistant in the library must obviously use these volumes very carefully when decoding messages. Sometimes the enquirer may not know which code has been employed to produce the message he has received, and this may involve laborious checking on the part of the staff, although the number of letters in the code words can provide a partial clue.

Trade or brand names frequently form the subject of enquiries in commercial libraries and many directories contain sections devoted to them; examples of such directories were noted in chapter nine. But, in addition, the librarian must use volumes which specialise in this kind of information. The weekly magazine *Trade marks journal* lists new British brand names and marks as they are registered at the Patent Office. This journal follows a classified arrangement and, because of the lack of a cumulative alphabetical index to its back issues, many commercial librarians have in the past compiled their own index to its contents for staff consultation. For some years now, however, an alphabetical index (in the form of flimsy paper slips) has been provided by the Patent Office, and several commercial departments in British public libraries have contributed to it. These slips will be heavily used, but the staff must still be prepared to extract information on trade names from directories, and there are a few directories, such as the *Kompass register trade names of the UK*, or the more specialised *Hardware trade journal register of trade names*, which are devoted entirely to these product names and signs. Sometimes the enquirer may want the name of an overseas firm which uses a particular trade name, and we must call upon a directory such as *Thomas' register of American manufacturers* for this. Or, again, if it is a 'mark' rather than a name that is the subject of the query, a serious problem can arise, for trade marks, unless obviously representing a particular word or accompanied by a word or phrase, have no obvious place in an A-Z index. Usually, however, the demand is for the user of a brand name and the sources described suffice. If they do not, the enquirer may have to pay an agent to search on his behalf and, even so, a few brand names may still be untraceable if they have never been registered.

The businessman is sure to need directories and indexes which will reveal the user of a particular trade name, but two other categories of material employed as sources of information in a busy commercial or economics library are maps and government publications. These categories are very different from trade names and from each other; yet it is one of the features of commercial library service, that a great deal of diverse material must be employed to satisfy managers, exporters, investors, advertisers, market research workers, statisticians, geographers and the host of other readers who may wish to utilise its resources. The public commercial library will thus stock economic and commercial atlases, a wide range of maps as indicated in the last chapter, and will also need government white papers, departmental publications and some publications of overseas governments and the international organisations. Most government publications are in pamphlet form and may well be housed in boxes in a departmental order or grouped in the boxes according to the system of classification in use, as a parallel arrangement with the bookstock. It may be pointed out, nevertheless, that some official publications are much larger—certainly in book rather than pamphlet form—and capable of being shelved with the other books in the library's principal classified sequence.

A primary requirement in the commercial department of the public library service is information on British and overseas companies. A request may be received for financial details of a firm, for facts about its range of products, or for both of these things. *Research index* is again helpful in pinpointing articles in recently published journals or current news items from the press, and, as we have seen, directories such as the *Stock Exchange official yearbook, Dun and Bradstreet's guide to key British enterprises,* or *Henderson's European companies* may be most helpful. They can profitably be supported by a file of the latest annual reports of British public companies if these are available, and by the news-sheets giving company information that are prepared by Moodies Investors Service Ltd, or by the Exchange Telegraph Daily Statistics Service. These sheets give details of directors, authorised capital, dividends paid in recent years and a mass of other information of interest to investors; one of the two services may be found in the fully developed commercial department.

In many such libraries we find too a collection of brochures and pamphlets issued by firms to advertise their services and products. These represent another important kind of non-book material, although a few of these trade catalogues, as they are called, will be in book form. A large collection of catalogues can be invaluable for finding details or even illustrations of manufactured commodities or other near-current data about a company's range of products, and also for historical research if back numbers of the trade catalogues are retained. The value of these catalogues in the latter sphere can perhaps best be gauged by a brief examination of the excellent *Guide to American trade catalogues 1744-1900,* compiled by L B Romaine and published in 1960. Yet it is necessarily the current trade catalogues that must be given priority. Most firms are glad of the publicity afforded by placing their literature in the public commercial library and will gladly send catalogues gratis on request. But the great difficulties in building up a really comprehensive and useful collection of such material in most libraries lie in the need to be highly selective in view of the time and room consumed by it, and the fact that it is constantly necessary to write for revised catalogues and leaflets and to give much thought to their effective arrangement. These factors must not obscure the great potential of trade literature of this kind, although many collections must be restricted to the catalogues of very important companies and those of local firms.

The public commercial library must also use a great deal of other pamphlet literature which will be provided free or at a very low charge by banks, chambers of commerce, the local stock exchange (if there is one) and by other commercial institutions. The joint-stock banks may be especially helpful in this way, distributing booklets, which are extremely informative and well produced, on matters such as exporting, starting a business or taxation problems. Some good examples of these that have been published or re-issued in recent years include Barclays Bank: *Foreign trade;* Lloyds Bank: *Priority target exports;* Martins Bank: *Starting a business in Britain, Finance for farmers and growers, The world is your market: a guide to overseas trading;* Midland Bank: *Setting up in Britain, Trading abroad;* National Provincial Bank: *Services for exporters;* Westminster Bank: *These are your markets.*

The last named title consists of booklets covering some fourteen overseas countries, including Japan, Latin America and most of the Scandinavian lands. The facts and statistics provided free in works like these can contribute a great deal towards commercial intelligence, as indeed do the articles and statistics in magazines issued by these banks. Barclays Bank also issues a journal giving a detailed review of current economic conditions in overseas countries.

Other pamphlet material may include periodicals insets or occasional booklets issued by a periodical or an organisation; examples are the survey of the commercial life of *The City of London,* issued as an inset in the *Stock Exchange gazette* of the 27th January, 1967, the *Board of Trade journal's* supplement on *Free trade in EFTA,* that appeared with the first 1967 issue of that journal, and the report of the 1965 export conference organised and described by *The financial times.* Yet there are many more. The commercial library must make strenuous efforts to acquire them, and may house them in boxes in a classified or other subject order, or may insert some of the smaller ones along with newspaper cuttings into a vertical file. The latter is an efficient way of organising certain forms of non-book material by the use of folders kept in a metal filing cabinet; a picture of the vertical file of cuttings and pamphlets in the Manchester Public Commercial Library appears on the cover of that library's official guide, *Commercial information* by A L Smyth.

There is, therefore, a vast range of material, much of it in pamphlet or journal form, that the public commercial librarian must try to exploit. He will need to compile many specialised indexes to organise his collection effectively, and may use published guides where possible to trace fugitive information sources, although potentially the best of these guides for indicating where statistics, commodity prices and other data could be found—*Verwey's economist's handbook* has not, alas, been revised since 1934, apart from the supplement that was issued three years later. In addition to compiling indexes to sources

142

of prices and statistics, to trade catalogues and other material, the librarian may well record the sources used to trace answers to some of the more difficult queries received. This can be useful in coping with future enquiries and may help the staff concerning the methods to adopt or the items to consult when faced with questions of an exacting nature. Certainly the staff of the public commercial library can never be content to wait for enquiries; if they are not directly engaged in providing information then they will be busy in supplementing, through their own industry in indexing, the published guides to commercial and economic literature.

It must be appreciated that, while the commercial departments of the public library service can be of great benefit to the reader, the general reference and lending libraries will still supply much of the material needed by students of economics, and the management literature that the businessman may require. We should not, therefore, in perusing the nature of public library services, consider only the work of the commercial or commercial/technical department, even though it deals with a wide variety of readers and material and is the most important segment of the public library service from the viewpoint of our subject field.

ACADEMIC LIBRARY SERVICES

We have considered in this chapter so far but one type of library; the detailed description of it can be justified in that much of the material discussed will also be employed in other libraries in the field and need not be reconsidered at length. Yet it is necessary now to turn to a consideration of the distinctive services provided by non-public libraries in the commercial and economic sphere, for these are far from inconsiderable.

The university library may well provide relatively little of the management literature that is accommodated in public libraries, unless it has a special school of business studies. It may also have comparatively few of the trade directories and trade journals that are demanded by the modern businessman. It must, however, be well endowed with social science material, including textbooks and learned journals on the various branches of pure and applied economics, in order to serve the undergraduate and the postgraduate scholar. It should be fortunate enough to have a good stock of overseas as well as British government publications that are of value to economists, and it will possibly be rich in older economic pamphlets, government

143

publications and manuscripts for the research worker to draw upon. Published literature is the raw material for research in the social sciences, especially if it can be supported by certain categories of unpublished information.

The British Library of Political and Economic Science at London University is the outstanding university collection in the field within this country, but many of the provincial universities are also extremely well endowed with literature and bibliographies on economic principles, social and economic history and applied economics. They will usually have good runs of statistical yearbooks and directories and of the scholarly periodicals. The college library will, on a less ambitious scale, be similar in scope and emphasis, placing great stress on modern textbooks and journals, appropriate government publications, pamphlet material and, perhaps, trade catalogues, but not normally supplying the telegraphic codes or foreign directories, for instance, that are a feature of the stock of the public commercial department. In general, college libraries are likely to be less stocked with large sets of periodicals or with other older material than the university collections. Management literature has, to date, been very unevenly reflected in many college libraries, but the new impetus given to higher management studies in this country should ensure that several stocks of textbooks in colleges will in future be as well equipped with these as with the basic texts on economic science.

College and university librarians may be called upon to provide short reading lists on economic themes for certain library users; from time to time this may be attempted by the public library too and, provided that the staff are well aware of information sources and have sufficient subject knowledge to approach their task intelligently, this can be an excellent part of the library service. An entirely different request and one which is quite unreasonable, is that the university, college or public library should buy numerous copies of basic or standard texts. No librarian can justify the acquisition of material which is merely satisfying a demand that students are expected to meet from their own pockets. Not the least objection is that many of these texts are quickly superseded by new editions and become 'dead stock' when examination demand has passed. Some purchasing of multiple copies may prove essential, but the student must himself acquire his key texts and leave the academic or public library to concentrate upon the acquisition of material which he cannot buy, but which is necessary to him.

When we turn our attention to the world of special librarianship, we find that there are many prominent libraries serving government departments, societies, or industrial firms which provide a good commercial and economic literature and information service. Indeed, although the special commercial library has been left until the latter part of this chapter, and although some of its stock is very much akin to that found in the larger public commercial department, it should be recognised that some of the outstanding libraries in Britain within this subject field are specialising ones. Some of them may be similar to academic libraries in that they are designed to help those workers who are carrying out advanced research in economics, but many of them will concentrate primarily on the provision of current economic and commercial facts for specialists in the institution served.

A government department library which has its stock heavily weighted towards the literature of this field of knowledge will offer an information service to professional economists, statisticians and others who work for the department concerned and many of these will be specialist practitioners carrying out advanced work on national income, on regional economic planning or on the application of econometrics principles. The library staff will need to be active in compiling reading lists on specialised branches of economic activity, in answering queries which will usually relate to some aspect of current economic affairs, in providing multiple copies of certain journals (a provision which is fully justified in some special libraries), in acquiring as many copies of new government publications as are necessary, and in ensuring that recent books and periodical articles are brought to the attention of those who are most likely to need them. The exact emphasis naturally differs from one government department to another and the categories of bibliographical material represented in such libraries will be influenced by the organisation's role. The Board of Trade Libraries, for instance, which are described in more detail in chapter 15, have very extensive collections of overseas trade directories, of government publications and of statistical material relating to the economies of various nations.

A library serving a society or research organisation may be performing a function which is partly similar to that of a university or college library. The main categories of material represented in the stock will then be journals, current and retrospective bibliographies, pamphlets, textbooks and government publications. Examples of such libraries include those of the Cotton Board, the Institute of Bankers and the National Institute of Economic and Social Research and, although these serve specialist readers of different kinds, they represent organisations where there is a demand for a first class information service to ensure that the subject experts within the institution are supplied promptly and reliably with appropriate data.

In industry we also find several examples of good commercial and economics libraries, although strictly speaking many of them are information bureaux rather than libraries in the usual sense of the word. It is true that the dissemination of technical information preponderates in most industrial libraries but there are some where the provision of commercial intelligence is more important and several where the economics and commercial information work is an important subsidiary to that of the company technical library. The fallacy that industrial librarianship in Britain is synonymous with technical and scientific literature needs to be exposed for, while a large proportion of the work does undoubtedly belong to these important spheres of activity, the thriving state of the Economics Group of ASLIB testifies to the interest of industry in commercial information. This testimony is supported by the fact that several firms who are not in that group nevertheless do receive a proportion of commercial queries in their library. The industrial library of a totally or partial economic character serves company economists and market research workers who are seeking new outlets for the distribution of the company's products at home and abroad. It also provides management information and literature to various levels of management ranging from company directors to a large number of specialised workers such as personnel managers, purchasing officers, accountants and those responsible for quality control or time and motion study. In addition, some workers in the technical field, such as chemists, may require commercial data like statistics relating to the production or sales of their products, or articles concerning changing trends in the marketing of those products.

The stock of the industrial commercial library gives journals, pamphlets, government publications and possibly other material, like trade catalogues or newspaper cuttings, preference over textbooks in many instances. It contains, however, a reasonable number of books and should be well equipped with appropriate bibliographies and, perhaps, with certain trade directories. The emphasis is very much upon current information (although there are good reasons for the library conserving a firm's business archives, especially if it is desirable for these to remain on the premises) and the librarian must be prepared here, as in all special libraries, to play a dynamic rather than a passive part in the distribution of information. This point is stressed because, although it is frequently made in connection with special librarianship, the student librarian with a public library background often fails to appreciate the steps which an efficient special librarian must take to provide an active information service. This is not to suggest that the reference staffs of public libraries are dormant individuals—far from it! But, in the public library, the clientèle is an extremely large and varied one and the exact needs of all the potential library users cannot possibly be known; the assistant librarian also tends to be sheltered from many of the more difficult aspects of the work by the fact that he can call upon a senior colleague for aid. But, in an industrial information bureau or a small research establishment's library, the young chartered librarian may be *the* librarian rather than one among many. He will come to know the potential and actual readers well, and the reputation of his library as far as information work is concerned will rest upon, to a very large extent, his own initiative and zest for developing and advertising the services. Special library work can prove interesting and rewarding and, while there are not so very many industrial libraries devoted to commercial information work, there are many where it does play a prominent part. Some good examples of firms' libraries with commercial materials and information services are the Dyestuffs and Fibres Divisions of Imperial Chemical Industries, the Market Research Department of the Co-operative Wholesale Society, Marks and Spencers, Metal Box Company, Renold Chains, Shell International Petroleum Company, and Unilever.

PUBLICISING THE COMMERCIAL INFORMATION SERVICE

This chapter has surveyed the work done and materials used in commercial and economics libraries of all kinds, an attempt being made to describe at some length the work of the public library in this sphere and then, more briefly, to comment on different emphases within special and academic collections. Yet there is one point touched upon near the end of the preceding paragraph which deserves some elaboration—the need to advertise economics and commercial library services. Many businessmen have used their public commercial library and commended it to others, and it is clear that the best form of publicity in this, as in other types of library, must be a good service to readers. Yet other avenues need to be explored to publicise the commercial services of the larger public library. These could well include advertisements in the press and by means of posters in the town centre, articles in the journal of the local chamber of commerce, displays of literature at industrial shows or exhibitions and the production and distribution of an information bulletin, book lists on selected themes, and/or a guide to the use of the library. The fact that a Reference and Special Libraries Conference in 1965 was devoted to a consideration of methods of publicising commercial and technical library services, indicates that, despite the heavy usage of such libraries, more could be done to make people aware of their public library's scope as an information bureau, particularly with regard to some of the more difficult problems that can be solved by assistants who possess a good knowledge of the literature.

In the college or special library, the prospective clientèle is, as already explained, usually known or calculable. Here the librarian, if he is to publicise his stock and its information resources, must be prepared to circulate bulletins indicating recent additions or recently published material of relevance which is not in stock but can be obtained comparatively easily. The special librarian may find it worthwhile to invite readers to inform him of any specific topics which are particularly relevant to their work, so that he can supply them regularly with references to newly published documents on this theme; this inevitably proves to be a time-consuming task, but it is most valuable to management or to the research worker. In addition, the librarian/ information officer must be prepared to leave his library to meet the specialists he serves, and to discuss with or even explain to them informally, their information needs. It is this kind of active publicity that can elevate librarianship to the position it deserves to hold in the eyes of the wide variety of experts who can profitably enjoy its services. Such publicity must necessarily be supported by a speedy and reliable supply of facts and literature and all this means hard work, whether in the commercial or the technical sphere or both. But the chartered librarian who is worth his salt will realise that it is only through good staff, a sound and up to date stock and effective publicity that the full information potential of published literature can be disseminated.

There is no shortage of information on commercial libraries, public and special although, unfortunately, it is scattered through many publications. The reader is urged to consult some of the following:

1 Bromley, D W: 'Publicity methods in a commercial and technical library' *The library world*, April 1963, *pp* 282-286.

2 Davinson, D E: *Commercial information: a source handbook*, 1965. (Chapter 14 deals with the work of chambers of commerce and similar bodies. The same author has also contributed useful notes in *The librarian*, March 1959, *p* 39 and July 1959, *p* 114, on bank and house journals respectively.)

3 Hanson, A O: 'Commercial and technical library services in Great Britain' *Special libraries*, January 1955, *pp* 29-38.

4 Henderson, G P: 'Commercial libraries' UNESCO *Bulletin for libraries*, March-April 1963, *pp* 77-81. (See also his earlier article 'Serving the businessman' *The librarian*, May-June 1956, *pp* 87-89.)

5 Hopkins, K: 'Commercial information'. (In *Information work today*, edited by B Houghton, Bingley, 1967, *pp* 43-52.)

6 Lowe, S J: 'The geographer and the commercial library: some unexplored sources' *Manchester review*, Spring 1962, *pp* 251-260.

7 Ross, I G: 'An economic information service to management' (at ICI Fibres Division) ASLIB *Proceedings*, July 1965, *pp* 217-227. (See, too, his paper 'The economics library and information service of an industrial firm' (in K A Mallaber (editor): *Conference on librarian-statistician relations* . . . 1966 *pp* 18-32).

8 Smith, A R: 'Economic and commercial intelligence work' ASLIB *Proceedings*, November 1956, *pp* 252-268.

9 Smyth, A L: *Commercial information: a guide to the Manchester Commercial Library*, 1964, should certainly be consulted. Other worthwhile readings by the same writer include his contribution on commercial libraries in *Five years work in librarianship 1956-1960*, edited by P H Sewell; his chapter on the same theme in the Board of Trade pamphlet *Aids to export* 1961 and the interesting historical article 'Forty years on . . . the (*Manchester*) Commercial library: a retrospect' *Manchester review*, Summer 1958, *pp* 187-192.

10 With regard to the publicising of commercial information services, see the papers in *Selling library services to commerce and industry: the proceedings of the thirteenth annual conference of the Library Association Reference, Special and Information Section*, edited by L R Stephen, 1965, 48*pp*.

It is noteworthy too, in this context, that LADSIRLAC now issue a monthly bulletin giving details of newly published books and articles on commerce and management, in addition to their technical documents bulletin.

CHAPTER TWELVE

ACQUIRING THE NECESSARY PUBLICATIONS:
BOOK SELECTION AND LIBRARY CO-OPERATION

NO MATTER HOW enthusiastic the librarian and his staff are, they will be severely handicapped unless the social science library is able to build up a good stock for the study of contemporary economic analysis and problems, plus a wide range of source material and specialised bibliographies to serve the research worker. Likewise, in the commercial library, the extensive acquisition of the publications described in the bibliographical chapters of this book, and the various types of material just discussed, will be vital to the provision of a fully developed information service. Sometimes, in this latter field especially, the demand for current information can only be met by the purchase of several copies of books, trade journals, or government publications. The whole task of book selection relates, as a consequence, to the working out of a policy suited to the functions of each library and the establishment of priorities within the various groups of readers served.

PRELIMINARY PROBLEMS IN BOOK SELECTION

Selection is governed to some extent by the funds available, and in some instances the amount of space that can be utilised may play a part in the acquisition policy. Equally important, however, are the needs of readers within a particular special, academic or public commercial or socio-economic library. The librarian must not merely think of the size of his budget and the value of published bibliographies in assisting him to select material. He must consider, too, matter such as obtaining and controlling the receipt of volumes of international and overseas trade statistics; the need to purchase a United States government publication quickly if it is to be of real use to the specialist reader as a source of current economic intelligence; and the value of publications which can be obtained gratis, or at a very moderate charge, from numerous organisations—local, national and international. Some bibliographies are reconsidered in this chapter from a book selection viewpoint, yet preliminary questions such as those stated above must necessarily be settled before the use of bibliographical material can be evaluated. It must be appreciated that, in many situations, selection depends as much or more on personal contacts and on a knowledge of the sources from which items appropriate to the library's functions can be traced and obtained, as upon the use of published bibliographies.

USE OF BIBLIOGRAPHIES, CATALOGUES AND REVIEWS
FOR BOOK ACQUISITION

Nevertheless, some bibliographies will be used and they are therefore discussed below. New books can be chosen from current issues of general publications—*The bookseller, British books* and, for the USA, *Publishers' weekly. British book news* may be of assistance too; its annotations are consistently good and sometimes the selected theme for a bibliographical article concerns a branch of economics. More than any other general source of reference, however, the economics or commercial librarian will rely on the coverage of the weekly *British national bibliography* and its cumulations.

While many new publications will be promptly noticed and ordered from the details given in BNB, this does not detract from the value of such specialised sources as the accessions lists of important libraries in the field. Thus economics and commercial libraries in this country may arrange to receive items such as the *British Library of Political and Economic Science: monthly list of additions, New publications in the Board of Trade Library* (twice each month) and, from overseas libraries, lists such as *New publications in the UN Dag Hammarskjöld Library* (monthly) and the *Selected acquisitions . . . of the International Labour Organization,* which is also monthly. In addition to scanning these lists for potential acquisitions, the librarian must use those published bibliographies which list and evaluate newly published books. The ILO is again to the fore with its *International labour documentation,* but the wider scope of the University of Pittsburgh's *International economics selections bibliography series I: new books in economics* may make this, despite the fact that it is a quarterly, the more generally useful tool in choosing new books. The annotations and the grading of material which is found in this latter publication are most helpful and it must be regarded as the best key we have to the current output of textbooks in the United States and, to an increasing extent, the publications of other countries. The series is also helpful for its discussion of new bibliographies and journals relating to economics.

The information gleaned from bibliographies of this kind can be supported by publishers' notices and lists of newly published or forthcoming books; the receipt of such lists helps to pinpoint quickly many important items and to order them promptly; occasionally, too, a visit from a publisher's representative may result in useful information about new books appearing under his firm's imprint. Yet another source of information are the reviews which appear in the scholarly journals and other periodicals on economics. Many of the learned journals are published quarterly and there is thus some delay before reviews of new books appear in their pages. No one, however, who has examined the long and authoritative reviews in journals such as the *American economic review, Business history, Economica, Economic history review, Economic journal, Journal of economic history, Oxford economic papers,* or *Review of economic studies,* can doubt the authority of such assessments, or their value for sifting newly published material and ascertaining its standard and emphasis. The journals quoted above will cover books on pure and applied economics and economic history, reviewing some and listing others as books received, but it must be remembered that several of the better known management journals also offer reviews and, for the field of applied economics, there are good ones in the weekly *Board of Trade journal.*

All the above sources are used when choosing new material, although the exact reliance placed upon any one source must vary from library to library. If intelligent use is made of information found in current bibliographies of a general or specialised character, in library accessions lists, in publishers' leaflets and in the reviews and notices of material that are found in journals, very few books of importance will be missed, and the problem of selecting the best available items in accordance with the emphasis and scope of the library will be partly solved; although it must be remembered that too much scanning of bibliographies and reviews may run up costs in staff time that are out of proportion to the savings made through wiser selection! Nevertheless, a good deal of this work must be done; in addition, copies of books may be sent on approval to the library, a representative may bring a selection of newly published titles with him, or the librarian may visit a large bookshop to examine items. The evaluation of new books from actual examination may prove invaluable, especially if many reviews in the learned and research journals come too late to be of great value for selection purposes. It may be argued that, in a field such as economics, the librarian cannot fully decide on the quality of a book unless he is also endowed with subject qualifications, and that there is some truth in this is hard to deny. But it is yet to be appreciated by many subject specialists that a librarian working in their field and with the necessary initiative and desire to learn can, unless the province is a highly technical one, gradually acquire a great deal of background knowledge and will assimilate, from the very nature of his work in helping readers, many facts about themes of current importance and about conflicting ideas and philosophies. As far as economics is concerned, it must surely be conceded that an information officer/librarian who keeps abreast of the current economic scene through newspaper reading, who knows the major divisions of the field and their relationships, as reflected in his readers' demands on the library, and who has some knowledge of major schools of thought in economics, can at least appraise most volumes for selection purposes.

Nor do specialists always understand that his bibliographical training equips a librarian to apply certain relevant criteria, quite apart from subject knowledge, to book appraisal. Thus, in evaluating a new book on economics, he may look for the qualifications of the author and the position which he holds, the titles of his past publications (one could even, time permitting, check reviews of some of these), and at the introduction and the publisher's summary; the latter, even allowing for commercial bias, will be of some use. Other factors which might help to indicate a book's worth, or possible emphasis and appeal, are the name and reputation of the publisher, the number of bibliographical references and tables and diagrams that are supplied, the quality of the indexing, and the extent to which statistics quoted or references to events within the text are up to date. All these things are, understandably, time consuming to inspect. Yet it is through considering the possibilities of a variety of methods such as these that the discerning librarian can, if necessary, endeavour to learn a good deal about the potential, for his collections, of a new book on economic science.

When the problem of acquisition concerns older, rather than newly published books, the emphasis being on stock revision or stock building, we have a vast range of bibliographies and a wealth of specialised aids to assist us. A social science collection may be improved and extended by using, for selection purposes, the larger cumulations of the *British national bibliography* and its indexes, the *Reference catalogue of current literature*, the *English catalogue of books*, the printed catalogues of large libraries and similar tools. At a more specialised level, the pamphlet bibliographies referred to in chapter four will give a good representative selection of textbooks on economics or on the branch of it with which they deal. The British Council publication *Economics: a select booklist* can be especially useful in this respect, although many of the others will prove of much value also. The more detailed and substantial bibliographies for retrospective searching will undoubtedly be of great assistance to librarians within this context. We must make good use, for stock revision purposes, of the *London bibliography of the social sciences*, the annual volumes of the *International bibliography of economics*, and the volumes of the *Bibliography on income and wealth*, the latter being generously annotated. One could go further and consult the works of *Cutlip, Batchelor, Stewart and Simmons*, the BIM's *Basic library of management* and, of course, the volumes in *Economics library selections series II*, as it was known, together with the index of publications in the first series covering the years 1954-1962, when the bibliography appeared under the imprint of Johns Hopkins University. These and other tools could all be cited as good examples for use in selecting older books when an intensive stock-building programme is being carried out. Wise readers of this chapter will re-examine many guides and bibliographies to assess their potential contribution to the acquisition of older items in the realm of economics or management literature.

Books published in earlier years may also be added to stock through the consultation of the catalogues and lists issued by booksellers and publishers. Many libraries retain a large number of these because of their scope and value for stock extension. Some outstanding British examples within the economics field include the 1966 *General catalogue of the social sciences* issued by the Economists' Bookshop (a shop, incidentally, which is situated alongside the British Library of Political and Economic Science), the 1966 catalogue of texts on *Economic history* issued by Dillon's University Bookshop (and their lists of recent and forthcoming books on economics and politics can be most useful when searching for new material), and the 1964 catalogue of books on *Industrial organisation and management* issued by a firm which has interests mainly in the medical and technical fields, H K Lewis. From publishers we have lists such as Blackwell's 1966-1967 catalogue on *Politics, economics and sociology;* the Longmans Green catalogues of the same date covering respectively

Geography, economics and related studies, and *Management, commerce, economics and business studies;* and the Macmillan 1965-1966 catalogue of books on *Economics and finance.* There are several others and they are of inestimable worth in revealing forthcoming volumes or which older books are still available and where they may be obtained. From the United States a similar example is that of the Bell and Howell Company showing out of print books reproduced by the duopage method. It is interesting to note that this catalogue contains many items on economics and business, including the Johns Hopkins produced volumes of *Economics library selections series I and II.*

SPECIAL CATEGORIES OF MATERIAL

We have, however, so far considered the choice of material in a manner which might suggest that books alone are involved. This is not so for, despite the importance of developing a rational technique for dealing with the selection of new and older books and knowing where to turn for reviews and lists of them, it is obvious that periodicals, trade catalogues and government publications, for instance, must also be acquired, and usually on a highly selective basis. Certainly in a social science library a good selection of learned journals will be essential; likewise the commercial information library must contain magazines of the type of *Investors chronicle* and *The economist;* also some management periodicals, trade and house journals and British and foreign statistical publications. In commerce especially, the journals are of most value for their current information and news service. Management and economics periodicals may well have a more lasting value and several of them can be almost indispensable for their back numbers as well as for the recent issues. The librarian must be continually on the watch for new ones and be prepared to assess their worth; he must recollect too that existing journals can change their character so much that the utility of subscribing to them needs to be reassessed. As is the case with books and pamphlets, there is sometimes an argument for purchasing two or more copies of journals that are in very heavy demand and cutting down on the number of marginal titles taken; it is impossible to legislate in this matter, for so much depends on the library and the requirements of readers. The exact range of journals held must vary greatly from library to library and, indeed, in large public libraries it is likely that journals of interest to our studies will be split up, some appearing in the technical and commercial department and others in the general reference library.

We have seen already that there are many aids which reveal the range of current economic and commercial journals available; they include general ones like *Ulrich's periodicals directory* and more specialised titles such as the UNESCO *World list of social science periodicals*. Because of the existence of aids of this kind, and because the older copies of journals are often scarce or out of print, the acquisition of back numbers is likely to prove more difficult than surveying current titles and reaching a decision as to which shall be purchased. It is possible to combat this difficulty by using lists of back number holdings that are available for purchase, such as those supplied by Kraus Periodicals Ltd of New York, while another American firm, the Johnson Reprint Corporation, issues catalogues showing reprints of reference works, books and periodicals in several subject provinces, including economics.

Directories create a difficulty in selection because they are relatively costly and usually appear annually; there are problems in ordering them and ensuring that they are regularly received—especially in the case of overseas directories. Yet no library with strong interests in commercial activity can evade its responsibilities for their provision. The amount of money spent on their purchase can be reduced to some degree through the co-operative acquisition of annuals and directories by libraries in a particular locality, or by a library buying a comparatively little-used directory only every second or third year. One could visualise, for example, a situation in which an industrial library in a particular region takes, say, *Food trades directory* each year because its firm has strong interests in some branch of the food industry, while the local public library receives only alternate issues of the work. If it is absolutely necessary to have information from the latest edition, the public commercial librarian can then turn to his specialising colleague for aid, while the company library can seek help from the public commercial department with regard to directories in fields marginal to those in which his firm operates—and this type of co-operation may have helped the public library to acquire more of the latter! There is still great scope in our libraries for the wiser integration of resources in this way; yet even so many libraries in our province must be prepared to expend a good deal of money on yearbooks and directories.

Government publications will usually be chosen from HMSO lists and monthly catalogues or, in the case of older items from the annual catalogues, sectional lists and similar sources; bibliographies issued by the various international organisations must, of course, be scanned also. The *Bulletin of the Public Affairs Information Service* may reveal some useful ones, especially from the USA and other publications may also be traced through this medium. Categories of non-book material such as pamphlets, trade catalogues and maps must also be remembered in the context of selection; trade literature is usually distributed free of charge by firms upon application, and selection here must be governed by space considerations and the amount of time available for the acquisition and indexing of the material rather than by cost. When these catalogues and brochures are received and acknowledged, a request should be made for the library to be placed on the mailing list for new or revised catalogues, if the collection of current trade literature is to be constantly replenished. Acquisition, therefore, involves both writing to firms for their literature and constantly checking to ensure that the collection is up-to-date. The library must also arrange to receive many pamphlets which are often not in the current bibliographies and publishers catalogues, but are donated or issued at a very small charge by such organisations as the Institute of Economic Affairs, the Economist Intelligence Unit, or by local chambers of commerce, banks, or the local stock exchange. Much useful commercial literature and many documents pertaining to applied economics or management can be acquired cheaply, or even at no cost whatsoever, if the librarian is alive to the value of these pamphlets and aware of the organisations from which they can be obtained. Sometimes the booklets and reports which emanate from societies are best traced through scanning the daily press for notices or short reviews.

Before leaving the question of acquisition and stock building, it must again be stressed that selection is needed not only on account of the monetary limitations that control the annual expenditure of most libraries, but because of the need to provide the library users with the best and most relevant material available and, often, to provide this material very soon after its publication. Bibliographies sometimes help the librarian, but he must mould his selection policy around a number of factors—some of which have no connection with the bibliographies or publishers lists, but are inherent in the nature of the demands made upon the library and the categories of material needed by specialists using it. Many items are not added to stock—simply because they are completely unsuitable. It is not, in this respect, works representing a minority or even a slightly eccentric viewpoint that are meant; these if relevant to the library should be acquired, for a social science collection should not discriminate against the unusual branches of economic thought—after all, annotation in the catalogue can reveal the emphasis of such works. The term ' unsuitable ', as used above, is directed towards items which, while excellent in many ways, would not be demanded by the readers of a particular library. User requirements also dictate that most collections should be weeded out regularly and stripped of items which no longer contribute to the efficiency of the stock. Thus selection is a continuing process for, when material is on the shelves, one still has to decide what shall be catalogued, which items shall go in the vertical file and so forth. Certain items no longer of current value can be retained in stackrooms as material of historical appeal, or offered to other libraries, but the open access collection cannot be cluttered up with largely obsolete material if a positive information service is to be provided. This dictum applies to all the subjects in our field, but it has especial force with regard to the literature of many commercial and business activities; the older literature often must be kept, yet it may pay to keep it apart from that used for providing current facts and statistics.

LIBRARY CO-OPERATION: LOCAL AND NATIONAL

Some libraries may be able to employ other ideas—such as the free exchange of publications issued by the institutions they serve—to augment the book selection programme and the policy for the acquisition of non-book material that is outlined here. But we must now turn to the other principal theme in this chapter, which is the need for library co-operation in this sphere. Probably all librarians nowadays would accept Vickery's statement that the time when a library could be self sufficient has gone and that the vital need for libraries to co-operate must be accepted as a law of library science. (See his article in the *Library Association record*, September 1964.) Co-operation is associated with a policy of acquisition in that, if a fully rational system could be developed for the integration of purchasing at a regional level, the amount of material which most libraries needed to buy would be considerably less. Even with the present, in some ways still rather limited, achievement of library co-operation in Great Britain, much saving in this direction has been effected. And it must be recognised that co-operation does not merely mean associated effort in the purchase and interlending of books; it essentially involves also the interchange of information and ideas, and co-operative storage, and it applies to periodicals and the many other categories of non-book material that we have encountered.

The traditional framework of co-operation in Britain involves the National Central Library acting as the co-ordinating centre for the various regional library bureaux. In addition, many important special libraries are designated as 'outlier libraries' of the NCL, and there is much direct inter-lending between university libraries. To what extent the regional system is satisfactory depends a good deal on the success of co-operative acquisition within that region; the better equipped regions are likely to be those which have developed subject specialisation schemes. The London system of specialisation initiated in 1948, in which incidentally Holborn (now part of Camden Public Library) takes books in Dewey classes 380 and 650 and Poplar (now part of Tower Hamlets Public Libraries) takes new British books classed in the 330s, is pre-eminent among these. When the NCL receives a request for a book which cannot be obtained through a particular region, it may try to satisfy this from the stocks of other regions (and union catalogues are available for most of these), or it may turn to outlier libraries, such as those of the Board of Trade.

The piecemeal development of co-operation in Britain has not prevented a certain amount of success being achieved. The large wheel of which the NCL is the hub is reinforced, as far as our own field is concerned by the informal and direct contacts made between various special libraries, by the work of ASLIB's Economics Group and by local co-operative schemes. The chief faults of the main pattern of library co-operation for the social sciences are much the same as those which exist for other subject fields—the process is often very slow and expensive, journals and pamphlet material are difficult to obtain, and certain libraries seek to borrow items they really ought to have bought, thus throwing an unfair load on to the better library collections. The working party on Inter-Library Co-operation in England and Wales, appointed by the Minister of Education, reported in 1962 to the effect that, among other developments, regional schemes of subject specialisation should be developed, that union catalogues should be streamlined to show the holdings of larger libraries and rarer items housed in smaller ones—thus enabling them to be kept up-to-date more readily, and that copyright libraries might lend some material with suitable safeguards. These proposals are not without interest when we consider the present problems of interlending in social science and commercial fields, but they have been overshadowed by the debate concerning the need for a National Lending Library for the Humanities.

The great success of the National Lending Library for Science and Technology has undoubtedly given much impetus to the idea of a parallel institution covering other subject fields, but it must be remembered that the pattern of lending is likely to be rather different in the sphere of economics and commerce than it is in the natural sciences; the stress on periodical literature, for instance, will not be so intensive. As S P L Filon and I P Gibb point out, 'a much greater proportion of requests in the humanities is for monographs than is the case in science and technology where there are nearly as many requests for periodicals as for monographs. The case of the social sciences lies somewhere between the two'. ('Inter-library lending; results of a survey of NCL loan requests' *Library Association record*, August 1966, p 291.) In *Journal of documentation*, December 1961, D T Richnell made out a case for the extension of existing co-operative machinery rather than for the setting up of a distinct Humanities National Lending Library; the present writer is inclined to agree that, at least, the time is not yet ripe for the latter. The greatest co-operative effort so far, within the province of commerce and economics, has been through the development of local schemes and it is a great pity that the co-ordinated plan of 'two tier' subject specialisation in the acquisition of materials in British public libraries, a blueprint for which can be found in the 1942 *McColvin report*, never came fully to fruition, for this essentially rests upon local rather than national initiative and would prevent a huge burden being placed upon a single, albeit vast, institution. However, when the contemporary scene is surveyed, it seems obvious that, rather than further developing local and regional subject specialisation and regional self-sufficiency along the paths envisaged by McColvin, the future lies more in national lending libraries as primary repositories of literature—although regional schemes can do much to augment these. The major problem for a national lending collection in the social sciences and humanities is very possibly, as P R Lewis has suggested, that these fields are not yet documented on a scale which is at all comparable with most of the natural sciences. The National Lending Library at Boston Spa could not function so effectively if its literature was not recorded in various abstracting and indexing services, enabling references to be speedily traced or checked. Meanwhile Dr Urquhart, having stated the case for another National Lending Library, is doing much to help the social science librarian by extending the range of sociological and kindred journals of which his collection has runs. A *Select list of the NLL social science serials* appeared in 1966 and, while it may be explained that the library has always held certain non-technical serials relating to topics that are likely to be of marginal interest to scientists, the intention is to develop the stock of social science periodicals and begin a lending service late in 1967. About 2,000 extra serial titles have been ordered since January 1966 to build up the collections to meet the envisaged demand, and the published select list shows that the library is now quite strong in economics and management periodicals.

Whatever the future may hold for the establishment of a national service of this kind, it is clear that there is, and will remain, great scope for library co-operation at a local level in commercial and technical fields. The Ministry of Technology has recognised the need for local information services by its appointment of regional liaison officers, who are charged with the responsibility of contacting local industry and inviting enquiries. The possibilities for co-operation of formal or informal kind between local public, university, college and special libraries has not, of course, been overlooked; indeed the number of local schemes for the dissemination of scientific and, often, commercial data and for the lending of material now cover many areas and are familiar to most librarians. These schemes usually employ the largest public library in the area as their focal point, but bring in a host of other libraries and, sometimes, industrial firms which have no library but which wish to borrow literature or to obtain information from other members of the co-operative scheme. A system of this kind opens up great possibilities for planned acquisition and storage as well as for the lending of material and the interchange of information. With regard to commercial material and facts, we should remember too that local banks, the chamber of commerce and other institutions may have much to contribute. The chambers of commerce, indeed, are extremely important organisations in the spreading of commercial information, and many of them issue valuable journals; their nature and role should be thoroughly understood.

Returning to the theme of libraries co-operating at a local level, it should be pointed out that several of the existing schemes give due place to commercial and economic subjects. The West London Commercial and Technical Library Service (CICRIS) is, naturally, one of these; others include LADSIRLAC, HADIS, and TALIC. The systems all have some individual features and, while several have an acknowledged headquarters, others do not. In some instances, it is necessary for a firm to have a library to participate, but in other schemes this rule is not introduced. Local initiative must be commended for the institution of such systems and, apart from their obvious functions in making available material and exchanging information between members, they have succeeded in many cases in producing union lists of members' journals or union booklists—an example of the latter being the Huddersfield and District Information Service list of holdings on management. In some cases these schemes have helped to make firms aware of the value of establishing their own commercial and technical information service while the pioneer scheme of this kind, the Sheffield Interchange Organisation (SINTO), did a great deal to persuade the Patent Office some years ago of the need for the issuing of a word index to trade names, an index which is now heavily utilised in commercial information work. Nor should we forget in this context the direct interlending between special libraries and the part played by the visits and conferences organised through the Economics Group of ASLIB in bringing together appropriate specialising information officers.

It is clear that with the NCL and the regional bureaux, the possibility of a National Lending Library (or at least a lending service) for the Social Sciences and Humanities, and the provision of commercial information in depth in several regions through the specially devised local co-operative schemes, we have the essence of an admirable system of library co-operation in our field. Much remains to be done, however. There is still scope for the more intensive pursuit of adequate schemes of subject specialisation in many regions to lighten the load of the NCL, and large special libraries; there is a need to pursue plans for the co-operative acquisition of material from abroad on the lines of the American Farmington Plan; there is also, with regard to economics literature and allied material from the social sciences, the fact to be faced that much of the material has a very long period of utility, and this gives rise to thought of the possible value of co-operative storage warehouses along the lines suggested in the article by H J Harrar in *College and research libraries*, January 1964.

There is also the question of the cost of loans and whether it is sometimes advantageous for the user rather than the material to do the travelling. Yet, despite the fact that some large and specialising libraries are still virtually exploited in our system of co-operation, in that they lend far more than they borrow, inter-library loans and the exchange of information have made a great difference to economics and commercial libraries, as indeed they have to other institutions. Provided interlending is not used to evade the problem of developing one's own stocks and services adequately, it offers the means whereby items can be selected according to a definite and systematic plan and the total resources of many libraries can be increased. The position may improve still further if, at an opportune time, a National Lending Library for the Humanities and Social Sciences can be created; Dr Urquhart once suggested that this might be done by increasing the responsibilities of an existing collection such as the British Library of Political and Economic Science, but it seems likely now that, if this is the road to the establishment of a vast store of social science monographs and periodicals on which all British libraries could draw, it is the stocks of the NLL at Boston Spa that must be extended.

SUGGESTED READINGS

1 Binns, N E: ' Co-operative schemes of library service for industry and commerce ' UNESCO *Bulletin for libraries,* November-December 1961, *pp* 310-316.

2 Maass, E: ' Inter-library loan work at the UN (Dag Hammarskjöld) Library ' *Special libraries,* October 1963, *pp* 517-520.

3 Mallaber, K A: ' Stock provision in the Board of Trade Library ' (in *Some aspects of stock provision,* Association of Assistant Librarians Greater London Division, 1964, *pp* 20-30).

4 Urquhart, D J: ' The NLL and the social sciences, *Journal of documentation,* March 1967, *p* 156.

The paper given at the 1951 LA Conference by B Kyle and A J Walford on ' Co-operation between libraries specialising in the social sciences ' may, although now inevitably somewhat dated, also be of interest and value.

CHAPTER THIRTEEN

ORGANISING THE PUBLICATIONS FOR USE—
CLASSIFICATION, CATALOGUING AND INDEXING

ONE PROBLEM THAT all librarians must inevitably face is that of arranging their literature and keeping an effective record of it. In this way documents containing information on a particular subject may be speedily traced; indeed, if the library is satisfactorily arranged, many of these related items will be conveniently housed together. The larger or more specialised a library is, the more important this principle of sorting and organising its collections becomes. The effective use of economics and commercial literature will demand the application of the well established library techniques of cataloguing and classification, and it will also call for an extensive amount of indexing, a procedure which has really only begun in recent years to receive the prominence and attention which it deserves. An index must be distinguished from the library catalogue in that, while the latter lists and describes publications, mainly books, the index is necessarily a terse record, often compiled only for staff use, of where information can be profitably sought. The multiplicity of indexes, usually subject indexes of various kinds, which are provided in public and special commercial libraries is mainly a reflection of the range of non-book material which these libraries possess.

CLASSIFICATION PROBLEMS

Library classification involves bringing together on the shelves, as far as possible, books and other documents relating to the same specific subject theme and the placing nearby of material on allied themes; if this is accomplished, a search for information can easily be widened or narrowed down. It will be profitable to consider this process and then the technique of orthodox cataloguing, before evaluating the part which indexing must play in serving as a key to commercial information.

Although classification can never be perfect because of the many relationships which exist between subject fields, or because a document itself covers more than one topic, it is an obvious economy in time and effort to utilise all the advantages that can be gained from a systematic subject arrangement of books on the shelves, and several libraries follow the classified order in arranging their catalogue entries also. For organisation of the literature of economics and commerce, a library may follow one of the established general bibliographical classifications, or a scheme which is restricted to the social sciences or to economics itself. Whether a completely general or a specialised scheme is used, the arrangement, if it is to be efficient, needs a certain amount of complexity; the classification of economic science and its ramifications is no easy task. One of the characters in T L Peacock's *Crochet castle* (1831), a political economist, remarks that his speciality can be simply divided into two great classes—production and consumption; he is immediately confronted with the retort that, if this is so, there are two great classes of men also—those who produce much and consume little, and those who consume much and produce nothing!

Political economy, it must be stressed, had many more than two divisions in the early nineteenth century; whatever our views may be regarding the validity of Peacock's comment, we must acknowledge that the classification offered is far too elementary. The modern successor to political economy is, however, much more vast again and many of its sections and sub-sections are intertwined in a very complex manner. The increasing stress on the relationship between economics and the other social sciences naturally tends to aggravate the task of arrangement and thus, as D J Foskett points out in his *Classification and indexing in the social sciences,* the general schemes of classification are now encountering serious difficulties in their attempts to cope with the literature effectively.

It is necessary to consider some of the problems that arise before evaluating the major classification systems for this subject field. One of these stems from the form in which the literature is published. The use of pamphlets, trade catalogues, maps, periodicals, government publications, company reports and other material, in addition to books, means that the librarian must have several parallel classified sequences and, in many cases, must fall back on subject indexing to provide support for the arrangement on the shelves. A brief consideration of two of these categories may serve to illustrate the difficulties involved. Trade catalogues are usually in pamphlet (but sometimes in book) form and they may be housed in a subject order or, possibly, they may be shelved in alphabetical order by the name of the issuing firm; in the latter case an alphabetical index will provide the key to what catalogues are available on a particular topic. In either case, the varied format of the catalogues will cause certain problems in arrangement. Government publications also can be small pamphlets or substantial volumes and their subject matter, even in a specialised economics collection, will range over a large number of themes. It is interesting to note that Professor Ford, in reviewing and describing past parliamentary papers, tells us that to follow chronological, alphabetical or sessional orders in his work would have been unhelpful, but ' conventional subject classifications such as the Dewey or Congress system . . . do not set out the documents so that they tell a story '. He thus attempts, in the volumes of his *Breviate of Parliamentary Papers*, to discuss and summarise the papers in ' broad subject groups in such a way as to exhibit the evolution of the problems and the development of thought concerning them ' (1917-1939 volume, page xii).

In addition to these problems arising from the diverse forms in which material is published and the especial requirements of categories such as government publications, there are other difficulties to be encountered and these stem from the complexity of the subject field. Lewis suggests that social science classification is difficult because of the increasing overlap that is now evident between the various major disciplines, the differences which exist in the aims and emphasis of different specialising libraries, and because the same term may be used with slightly different meanings in different social science disciplines. This last point is echoed by Barbara Kyle and the American writer, J H Shera. It is certain that a greater standardisation in social science terminology would do much to promote the effective classification of economics and kindred social science disciplines. However, the subject encroaches beyond the social sciences in the strictest sense of that term, taking in commercial and entrepreneurial activity and the libraries within this subject field comprehend several examples of both general and specialised collections, ranging over academic libraries with strong social science interests through the public library, which caters for both economics and commerce, to the special library providing an intensive service in commerce, management, or some branch of applied economics.

The cumulative effect of these difficulties—diverse forms of material, imprecision of terminology, and differences between emphasis and depth of coverage in various libraries—means that there is no one classification that can confidently be recommended for the majority of the collections within the broad field of our interests. It is possible, of course, that the modern technique of subject classification through facet analysis, whereby a scheme lists merely basic constituent elements in appropriate categories rather than enumerating compound subjects, might be helpful. Yet, as Foskett points out, these methods are only just beginning to make an impression on social science literature and, rightly or wrongly, faceted classification tends to be associated with detailed arrangement. Some economics documents will demand precision in arrangement, but detailed classification throughout may not be as necessary as it is in the physical sciences. Commercial libraries (and many of the libraries considered in this book have at least a partial interest in commercial documents) have traditionally tended to rely on broad classification. Both Lewis and Kyle have expressed misgivings about precise arrangement and the latter suggested that 'detailed classification is only applicable to factual and precise information which, at present, is only a small proportion of social science literature '.

TREATMENT OF ECONOMICS AND COMMERCE
IN THE GENERAL CLASSIFICATIONS

The extent of these problems may be more precisely understood after the general and special schemes which compete for the favour of social science and commercial libraries have been briefly discussed. It is naturally assumed that the student will use these comments in conjunction with his own examination and appraisal of two or three of the major schemes involved, for first-hand critical assessment is very necessary if problems of classifying economic and commercial literature and the merits of the rival systems are to be truly understood. The best known classification is undoubtedly the *Decimal classification* (DC) of Melvil Dewey, first published in 1876 and now in its seventeenth edition, 1965. It is the most widely used book classification in the world and, although many competent modern critics argue, with justice, that it betrays increasingly its reliance on an outmoded organisation of knowledge, librarianship still lacks a scheme which most general libraries could confidently accept in its place. With regard to the subject field of our own interest, the separation of history and the social sciences at main class level is most unfortunate and, within class 300, there is a scattering of closely related material. Economic theory and history, labour economics,

168

money and banking, taxation and a number of other topics are collocated in the 330 class, but related themes are found elsewhere; insurance, for instance, at 368 and international trade at 382. The commercial subjects, which might well have taken in insurance, are in the applied sciences class. The divisions of class 650 here encompass general commercial practice, management in its various forms, and themes such as accounting and advertising, but the order in which they appear is very unhelpful. To some extent, this criticism must apply to the DC arrangement of economics also. Here the apportionment is often poor, some divisions being overcrowded while others are rarely wanted.

Not all comments regarding DC should be directed to its weaknesses, and it may be remembered that many of the latter arise because drastic reconstruction of class 300 is now impossible. The seventeenth edition gives thirty-nine pages of tables for 330 which, with the addition of the divisions for commercial and management material, should be detailed enough for even a fairly large collection. The scope notes given by the editors, and the frequent use of synthesis, through the instruction ' divide like . . .', are also commendable features. This latest edition has introduced some useful new themes, for example the causes and effects of unemployment at 331.1372 and 331.1373, and some transfers, such as the movement of the International Monetary Fund to 332.152 and the removal of consumer education to class 640. There is, as in the sixteenth edition, an attempt to reflect modern needs with places for themes like Keynesian economics, although the sixteenth edition's useful location for mathematical economics has now disappeared. It must be confessed that there is still no place for several topics of intense interest in the light of recent events in the British economy—capital gains taxation and the freezing of wages, to name but two. The indexing in this latest edition has also proved unsatisfactory in many respects. The conclusion must be that, while some parts of the scheme may prove useful, the classification as a whole cannot be commended to special libraries in the realm of economics, although general libraries with socio-economic or commercial interests may use it on account of the great administrative benefits which can be reaped through its adoption.

The European offspring of DC, designed for the exact classification of specific and complex literature, is the *Universal decimal classification* (UDC). Libraries in this country are most likely to employ the third edition of its abridgement in English; this is published as British Standard 1000A : 1961. The great argument for UDC has concerned the possibility it offers of international uniformity in classification at the documentation level; it also has the benefit of being continually scrutinised and amended by a body of experts. The traditional query placed against it arises from its obvious debt to the fundamentally enumerative structure of DC, plus the fact that it repeats some of the weaknesses of order that are apparent in its American parent. It has been used by libraries in our field, that of the British Institute of Management and some UN libraries, for instance, and is employed in the Dutch *Economic abstracts*. It possesses a tremendous apparatus for exact classification through notational synthesis and the provision of a number of auxiliary signs and symbols, and has striven hard to overcome several of the more apparent limitations of DC. The English abridgement offers places for subjects like the taxation of capital at 336.217 and econometrics and mathematical economics at 330.115, and there is now a considerable difference between the sequence of topics in the economics classes of DC and UDC. Yet, despite the international appeal of the notation, when it was considered for the arrangement of the UNESCO bibliographies in the social science documentation series Miss Kyle decided that it could not be recommended and that a new international scheme for social science literature ought to be created. In recent years, there has been recognition of the fact that UDC ' has lagged behind in the social sciences ' (M Schuchmann: ' The UDC; yesterday, today, tomorrow ', in *Proceedings of the 1964 Elsinore conference on classification research*, edited by P Atherton, 1965, *pp* 113-117). A committee on the UDC social science schedule was formed in 1959 and there have been great efforts to make a full edition of the schedules for class 33 (economics) available. Proposals to merge classes 33 and 38 and to blend 332 and 336 are bound to arouse our interest, and it is plain that UDC wishes to be a modern dynamic scheme, even if this causes a certain amount of complaint from established users who are firmly committed to the conventional order. The conclusion with regard to this scheme must be that, despite the efforts to effect reforms and the international renown of the system, it is facing immense difficulties in emancipating itself from the shackles of the original DC framework. We must assert, rather reluctantly, that this is not really a suitable classification for the arrangement of economics and management literature.

A scheme that warrants close and serious attention is that designed for use in one of the world's greatest libraries, the *Library of Congress classification*. Social sciences and commerce are brought together in its gigantic class H, the largest class in the scheme and one which, like the others, is published separately with its own relative index. The scheme scorns the synthetic approach that is so much in vogue in Britain nowadays, but enumerates topics in tremendous detail, and often makes use of alphabetical order by topic, within a class, if it is considered that further systematic division would be fruitless. The general outline, as far as it concerns us, is as follows:

H Social sciences in general

HA Statistics

HB Economic theory

HC General economic history; economic geography

HD Economic history and development—including agriculture, labour and industries

HE Transport

HF Commerce and business—including topics such as retailing, accountancy and advertising

HG Finance—money, banking, some aspects of taxation

HJ Public finance

and these classes are followed by material on sociology. It will be perceived that classes H-HB are comparatively small, whereas a wealth of detail, no doubt reflecting that of the Congress collections, is found in classes such as HD and HJ. The collocation of economic history and geography is to be commended, especially when one considers how, in DC, this has only been recently achieved. Equally commendable is the association of commercial topics with economic literature, although it must be confessed that, in several libraries of a commercial character, classes other than H, S (agriculture) and T (technology) for example, would also be needed to cope with the material acquired. On the debit side, we have the fact that, while revision is continuously effected through the *Additions and changes bulletin,* the class as reprinted in 1959 still manifests a somewhat antiquated appearance and seems to ignore certain topics pertaining to recent decades; also the notation is awkward in its provision for expansion and the arrangement is often complex. The indexing is good, if unnecessarily repetitive at times. It does not, however, always enable us speedily to trace topics on the border of economic activity that are inevitably located in classes other than H.

The use of this scheme in libraries such as the British Library of Political and Economic Science, the Board of Trade Library, and several universities is a powerful testimony to the fact that it is suitable for employment in British libraries and caters for both commercial and economic interests. It must be concluded that, despite certain archaic traits and one or two examples of dubious order, the scheme will be the best available for many large social science collections.

A challenger in this respect could well be the *Bibliographic classification* compiled by Henry Evelyn Bliss, an American, over the period 1940-1953. It is more exact to speak of BC as being ' published ' during these years, for Bliss's research into classification and his outline of the scheme belong to the earlier part of the century. Class T (economics) is the central one for this field, although some aspects of the subject will be found elsewhere. Bliss was assisted in his labours over the construction of this class by his fellow-countryman, F W Weiler, and by the British classifier, J Mills. It begins with theoretical and descriptive material and takes us through land and industrial economics, business methods, and money and banking to the economics of the state and public finance. Economics and commerce are viewed as an acceptable unity, and the order within class T is to be commended. The introduction to this class is also useful in explaining, rather better than do some economics textbooks, why the old term ' political economy ' became unacceptable as a name for the subject. Places are found in the scheme for some comparatively modern topics —an instance being economic planning.

The weaknesses of this system lie in the all pervasive fault of its doubtful revision policy—despite the energies of Mills and others there is no certainty of a new full edition of the schedules—and a few unsatisfactory separations. It may be asked, in the latter respect, why international economic organisations are under applied social science in class QY? The economic statistician, too, will surely find statistics in class A too far away for his liking. Despite these things, the scheme may be praised, and in BC we have a scheme which is potentially the best classification of a general nature for the social sciences. The order is good, although a special library with a particular emphasis might be inclined to make some slight modifications to it, and the indexing, despite a few minor irritants, is thorough. A number of systematic schedules permit precise classification if needed, and certain themes (economic history is an obvious example) have the requirements of various libraries recognised through alternative locations. Communism, as in LC, is treated as a social ideology not as, alas, in DC and UDC a branch of economic activity. It must, in short, be regarded as the major rival to the Congress classification, although this claim, in part, assumes that plans for its revision materialise.

The other well known general schemes are the *Subject classification* of J D Brown (SC) and S R Ranganathan's *Colon classification*. Of these, the former was last revised in 1939; in spite of some commendable synthetic features for the linking of concepts, it is now almost useless for our purposes. It enumerates, in fact, only sixty six divisions for economics and these include such specialised historical terms as sweated labour and feudal serfdom! SC cannot thus be commended at all nor, although for very different reasons, can CC. This Indian scheme is now in its sixth edition (1960), and a seventh is being prepared. It has reshaped classification theory through the clear recognition of the outstanding possibilities of the entirely synthetic system, but although it groups economic and commercial themes usefully, its class X is in need of expansion and has a strong leaning towards the literature of the East. The only British library employing the scheme has reported that the economics class is difficult to use, and this classification must be thought of as a pointer to the future rather than an effective rival social science classification to the other systems described.

SPECIAL CLASSIFICATION SCHEMES

Many libraries may decide that none of these schemes are fully suitable for their own purposes, particularly if they are specialising in a major branch of economics. The general schemes are bound either to lack detail, to obtain the necessary minute classification only at the expense of cumbersome notations, or to have an emphasis which does not reflect that of either a large library with economic or sociological interests, or libraries providing an information service in the sphere of applied economics and commerce. We find, therefore, that some libraries and bibliographical services are arranged by a scheme of their own devising; British special libraries in this category which may be instanced here include those of the National Institute of Economic and Social Research and the Market Research Library of the Co-operative Wholesale Society, while among important bibliographical tools the *Index of economic journals* uses its own classification, while *Market research abstracts* has been striving to develop a classification and indexing system which will suit its special requirements and the Anbar classification has been recently revised.

It is impossible to legislate in this matter, in view of the diverse functions of economics and commercial libraries, but although the present writer has elsewhere expressed doubts about the wisdom of adaptation, it would seem that for academic libraries the use of DC or LC with some slight modifications is the best solution at present available. Public libraries will almost certainly use DC and its attendant administrative benefits. In some special libraries, however, the adaptation of a general scheme certainly will not do, and the modern technique of faceted classification seems to provide the basis for the construction of appropriate special schemes. Some faceted schemes of relevance include:

D J Foskett: *Occupational safety and health classification.*
B Kyle: *Classification for the social sciences.*
J Mills: *Classification for office management.*
O W Pendleton: *Classification for insurance.*

These, with the obvious exception of Miss Kyle's classification, are too restricted to be used by any library other than a highly specialised one; Foskett's scheme, for example, was made at the request of the International Labour Office. But they may be important to other special libraries in suggesting how effective schemes can be made, and the advantages of an entirely synthetic classification in offering helpful order plus the ability to classify accurately highly specific topics. One might mention also in this context the work of S R Ranganathan and D W Langridge towards the production of a faceted scheme for management, the scheme for demography devised by the Indian B I Trivedi and the proposed expansion of class X of the Colon classification which has been drafted by his compatriot, H C Jain. For our purposes, the Kyle classification (KC) is the most important of these systems, although it does not deal sufficiently fully with the principles of economics to be entirely satisfactory in a library with strong general economic interests. The insistence here on treating the social sciences as a unity and the ingenious retroactive notation are among the major points of appeal. It was designed for the UNESCO International Committee on Social Sciences Documentation, and its use is illustrated in some of the volumes of their annual bibliographies covering major social science disciplines.

More widely known in libraries with business and commercial

174

interests is the Harvard University: *Classification of business literature,* second edition, 1960, and, as this has a strong emphasis on economic principles and affairs as well as commercial matters, it is the special scheme we must consider most fully. Intended for the arrangement of material in the George F Baker Library of Business Administration, the first edition (1937) was chiefly the work of W P Cutter who developed it in conjunction with specialists at the Harvard Business School. In the choice of a basic notation of letters, with numbers as form divisions and another set of numbers serving as a ' local list ' for common geographical subdivision, the scheme resembles the principles behind his more famous uncle's ' Expansive classification '. The business classification is very detailed and, although there is not a conscious attempt to practice facet analysis, it has a strong synthetic element. This is seen in various ways, for example in the form divisions where recurring modes of presentation are constantly introduced in the same way. Thus, in class B (economic theory), an abstracting service dealing mainly with the principles of economics would appear as B.14 (.14 being the form division for abstracts). Numbers representing localities serve as another synthetic device and are added directly to class numbers where necessary, without an intervening point. We have, to quote again a specific instance, ' MD Theory of rent ', ' MD 75 Theory of rent in the USA ' (75 is the local number for the United States). Finally there is a set of industry numbers introduced by a colon. In this third series, the clothing industry is represented by 45 and, as NGE stands for the working week, we could classify the ' working week in the clothing industry ' as NGE : 45. There are also some instances where the instruction ' divide like ' appears in the main tables and permits further synthesis; its use is very much akin to that of the same advice which is so liberally provided these days in the Dewey decimal classification.

The Harvard scheme must be considered as basically enumerative despite these synthetic features. It is specific enough to cope with precise classification of non-book material if need be, has a good index with a wealth of helpful detail, and caters for many topics of great interest to modern economists—devaluation, welfare economics, job evaluation, to name but a few—that have no place in several of the general systems. For these reasons it has been used by some special libraries in the USA apart from the Baker library. Its faults lie in the fact that ' non-business ' topics are herded together in class z, where they are given the appropriate Library of Congress notation, and in the rather annoying decision to publish synthetic tables separately from the main volume. Casellas, in an article quoted at the end of this chapter, believes that the greater detail given to the technical as well as the economic aspects of industries in the Congress system, and the administrative advantages which LC affords, would make it superior to the Harvard system for the arrangement of a marketing library. She may be correct in this assertion; certainly the Harvard business classification has been shaped very much by the Baker library collections. Nevertheless it is an important special scheme which is remarkably up-to-date, despite the lack of regularly revised editions. The major changes in the second edition appear to involve class B (business and economic theory).

At present, it is clear that many libraries of a specialised kind will encounter great difficulty in selecting an appropriate scheme, and it will be interesting to see if more faceted systems are developed in branches of business and economics, and to what extent the Kyle classification may, in the future, be reappraised or revised. A final word on classification must, however, point out that the making of systems for the arrangement of this sphere of knowledge is not the monopoly of librarians and information officers. The helpful grouping of British industries that is provided in the Central Statistical Office's *Standard industrial classification* and the United Nations *Standard international trade classification* with its detailed analysis designed to promote the helpful layout of volumes of trade statistics, are cited to show that within the published literature itself the need for systematic grouping is fully appreciated; the former system is, in fact, used for the grouping of British trade directories in the library of the Board of Trade (where the main system in use is, of course, that of the Library of Congress) while the latter scheme has assisted there in trade catalogue arrangement and in the classification of commodity statistics.

CATALOGUING

The cataloguing and indexing of publications must also receive a good deal of attention; however effective the classification, it can be no substitute for the range of entries offered in a catalogue, and some indexing of the information that lies buried in pamphlets or periodicals may also be essential. Author cataloguing will normally be orthodox, as far as books and pamphlets are concerned, although

176

some simplifications or minor adaptations of code rules may be made. In social science and commercial libraries a subject catalogue of some kind would seem to be essential too and here, as most readers of this chapter will be aware, the choice is virtually between the alphabetical dictionary catalogue, which includes subject entries and references with others in a single alphabetical sequence, and the classified catalogue, which repeats the systematic order of the classification but can provide entries for a book under more than one class number if these are necessitated. Arguments concerning this rivalry may be found in profusion in other texts, but it is necessary to say that the classified catalogue has the advantage of bringing many more allied subject entries together than is possible in catalogues of the dictionary type, that it relies far less on ' see also ' references, and that it obviates many of the terminological problems which, as we have already seen, are apt to be particularly acute in the social sciences. A certain measure of confidence in the classification must be a *sine qua non* in electing to employ a classified catalogue, but if this is rejected we have, as a major difficulty, to contend with changing terminology and ambiguity manifested between certain technical terms used by economists, and the same terms as used by other social scientists.

Nevertheless, some prominent libraries in the field, among them the British Library of Political and Economic Science, do use dictionary catalogues, and this type of catalogue is the established norm in the USA, although one American writer (Alex Ladenson: 'Application and limitation of subject headings ', in *Subject analysis of library materials,* edited by M Tauber, 1953, *pp* 64-72) has pointed out that the subject headings used for social science literature in library catalogues in his country have serious limitations. If a classified catalogue is used, the chain procedure may be employed to ensure that the A-Z subject index collects related material which the classification has separated. If, however, the dictionary catalogue is used, great care must be exercised in choosing headings and adhering to them consistently. The dictionary cataloguer in a large social science or economics library will most certainly need the Library of Congress *List of subject headings* (seventh edition, 1966), and may possibly endorse the working copy to indicate deviations from its practice or the rejection of terms which would not be suitable in a British library. As an alternative to the annotation of the list itself, many libraries will keep their own authority file showing their established procedure with regard to subject heading work. Other published aids must be used also. At a more specialised level are lists such as the Special Libraries Association's *Subject headings for financial libraries*, 1954, and the same organisation's *Subject headings in advertising, marketing and communications media*, 1964. Bibliographies may be helpful in this respect, for if they provide a detailed survey of past literature under alphabetical subject headings, they must necessarily meet the same problems as does the dictionary cataloguer. In various libraries, tools such as *Business periodicals index and Index of economic journals* could be used for this purpose, but pre-eminent in this respect must be the great *London bibliography of the social sciences*, despite the fact that it reflects Congress practice to a large extent. It is virtually a record of the solution adopted for subject headings at Britain's largest social science library, which smaller institutions may use as a guide, making modifications of its great detail as necessary.

Analytical cataloguing is also of interest in our studies, although the amount of it done in social science libraries must, as in many other cases, depend on the number of published bibliographies available which do work of a similar kind. With regard to journals, most libraries will have a good number of these bibliographies; certain books of a composite nature in the economic field may, however, provide scope for subject or author analytics. P A Samuelson and others: *Readings in economics*, which includes such classic writings as the French economist Bastiat's attack on the opponents of free trade; the American Economic Association's series of volumes, which gather together carefully selected key readings on price theory, trade cycle theory, international trade and so forth; the essays on economic history collected by Miss Carus-Wilson; M W Flinn's *Readings in economic history*, 1964—these are examples of economics texts that might warrant judicious analytical cataloguing. In the commercial and management fields examples are more rare perhaps, as information in book form here tends to date rapidly, but in many libraries chapters relating to the management pioneers might be dealt with in this way, and there are bound to be some other items which lend themselves to a similar treatment.

So far, we have really only considered the cataloguing of textbooks or journals, and it has been shown in earlier chapters that an economics or commercial library will contain a very wide range of material other than these. A brief word must be said about the cataloguing of government publications—perhaps the most significant of the other categories from the cataloguers viewpoint, as many specialised types of material must be dealt with through subject indexing rather than by the provision of entries in the library catalogue. Government publications can be traced through official indexes, but these have their faults and, in any case, it may be necessary to indicate clearly by means of catalogue entries which of them are in the library. It is customary and practical to enter the publications of British government departments directly under the name of the issuing department and not under 'Great Britain' or a similar heading. The amount of descriptive cataloguing provided will differ, perhaps considerably, from one item to another; this is probably a reflection of the tremendous difference in length, format and subject content which can exist between different government publications. The catalogue must show too, naturally, which parliamentary papers are held, but many command papers and other substantial pamphlets in this sphere will also call for individual treatment. It will be important to provide entries under the names of the chairman of commissions or committees, if it is at all likely that blue books or white papers might be searched for under these names; thus we might expect an entry under 'Radcliffe' for the 1959 command paper on Britain's monetary policy or under 'Barlow' for the 1939 report on industrial population. Many of the older HMSO indexes tend to be deficient in this respect.

Documents issued by overseas governments and the publications of OECD or the United Nations and its agencies must be catalogued with great care. The idea of entry under country, followed by the name of the issuing department is more practicable for the former than it would be for the publications of the 'home' country. The publications of international organisations are expanding rapidly in number and, even if they are acquired on a highly selective basis, libraries in our sphere are likely to encounter cataloguing problems. With regard to United Nations material, it is probably best to sacrifice collocation to some degree and enter, in author cataloguing, publications directly under 'Food and Agriculture Organisation', 'International Labour Office', or whatever the appropriate body may be. Finally, with regard to all these publications, British and overseas, it is wise to remember that when an organisation or department changes its name, service to the reader demands entry in the catalogue under the latest name or, better still, entry of the publications under

179

the name held by the organisation when they were issued, with references to earlier or later names.

In public, most academic, and some special libraries, the cataloguing will be carried out by specialists in this work rather than by the librarians who are on the staff of the department dealing with economic and commercial literature. But, in any of these institutions, and especially those where commercial information of a current nature is demanded, there will be great scope for the compilation, by those who are dealing with the literature, of specialised indexes. These alphabetical indexes, if a point made in the introductory paragraphs to this chapter can be repeated, will be designed for use by the staff in finding information for readers, and will not possess the formal description of publications and other refinements which usually appear in catalogues intended for the purposes of both enquirers and librarians. The staff of a public or special commercial library might, for instance, compile an index—probably on selective lines—indicating where statistical data may be found in the library. Such a compilation will mean a good deal of labour in checking various British and overseas statistical publications and recording the scope of various statistical series, but it will prove an excellent aid in tracing published economic statistics. Thus if a reader asks for figures relating to, say, the average 1965 earnings of female salaried local government employees, the index might refer the librarian to a source such as the Ministry of Labour quarterly magazine on *Incomes, prices, employment and production*. Such a tool can, if kept up-to-date, be useful to all librarians but it may be especially helpful to those members of the staff who are relatively new to commercial information work. If it proves impossible to build up a full index of this kind, at least information housed in unlikely sources should be indexed.

Other such indexes may include a general index to news items in comparatively ephemeral pamphlets, in *The financial times*, or in other commercial papers; and possibly an index to commodity prices, similar in design to Wasserman's *Guide to USA commodity prices,* 1959, but based on the literature actually held by the library. From the latter type of index the staff may discover that the price of rosewood oil, for instance, is given in the current *Public ledger*, a useful daily bulletin issued by UK Publications Ltd. It is certainly very important that indexes of this kind be maintained as a key to the scope of a trade catalogue collection, if the latter is held in a public or special commercial library. The catalogues are best arranged in some form of subject order, those in pamphlet form being housed in boxes. The librarian will need an alphabetical key to the products and services represented in this subject arrangement plus an index of firms whose catalogues are held. The collection of catalogues cannot possibly be fully utilised unless supported by such indexing. Lastly, we may note too that in some commercial libraries one still encounters staff-compiled indexes to British trade names, which have been meticulously built up over the years to support the information on trade names given in directories, in the days before the Patent Office's service of trade names slips was available.

The value of this indexing should be clearly apparent; sometimes indeed it may be more useful and rewarding than entries in a commercial library catalogue, at least from an information viewpoint. Yet it is also clear that the hours consumed by the compilation and maintenance of indexes of this kind must be considerable. Often, therefore, the indexing of such information as sources of market prices and statistics must be selective and the range of the indexes provided will depend upon staff numbers and pressure of work, as well as on the potential utility of the operation; it may then be necessary to rely as much as possible on published alternatives—*Research index, Fenelon's Economic intelligence sources* or *Keesings contemporary archives* cover some of the ground we have been considering for library indexing, although these may be imperfect substitutes for the indexes that are modelled upon the library's own stock and requirements. In many academic libraries also, several of these indexes would not be made, since the categories of material concerned might not be well represented, the library dealing with pure economics rather than with its commercial ramifications.

A different kind of indexing altogether which has not yet had much opportunity to prove its worth in the province of economics is the technique known as post co-ordinate indexing. This is really intended for non-book material and it involves the analysis of a document's subject into its key terms and the allocation of a series of running numbers to the documents. A card is made out for each of the appropriate terms and the relevant number is placed on these. Information is later retrieved by searching for common numbers, although it is now more customary to find punched cards of the optical coincidence kind facilitating the co-ordination of concepts. Special libraries employing one of the many varieties of this process have sometimes had commercial interests, but have been predominantly concerned with technical literature; it would indeed be interesting to know to what extent a post co-ordinate method of this kind, so called because the cards are filed in alphabetical order of concept and co-ordination takes place only at the time of search, could be successful for information retrieval in social science and commercial subjects. The work of the International Labour Organisation in this sphere has already been mentioned but, within Britain, there are now signs of greater interest in experiments in this direction. The Shell International Petroleum Company have retrieved economic data by this method for some time and now the graduate business schools at London and Manchester have bravely resisted the temptation to adopt an existing classification like the UDC, and are working on the construction of faceted schemes, although at the time of writing these are only at an embryonic stage. They are also contemplating supporting such a system with the post co-ordinate indexing of non-book items; it is clear that, in some respects, co-ordinate indexing and faceted classification are complementary, and certainly the concepts which are isolated for the one may serve as terms for the other. Progress at these institutions must be regarded with keen interest, as indeed must be the work at the British Institute of Management Library, where, as a starting point in the application of such indexing, the contents of *Management abstracts* are being allocated terms and phrases for entry into a retrieval system.

The present writer's interest in the possibilities of these methods for non-technical fields led to the initiation in late 1966 of a project at the Liverpool school of librarianship involving the selective co-ordinate indexing of some fifty journals and many pertinent British government publications. The chief object is to examine the vocabulary problems in spheres where terminology is often ambiguous or vague with a view to assisting in the clarification and eventual solution of difficulties that are likely to arise when, as must surely happen, the process achieves greater vogue in commercial and social science libraries. The periodicals being indexed include both research journals on economics and commercial and management magazines. It is hoped that, during 1968, this index on punched cards will have assumed proportions substantial enough to justify the carrying out of thorough testing. Some liaison is taking place between the school, the graduate business schools and the BIM Library with regard to the compilation of thesauri and the structuring of vocabulary, and this should be of mutual benefit with regard to the elimination of synonyms in management literature, while preventing the library school project from becoming merely indexing *in vacuo*.

It is evident that, while some of the ideas discussed above are inevitably in conflict with each other, the three techniques of classification, cataloguing and indexing all have their part to play in arranging stock advantageously and enabling commercial and economic information to be speedily traced. Their interdependence is revealed by the part that classification can play in the shaping of a systematic subject catalogue or an indexing system's terminology. It should be obvious that, within our province, as in any fluid and expanding area of knowledge, the librarian of a large collection cannot glibly accept or reject conventional methods but, bearing in mind the needs of research workers and all other serious enquirers in economics and kindred social sciences, and the information demands of businessmen, should select for the various categories of material that combination of the three techniques which is compatible with maximum efficiency. Advances in knowledge and the constant introduction of new ideas and phrases are making librarians reappraise methods for achieving the organisation of documents, and it would seem self-evident that an economics or management library should be well to the fore in using the techniques most helpful and acceptable to its readers, and in proving that the librarian is actively concerned with controlling and exploiting efficiently the store of information with which he has been entrusted.

SUGGESTED READINGS

1 Casellas, E: 'Relative effectiveness of Harvard Business, Library of Congress and Decimal Classifications for a marketing collection', *Library resources and technical services*, Fall 1965, pp 417-437.

2 Coates, E J: 'Decimal classification class 300', *Library Association record*, March 1960, pp 84-90. (A thorough critical analysis based on edition 16.)

3 Foskett, D J: *Classification and indexing in the social sciences.* Butterworth, 1963, 190 pp. (Chapters 4 and 7 are especially relevant.) Note, too, his periodical articles: 'Information retrieval in the social sciences', *Wilson library bulletin*, May 1964, pp 755-762; 'Information problems in the social sciences with special reference to mechanisation', ASLIB *Proceedings*, December 1965, pp 328-342.

183

4 Kyle, B: 'Towards a classification for social science literature ',
  American documentation, July 1958, *pp* 168-183. This is supported
  by her critical article ' The merits and demerits of various classifications for the social sciences ', UNESCO *Bulletin for libraries*,
  March-April 1960, *pp* 54-60.
Of the above, Foskett's book is obviously a major source of reference
but these readings must be supported by an examination of classification schemes and lists of subject headings.

CHAPTER FOURTEEN

MAJOR ORGANISATIONS IN THE FIELD AND THEIR WORK

EARLIER CHAPTERS HAVE necessarily referred, often in a somewhat cursory manner, to the work of organisations—local, national and international and the publications that they produce which are likely to be of value to economists or to those with similar interests. We now consider in rather more detail the very wide range of corporate bodies that exist within our specialised area of interest, and the diverse publications and services which they can offer. Several of these bodies are learned and most are highly specialised institutions; as A D Roberts pointed out in his *Introduction to reference books,* their works sometimes escape many of our bibliographies and present cataloguing problems in that they have no personal author. We are concerned with British and foreign societies, government departments and international agencies and their output of publications. Many of the documents and journals which they issue may be of the highest authority, particularly where the organisation from which the publications emanate is recognised as the most scholarly or expert source of knowledge within its own province; thus we must often look to societies and other corporate bodies when considering how the gaps in economics, commercial and management documentation can best be filled.

These organisations are also of great value as specialised sources of information. If a library's resources have only been partially successful in answering a query and the aid of other libraries in the area cannot advantageously be called in, the librarian should consider approaching a local or national body which has interests pertaining to the enquiry, or should put the reader in touch with the organisation concerned. Thus it is legitimate to mention the Board of Trade or even the advice available from commercial banks to the reader wanting detailed information on marketing opportunities abroad, in addition to utilising directories, government documents and other material; or to advise the enquirer who is seeking old documents about the origins of a certain company to contact the Business Archives

Council. Examples such as these could be multiplied, but it should be obvious that societies, apart from their publishing activities, are important for the way in which they can be called upon to supply expert knowledge and advice. Many of them are supported themselves by a good library and information service.

The names of appropriate societies can be traced from various sources; many of them are listed in booklists and pamphlet bibliographies, or both listed and described in guides to the literature. We can find their names and addresses also by using publications like *The world of learning* and the *Yearbook of international organisations* or, at a more specialised level, Allen & Unwin's *Scientific and learned societies of Great Britain* and the UNESCO *International organisations in the social sciences*. It is important that these sources be properly utilised, for when we consider the role of organisations in publishing, organising lectures and conferences, giving advice and disseminating information, it is obvious that we will often need to know the name of a British or overseas body in some highly specialised area of our wide field of interest and be able to locate its headquarters.

In this chapter some important societies and other organisations are mentioned and their work discussed, but it is impossible to be exhaustive in this respect or even to treat fully all the activities of the bodies that are mentioned by name; an attempt has been made, where possible, to make the information given complementary to that found in easily accessible readings—especially Bakewell's *How to find out: management and productivity* and Davinson's *Commercial information;* such texts prove a good starting point for the investigation of the multifarious activities of these organisations.

BRITISH ORGANISATIONS

Beginning with economics as such, the outstanding learned body in Britain is the Royal Economic Society which publishes the excellent, although very advanced, *Economic journal,* and which has fostered the publication of commentaries on classics such as the *Sraffa 'Ricardo'*. From a bibliographical point of view the society is dormant in comparison with, say, the American Economic Association, but it is nevertheless an important organisation which has done much to unite economists and to disseminate information, particularly on economic theory. Other societies in this country which publish journals are the Economics Association and the Scottish Economic

Society; the objects of the latter are stated to be ' to advance the study of economic and social problems in accordance with the Scottish tradition of political economy inspired by Adam Smith and to encourage the discussion of Scottish economic and social problems '. It has been concerned with the reprinting of some Scottish economic texts of importance and issues, three times per annum, its magazine the *Scottish journal of political economy.*

A body which depends for its success largely on the subscriptions of members, but which has contributed a great deal to the literature of economics is the organisation entitled Political and Economic Planning. It publishes reports upon economic and social questions and is particularly concerned with the investigation of problems on which present knowledge is inadequate or totally lacking. Its monthly journal *Planning* devotes each issue to the study of a particular problem or theme and is very useful; indeed, in an economy where more and more emphasis is being placed upon economic control and co-ordination, the whole programme of the PEP is important in the influence of government policy. A different body, founded to increase public knowledge of economics and its application, is the Institute of Economic Affairs. Its publications include the introductory text-book on economics, *Getting and spending,* by J W Roche and G R James, second edition 1965; detailed studies such as R Harris and M Solly: *A survey of large companies,* 1959; R Harris and A Seldon's *Advertising in a free society,* 1959; and the same authors' *Advertising in action,* 1962; also numerous papers such as Sir Sidney Caine's *Prices for primary producers,* 1963, and F R J Jervis: *The company, the shareholder and growth,* 1966, both of which appeared in the regular series known as Hobart papers.

An organisation which should be carefully distinguished from the Institute of Economic Affairs, for the two are often confused, is the National Institute of Economic and Social Research. This body is financed by the subscriptions of interested individuals and organisations and also receives grants from various sources to enable it to carry on the programme of work effectively. NIESR employs research staff and often collaborates with universities in the investigation of economic problems. It publishes occasional papers and detailed studies as the fruits of this research. The more detailed studies have included J B Jefferys' historical investigation, *Retail trading in Britain 1850-1950,* 1954; D L Burn's the *Structure of British industry,* published in two volumes in 1958, an excellent sourcebook on the growth

187

and decline of various major industries; G Routh: *Occupation and pay in Great Britain 1906-1960,* 1965; also published in 1965, *The British economy in 1975,* by W Beckerman and others. Above all, its quarterly periodical *Economic review* has excellent articles and valuable comments and tables relating to the current British economic scene.

Often our interest may shift from those societies that deal with economic principles and practice to those that are more concerned with the historical side of the subject. The Economic History Society, which meets regularly at Cambridge, has promoted much advanced study and research, and is responsible for the production of the invaluable journal *Economic history review.* Historical research pertaining to economics is sometimes reflected in the journal of a body like the Royal Society of Arts and, of course, with regard to the preservation of industrial documents, there is the Business Archives Council, with its brochure giving advice on which items can profitably be retained and its magazine *Business archives,* which appears quarterly.

Returning to organisations that are involved much more with current economic problems, we may note the Economic Research Council, which has been particularly active in promoting the publication of material relating to financial and labour economics and to management problems, and more specialised bodies that contribute to economics documentation. In the latter respect, attention may be drawn to the work of the Royal Statistical Society, which published M G Kendall's *Sources and nature of the statistics of the United Kingdom,* and has co-operated with the Library Association in examining the ways in which library services for economic statisticians can be improved. Almost as important, among the more specialised organisations are the Agricultural Economics Society with its quarterly *Journal of agricultural economics;* the Commonwealth Bureau of Agricultural Economics, which issues quarterly abstracts relating to *World agricultural economics and rural sociology;* the Market Research Society with its valuable abstracting service, plus publications like *Statistical sources for market research 1957;* and the Fabian Society. The last named body is concerned with labour matters and was founded in 1884 to promote research and publish material on democratic socialism. Its name is derived from the fact that it opted for steady and persistent persuasion rather than militant tactics, methods made famous by the Roman general, Fabius Maximus—a great believer in what has been described as 'the inevitability of gradualness'. Economic problems tackled by the Fabian Society concern matters like redundancy and part-time employment and many research monographs and tracts have been issued. Some of the more interesting ones in recent years have come from the Young Fabian Group and they include a study group report on *Womanpower*, 1966, and D Steele's *More power to the regions 1964*.

Other organisations concerned with economics in Britain to some extent include the Acton Society Trust, the Tavistock Institute of Human Relations, the Royal Institute of Public Administration and the Royal Institute of International Affairs. The last named has recently co-operated with PEP to produce publications on economic and other trends in Europe. The interests of these institutions in our sphere of study are often rather marginal, however; of more importance is the contribution made by the universities and other academic bodies. Recently in this context the collaboration of economists and statisticians at the London School of Economics and the Department of Applied Economics at Cambridge University resulted in the publication of a valuable series of economic statistics—a guide to long term trends in the British economy as reflected in statistical tables. The LSE has also been responsible for the reprinting of many valuable older economic works and it issues the journal *Economica*.

In addition, many more colleges are now offering advanced courses in economics while, in the universities, there is more evidence of opportunity to study subjects like market research, and statistical sampling so the training of economists is undoubtedly improving. One academic institution, the Woolwich Polytechnic, has issued a series of economic papers and is to be commended for its initiative in this respect; it is perhaps unfortunate that the research work pursued by students at universities and colleges does not reach a wider public. On the subject of management, it is most important to appreciate that there has been a belated attempt to set up graduate schools of business management in this country along the American pattern and these now exist in London and Manchester. The Oxford Centre for Management Studies which, unlike the two schools just mentioned, is independent of the nearby university, also merits a mention here.

The government departments make a great contribution to economics literature, as we have seen in earlier chapters, and they must be borne in mind as information sources, or potential ones, for enquiries of a more difficult nature; the Board of Trade—for both home industry and export services, the Ministry of Labour, the Central Office of Information and the Department of Economic Affairs can furnish the businessman or specialising economist with facts that are difficult to obtain from other sources. Government literature, it need hardly be reiterated, makes a most important and highly distinctive contribution to our knowledge of the current economic situation; by its very nature it provides much data, statistical and otherwise, that no British society is able to collect and disseminate.

One interesting organisation in Britain that has not yet been considered is the Economist Intelligence Unit; this is a subsidiary company of *The economist* magazine, but it operates independently as an international consultancy service. It provides its clients (who may be individual businessmen, firms, or even government departments) with expert information on many matters, but particularly marketing and statistical topics. It has built up, since its creation shortly after the second world war, a high reputation for value for money. The publications are many, but perhaps especially worthy of mention are the quarterly review *European trends*, the monthly *Marketing in Europe* (designed to help those who wish to export to common market countries), and the publication *Retail business*, also monthly, which gives data of value to overseas companies concerning export markets within the United Kingdom. In addition there are quarterly reviews on economic conditions in a number of countries, notably member countries of the common market and the European Free Trade Association. The reader may also be reminded of the fact that the *Oxford economic atlas* is compiled by EIU personnel.

It is difficult to draw a clear distinction between societies and other bodies concerned with applied economics and those engaged in publishing material and spreading information about commercial activities and management. The Confederation of British Industries resulted from a 1965 amalgamation of three important organisations which, between them, had published many important documents on management and economics. The new organisation is continuing this work and its *British industry week* is a medium for the dissemination of much useful information on exports and other economic topics. The Institute of Marketing publishes some valuable material too, such as the maps and regional statistics of market prospects that are to be found in its *Basic economic planning data*, compiled by E B Groves, second edition 1966. On exporting, in addition to the work of the government's Board of Trade and Export Credits Guarantee Department services, the publications of the commercial banks and those of similar bodies, we have organisations like the Institute of Export spreading information through its occasional publications and, more especially through its magazine *Export*, the Institute of Directors, and the British National Export Council. Another useful magazine on this theme is the *British export gazette*. The Institute of Directors is naturally concerned with many other business and economic matters and publishes the monthly magazine *The director*. The work of these organisations is supported by that of bodies like the Association of British Chambers of Commerce and various professional associations —the Institute of Bankers or the Institute of Cost and Works Accountants, for example, and other institutions like the Advertising Association, which seeks to improve advertising standards and to watch over advertising ethics.

Pre-eminent among the management societies is the British Institute of Management with over 5,000 member organisations and more than 14,000 individual members. Executives in Britain have had the benefit for over twenty years of its reports, pamphlets and conferences and also, of course, of the magazine *Management today* (formerly *The manager*). The BIM also produces the abstracting service *Management abstracts* and awards associate membership, membership and fellowship to those of suitable attainment and experience. It is a non profit making body, supported by the contributions of individual and collective subscribers in the main; meetings and seminars are held and information and advice given, although some of this is only available to the collective subscribers. The latter receive news and announcements in a bulletin entitled *Notes for collective subscribers* and there is also a bulletin circulated to individual members. A good description of the Institute's functions is given by its former librarian, K G B Bakewell, in his book *How to find out: management and productivity*. His account draws attention among other matters, to the important fact that the BIM is the British agent for the publications of the National Industrial Conference Board, an important North American economics and management body.

The work of the BIM, in providing an advisory service to industry and in making management information and progress available, is supported by a number of other British societies. These include the Institute of Office Management; the Institute of Personnel Management, which formerly shared the BIM premises and library services;

the Industrial Society (formerly Industrial Welfare Society); the National Institute of Industrial Psychology; and the British Productivity Council, which publishes a monthly magazine entitled *Target*. Management data is, of course, also available through reliable consultants like Urwick Orr and Partners and, often, from bodies which are primarily technical in nature, such as the Institution of Production Engineers and the British Standards Institution.

INTERNATIONAL SOCIETIES

In any review of organisations it is necessary to consider some international societies or agencies and prominent national institutions from other countries. The British librarian may rarely, if ever, contact these for information, but their importance to him with regard to authoritative publishing is certainly no less than that of the British societies, especially if the documents they issue appear in the English language. Indeed, at times, their publications may be of greater significance than those of our own organisations, because they put a particular matter into international perspective or present a picture of economic conditions in an overseas country in minute detail which could not be equalled by surveys carried out by the British societies and institutions. The United Nations Economic and Social Council and the UN Statistical Office have, over the years, produced a phenomenal number of publications concerning the world economy and the growth rate of individual countries. On specialised aspects of economics, the various UN agencies have published, usually as regular serials, detailed accounts and statistical surveys. The reader should therefore reconsider the output of UNESCO, the International Labour Organisation, the International Monetary Fund, the World Bank, the General Agreement on Tariffs and Trade, and the Food and Agriculture Organisation, in addition to those of the UN itself and, if it is at all possible, re-examine some representative items from their very wide range of published documents. OECD, the European Economic Community and EFTA and their economics documentation programme also merit further appraisal here; in many cases their publications examine economic trends in Europe or offer detailed statistical investigations in an even more intensive fashion than the works of the United Nations and its specialising agencies. Nor should we ignore the achievement of other international organisations; the International Economic Association has done much valuable work in holding conferences, in publishing English translations of important writings in its *International economic papers* and in assisting UNESCO staff in the compilation of the annual *International bibliography of economics*, while the International Bureau of Fiscal Documentation has initiated several important services. This latter corporate body has its headquarters in Amsterdam and its publications include *European taxation*, a monthly journal, and *Guides to European taxation*, two loose leaf volumes, the second of which deals with company taxation in the common market countries; the twice monthly loose leaf *Tax news service*, which reports new taxation developments throughout the world; and the general monthly *Bulletin for international fiscal documentation*. The bureau also publishes specialised monographs and studies. There is, too, the achievement of the International Council for Scientific Management (known as CIOS) and that of the International Association for Research in Income and Wealth to be considered. A number of detailed papers on macroeconomic problems with special reference to income and financial accounting have been published in the latter's *Income and wealth series;* it has also issued papers presented at conferences, for instance the selection of papers studying income and wealth in Asia given at the Hong Kong Conference of 1960, and produces the *Bibliography on income and wealth* that has been described in an earlier chapter.

It would be futile to attempt to describe the work and output of the major economics organisations in the European countries; the reader should, however, seek information on a few of these institutions, perhaps concentrating upon those of one European country. Outstanding societies and other corporate bodies include the French Institut National de la Statistique et des Études Économiques, the German Institut fur Weltwirtschaft and, in Italy, the Istituto di Economia Internazionale. There are many of these organisations and they are often prolific contributors to the documentation of our subject, yet it must be remembered that, within each nation, there is also bound to be a high output of publications on economics and commerce issued by the central government and, to a lesser extent, by banks and by local commercial bodies.

ORGANISATIONS IN THE USA

The study of the achievement of United States organisations is perhaps more profitable, due to their number and importance, the range of their subject coverage, and the fact that their works are in the English tongue and a good selection of them is often to be seen in larger British libraries. Outstanding, from our viewpoint, is the American Economic Association. Its more obvious bibliographic achievements lie in its initiation of the retrospective bibliography of periodical literature, the *Index of economic journals,* its contribution to the *Journal of economic abstracts,* which although produced at Harvard University is published under the AEA's aegis, and the value of the scholarly articles and book reviews found in its *American economic review.* The latter is supported each year by a special issue embodying the proceedings of the association's annual conference. It must be realised too that the association is also active in economics documentation through the *Survey of contemporary economics,* published some years ago; the *Surveys of economic theory,* published in association with its British equivalent the Royal Economic Society; and on account of the volumes which have collected basic readings on major segments of economic activity conveniently into a composite collection—these have already been mentioned as items which may merit analytical entries in the library catalogue. The AEA must be regarded, among national societies which seek to unite academic economists and to promote the study of economic problems at the research level, as the foremost with regard to the initiation of bibliographical services and a documentation programme. It is perhaps natural that this should be true of the most important economics society in the United States, yet it is evident that some of the learned societies in our field in other countries might well strive with profit to emulate the American Economic Association's output and initiative.

Other American organisations which certainly deserve some mention are the Economic History Association with its *Journal of economic history;* the American Marketing Association; and bodies like the National Association of Business Economists. The National Bureau of Economic Research carries out studies, mainly with regard to capital and wealth, growth and productivity, and international economic relations; although this body is not attached to the US government, its publications have, at times in the past, influenced government opinion and the content of documents issued by official bodies like the Department of Commerce. In the management field, American societies are even more plentiful. The American Management Association publishes a wide range of reports and other documents and has helped to make available the writings of some management pioneers. A bibliography of much utility is its ten year index of AMA publications 1954-1963. The scope of the reports and documents often ranges beyond the subject of management as such and covers many aspects of the broad field of economics—we may cite, for example, its *Guidelist for marketing research and economic forecasting*, by R N Carpenter, 1961. The AMA issues no less than five journals on various facets of management activity. Then, among other important managerial associations and groups, we ought to note the National Industrial Conference Board, already briefly referred to in conjunction with the BIM, the Administrative Management Society, the Industrial Management Society, the National Association of Manufacturers and the Society for the Advancement of Management which issues the journal *Advanced management*. The American Institute of Management also publishes some important management periodicals.

The quantity and variety of the work and publishing activities of the United States government departments and of American universities must be recollected too. Among the universities, one might single out the work being done by Paul Wasserman at *Maryland*; the *Business history review, Harvard business review* and the various other publications and bibliographical guides emanating from Harvard (some Harvard bibliographies are concisely described in C M White's *Sources of information in the social sciences,* 1964, *pp* 162-163; more recent ones are recorded in the pages of the quarterly *International economics selections bibliography*) not to mention its contribution towards *Journal of economic abstracts;* the revival at Pittsburgh of the two *Economic library selections* (now *International economics selections bibliography*) series; and the bibliographical and documentation work that is pursued at several other universities, such as Columbia and Cornell. Indeed it is not without significance that this chapter should close with the consideration of these American academic institutions; while their work may seem rather remote to many British librarians, together with societies like the American Economic Association and the United States government departments they show us, better than the equivalent bodies of any other country, the unique contribution which well developed and literature-conscious organisations can make towards the elimination of gaps in social science documentation and bibliography.

SUGGESTED READINGS

Information on the major societies in economics may be obtained from guides to the literature such as those of *Bakewell* and *Davinson;*

from standard reference tools which are general in scope like *The world of learning;* and in the case of the American organisations, from the *McGraw-Hill dictionary of modern economics.* Other sources include:

1 Michalski, W: 'Work of the Hamburg Institute for International Economics', ASLIB *Proceedings,* March 1965, *pp* 83-87.
2 *Scientific and learned societies of Great Britain,* Allen & Unwin, 1964, *pp* 167-172.
3 UNESCO: *International organisations in the social sciences,* 1961, 145 *pp.*

CHAPTER FIFTEEN

SOME IMPORTANT ECONOMICS AND COMMERCIAL LIBRARIES

ONE OF THE MOST interesting aspects of investigating the librarianship of a specific subject field is visiting some of the great libraries that have made that sector of knowledge their speciality. A description of important economics and commercial collections cannot really hope to compete with visits, but at least it makes a contribution towards an increasing awareness of the high standard of library service that can be, and indeed is, given in the larger specialising libraries that have a long history—this helping to ensure good runs of periodicals and valuable older research material—and are supported by adequate funds. It might not be true to argue that all the libraries described in the present chapter have really ample funds, but several of them are most liberally endowed in comparison with many collections. An investigation of their resources can be of utility to us for various reasons. It may help to reveal, as already suggested, the range of material and services that are a part of a fully developed library within our province; it may indicate libraries which can be contacted for the lending of certain items or the passing on of specialised information that is inaccessible or, more likely, non-existent, in less ambitious collections; and it can draw attention to valuable catalogues, bulletins and accessions lists issued by these great libraries which can be acquired to serve as current or retrospective bibliographies elsewhere.

It will soon become evident that, just as there are an extensive range of societies within our branch of knowledge, so there are very many libraries; but, in the case of the latter one or two stand out in Britain as being supremely important and these receive the most attention here. It is essential, nevertheless, to survey the work of other libraries both in Britain and abroad and to remember the variety of these. They include public and academic libraries and a host of special ones, comprising the libraries of government departments, firms, professional bodies and many of the societies mentioned in the last chapter.

197

The fact that economics libraries are usually, in reality, social science collections which give a strong emphasis to economic literature has already been stressed. Among these, the *British Library of Political and Economic Science* must be singled out for particular mention. Founded in 1896, chiefly due to the enthusiasm of Sidney Webb, it is unique among British academic libraries in that it serves a dual role; its most obvious task is to serve the London School of Economics, but it also acts as a collection which can be utilised by research workers who cannot readily obtain their materials elsewhere. Within its vast resources there is a separate teaching library, where the London undergraduate will find much of the social science literature that he needs. The stock now is in the region of some 460,000 volumes including pamphlets, and some 9,000 journals are currently received. These riches are augmented by special collections and the library is thus regarded as the largest in the world confined to the social sciences. It covers a much wider range of social science literature than its name might indicate but it is especially strong in material on the principles of economics, on British and overseas government publications past and present, on statistical items and on overseas bank reports. The collections have been built up over the years by purchase, exchange and donations (Sidney Webb gave the library his books on trade unionism, for instance, including many rare items), while the enthusiasm of past librarians like B M Headicar, of whose ' energetic librarianship ' a successor has written appreciatively, has done much to ensure for this library its present day enviable prestige and efficiency.

The special collections mentioned include extant letters, diaries and other manuscript material relating to such eminent names as J S Mill, W H Beveridge, R H Tawney, the Webbs and the social scientist Charles Booth. Subjects are also represented among the special material; there is, for example, a collection of central and local government reports and pamphlets on unemployment published during the period 1886-1914. From the more general material, the library will lend, when possible, through the NCL or directly to other libraries, as well as to the London University student. Its publications include the vast *London bibliography of the social sciences*, a pamphlet *Notes for readers*, which is frequently revised, and the 1948 *Guide to the collections*, which is now very dated. Current developments are indicated in the library's annual report. The bulk of the stock is classified by the Library of Congress system and the shelf arrangement is supported by an author catalogue on cards, plus the card continuation of the dictionary cataloguing in the London bibliography. Current acquisitions are recorded in the *Monthly list of additions.*

The future of the library is well assured on account of its financial resources and heritage and also because of the calibre of the present staff. The deputy librarian, Majorie Plant, may justly be singled out here for her compilation of bibliographical guides and contributions to library literature. Development and growth within the library is constantly taking place; a few years ago, for instance, the management consultants Urwick Orr and Partners were commissioned to undertake a survey of the library and their report led to certain changes in its administration. In a library of this kind the very strength of the resources and the bulk of accessions can be almost embarrassing, but it is clear that the high standards and traditions are being maintained and strengthened.

Other British academic libraries must obviously be reviewed more briefly. Also serving London University is the *Goldsmiths' Library* which is the largest of the university library's special collections. This is complementary to the library just described in many ways, and is extremely strong on material on economics published before 1850. It has some 70,000 volumes, and rarities include items from the private libraries of Adam Smith and David Ricardo. Most of its resources are to be found recorded in the *London bibliography,* and it should be stressed that they include many older items that are not in the British Museum collections. Most of our university libraries, while they cannot equal the wealth and unique character of the London collections in the economic field, have excellent resources to call upon. Leeds, Leicester and Glasgow can be singled out for various reasons as being among the best, and there are excellent libraries for the economist, of course, at Oxford and Cambridge. It may be mentioned that the latter university's Kings College has a special Keynes Library. The universities have not normally been so well endowed with management and commercial literature as with that of pure and applied economics, but the establishment of business schools within the University of London and the University of Manchester—arising out of the BIM-produced Franks report of 1963— points the way towards the gradual emergence of excellent libraries on management resources at these establishments. The Manchester

Business School hopes to have, by the early 1970's, a management information centre and library of some 30,000 volumes. College libraries cannot hope to compete with the rate of expansion we are witnessing in these and other universities, yet the increase in further education and the introduction of Council for National Academic Awards degrees is providing the necessary impetus for the improvement of these libraries too, for economics literature as for other fields.

PUBLIC LIBRARIES OF IMPORTANCE IN BRITAIN

Turning from the academic collections to public librarianship, it is immediately apparent that the holdings of scholarly works and rare documents will be far less. Nevertheless our public libraries provide very good services for students of economics and, in certain towns, have achieved a great deal in the building up of a thorough and most valuable commercial information service. There are good commercial or commercial/technical libraries in Belfast, Birmingham, Liverpool, Manchester, Sheffield, Southampton and some other provincial cities, while some other libraries are strong in commercial or economics literature because of their participation in subject specialisation schemes. In London there is the *Guildhall Library*, which has a special commercial reference room. It has an extensive range of trade and professional periodicals, of British and foreign newspapers, of statistical material and of timetables, although it is most renowned for its trade directories. Its strong and varied collections make the Guildhall one of the country's most important reference libraries and enquiries are received by it from many other institutions. There is issued twice each year a *CRR courier* showing additions made to the commercial reference room and indicating the character of its contents. Like other public libraries, the Guildhall is usually most generous in lending material which is not easily available elsewhere, if this can be spared from the library.

SPECIAL LIBRARIES

It is the number of special libraries within our broad field and the different emphases of these British collections that, however, most engage our attention. Beginning with the government libraries, the economics and statistical holdings of the *House of Commons Library* merit consideration. According to a House of Commons paper from the 1945-46 parliamentary session and concerned with this library's work and development, its purpose is to 'supply members with information rapidly on any of the multifarious matters which come before the House or to which their attentions are drawn by their parliamentary duties'. This statement led to the development of a research division of the library, and within this there is a statistical section strongly equipped with periodicals and British and overseas government publications and having trained statisticians to pursue research for members. Within the main part of the library the bookstock is well equipped with textbooks and other material on economics and economic history but, from our viewpoint, it is the library of statistical sources within the research division that is of greatest interest; it is possible that in the future the research programme for members may be extended to cover the broader field of economic science as a whole.

Of the departmental libraries, we might naturally expect that of the *Board of Trade* to be the best equipped for our province and indeed it is. The board's library had a chequered and most interesting history in the nineteenth century, and today we find that it is organised in two parts, these being the *Headquarters Library* and the *Statistics and Market Intelligence Library*. The main library covers all the social sciences but places great emphasis on international trade and other economics literature. It has about 250,000 volumes and receives some 3,000 current periodicals. The emphasis is very much on current material; multiple copies are provided of certain periodicals and of many recent British government publications to cope with the tremendous demand for these items. Readers and enquirers include government economists, econometricians, statisticians, administrators and other civil servants and some subject themes—such as regional economic development—are very prominent in the work of the library. As far as possible, enquiries from industry are also dealt with and, of course, the library is an NCL 'outlier'. Internal loans, excluding 'hand outs' of pamphlets and government papers that have been purchased in bulk, are in the region of 16,000 per annum and the library has a staff of over sixty. Staff numbers are fully justified, considering that the library is responsible for a first rate information service; the acquisition and cataloguing of its own stock, that of the *Statistics and Market Intelligence Library*, and the items housed in various small branch libraries maintained by the board in various parts of the country; services to the comparatively new Department of Economic Affairs and the Prices and Incomes Board as well as to the specialists of the Board of Trade; the production of some 2,000 photocopies each year; the compilation of bibliographies and many other tasks.

Many of the enquiries received are from the board's staff in other parts of Britain or in overseas countries and the main demands are for up-to-date and accurate information, whether the enquirer is from this country or an office abroad. Information is disseminated by bulletins compiled by the library staff. *New publications in the Board of Trade Library* is produced and circulated twice each month and a weekly service *Contents of recent journals* eliminates many of the problems associated with the circulation of periodicals in a large institution. The library staff participate in other bibliographical ventures—for example the booklet *Commerce, industry and HMSO* and the contributions to the *Board of Trade journal* noted in an earlier chapter—produce guides to particular subject matters, like their 1965 list of the *London trade enquiry offices of overseas countries,* and are responsible for liaison with the stationery office on questions affecting the printing of the Board of Trade publications.

The chief classification in use at the headquarters library is the Congress system and alphabetical subject and author catalogues are maintained. Card indexes to the current content of the *Board of Trade journal* and the Board's *Census of production* are provided. Specialised material in the library includes the selective collecting of the government publications of overseas countries and the acquisition of their catalogues. Despite the tremendous emphasis on recent developments and information and the weeding of dated stock that takes place, the library is rich in valuable older material although, for space reasons, much of this is shelved elsewhere.

The *Statistics and Market Intelligence Library* of the Board is located with the department's Export Services Branch. It is particularly strong in overseas directories and statistical publications. It is estimated that the former cover some one hundred and seventy countries, while there are over 85,000 volumes of overseas trade and other statistics. Another feature of this library is the growing collection of trade catalogues of overseas firms, numbering at present over 13,000, which is housed there. The library has a staff of about thirty and is classified by a special scheme, which utilises some of the divisions of the UN Standard international trade classification. Its main wealth lies in its statistical publications, which cover not only those of Britain and overseas countries, but the variety of statistical yearbooks and bulletins emanating from the United Nations Statistical Office, the UN economic commissions for various regions, the UN agencies, the OECD and the European communities, especially the economic community. This is one of the two or three largest libraries in the world in the field of economic and kindred statistics. A notable feature of its activities is that, unlike the headquarters library, its stock and services are available directly to the public for reference as a part of the board's services to businessmen and exporters; it thus serves a wide range of enquirers from industry as well as the staff of the Board.

These Board of Trade libraries have been discussed at some length because of the excellent standards they maintain as communicators, as well as custodians, of information and because they indicate the demands made upon and the variety of work done by a special library of this kind. Many of the other government departments have good libraries from an economic viewpoint, too, although their active information services are not as well developed as those we have just been considering. The *Ministry of Labour Library* has about 35,000 volumes and is especially strong in matters relating to employment, the cost of living, prices, and trade union and labour problems; the library of the *Foreign Office* is a good deal larger and has much material pertaining to the economics field, while the *Ministry of Social Security* and the department of *Customs and Excise* both have libraries of approximately the same size as the Ministry of Labour. The Customs and Excise Library has a good deal of manuscript material and is especially strong on financial economics, taxation and many aspects of trade. The *Treasury* and the *Board of Inland Revenue* also have libraries worthy of consideration and it seems certain that, when its resources have had more time to develop, the *Department of Economic Affairs* will have a library that is of major stature for its subject in the United Kingdom. Many of these departmental libraries will lend material to each other but are often rather diffident, for understandable reasons, about entering into the field of library co-operation on a very large scale. Some of them, for instance the Foreign Office Library, which does so annually for the benefit of its own and other government departments, produce useful accessions lists.

There are many other special libraries to be considered. The *Bank of England* has very large reference and lending libraries and, as one would expect, these are strong in applied economics and, with regard to economic principles, on monetary theory. It has very good holdings of periodical literature too, especially from overseas countries. The Bank of England Library is generous in lending books and, more occasionally, periodicals to other libraries for short periods if the items concerned are difficult to borrow from other sources. A library of a professional association that is naturally similar to it in subject coverage is that of the *Institute of Bankers*. This has over 50,000 volumes and is divided into reference and lending sections. The former is particularly strong in bank reports and in runs of economics and banking journals; the latter, although intended for the professional banker, is quite generous in lending to others, when possible, through the NCL. The general coverage of these collections ranges over economics, law, accountancy and statistics but naturally financial publications are well to the fore. Several other societies catering for professions have good libraries also; we may cite, from among many examples, the *Institute of Chartered Accountants* and the *Chartered Insurance Institute*. The last named body has a library which is of interest to us mainly on account of its faceted classification and its collection of early books on insurance, including a file of insurance policies that are of considerable historical interest. It has over 20,000 items in stock and lends to other libraries.

A comparatively small but important special library within the province of economics is that of the *National Institute of Economic and Social Research*. This has a stock in the region of 25,000 books and other documents and covers the broad field of economic science with a particular emphasis on the literature of more recent years. It exists chiefly for the institute's research staff but will consider lending books to other organisations. A feature is the distinctive system of classification; this has not proved altogether satisfactory and a change is contemplated. It is a collection that contains, in an embryonic state, the foundations of a really excellent economics library and it is to be hoped that it continues to develop and that its staff have the opportunity to build up a fuller information service for the specialists at the institute.

Several periodicals and newspapers, notably *The financial times*, have libraries which are strong on economics literature also; the book stock of such libraries is nearly always augmented by an excellent collection of newspaper cuttings, pamphlets and similar material. But, with regard to economics and commerce, the other special libraries that most engage our interest are the ones to be found in industry. In chapter eleven, the names were given of some of the industrial firms which have libraries or information centres specialising to a great extent in commercial as well as, or even rather than, technical material. In *Imperial Chemical Industries Fibres Division* (previously British Nylon Spinners) there are three distinct libraries, one of which covers economics and is concerned with commercial information work. It has been well described already by its former librarian I G Ross, but it should be mentioned that this library contains many journals, newspapers, pamphlets, and government and statistical papers and bulletins in addition to books. It provides an information service to company economists, market research workers, statisticians and others and issues an information bulletin, as well as contributing to the general bulletin of the three divisional libraries— *British and foreign news review*. It is active in co-operating with other libraries both in relation to loans and the interchange of information and is obviously a company library with a first rate commercial intelligence service. Another excellent library in this respect is that of the *Co-operative Wholesale Society's Market Research Department* in Manchester. This library has some 14,000 books and over 20,000 pamphlets and news cuttings. It contributes to its department's *Weekly digest* which is an information bulletin pinpointing new books and, more especially, articles in a whole host of journals that are likely to be of current value to research staff of the society. Like most well developed industrial commercial libraries, that of the CWS is very strong in trade journals, statistical periodicals and abstracting and indexing services for the emphasis is very much on recent material relating to the marketing of various products in Britain and abroad. The excellent classified file of news items and articles extracted from periodicals and the daily press indicates how much information a company economics library can gather from such sources.

Among libraries chiefly of note for their management collections, that of the *British Institute of Management* is an outstanding and obvious example. With a stock of some 40,000 books and pamphlets it is Europe's largest specialising management library, although within the next decade the growth of the libraries of the British graduate business schools could challenge its supremacy in this respect. The steady development of this library over the years since the BIM's initiation in 1947 has resulted in the present day first class collection which includes about 400 management journals and some unpublished material. A service is provided to BIM members and to the institute's own staff and many enquiries or requests for material are received through the post or by telephone. Books are normally lent out for one month and there are sometimes over 30,000 loans within a single year; it may be mentioned, however, that the BIM library staff must discriminate to some degree between corporate and individual members, the former receiving the fuller service. Much important management literature is published in the United States, so it is not surprising that American texts loom large in the BIM stock. This is yet another example of a library where a certain amount of multiple purchasing of particular texts takes place to meet the demand for recent material from the library clientèle. Some of the duplicate copies purchased may later become superfluous, but without them the library service with regard to new material and current information would have been retarded.

The BIM library staff compile at intervals the valuable management bibliography *A basic library of management,* and they have also undertaken over a period of years the preparation of numerous bibliographies of specific management themes. A translation service is available to the institute's members and, to some extent, the library lends and borrows material through the usual channels of inter-library co-operation. The classification used is the UDC, but the present librarian is enthusiastic about the possibilities of post co-ordinate indexing in the management field and it will be interesting to see to what extent this can complement, at least with regard to non-book literature, the more traditional methods of organising material.

The other management societies and organisations in Britain, several of which were mentioned in the last chapter, also in many cases have libraries to support them, although these cannot be compared with the stock and services of the BIM. It is interesting to note that one of these libraries, that of the organisation now known as the *Industrial Society,* was once arranged by Bliss's bibliographic classification, although the system was abandoned as it was believed to be too complex for the library's needs.

THE LIBRARIES SERVING THE UNITED NATIONS

We must again switch our attention to the United Nations and its agencies, this time to examine their excellent library resources. Some of the very best libraries developed by the United Nations in its twenty or so years of existence have truly fulfilled the statement in one UN document that they should become 'real centres of learning and research and the world's most reliable information centres in their respective subjects. '. Outstanding is the headquarters library in New York which dates back to the mid-nineteen forties, but was dedicated in 1961 as the *Dag Hammarskjöld Library*. This contains some 300,000 volumes, has a staff of a hundred representing thirty five nationalities and is estimated to answer 100,000 queries during each year. It operates both as a lending and reference library, but is mainly for the UN staff; research scholars and others are allowed access to its collections only if this can be done without impeding the library's primary responsibilities. In the economics field the collections relate mainly to applied economics and literature reflecting current international economic relations. The whole object of the library is on utility and there is little attempt to build up material for historical research.

The Dag Hammarskjöld Library issues a monthly list of *New publications* and its staff have compiled many specialised reading lists and bibliographies. The latter include one on *Industrialisation in underdeveloped countries*, 1956, plus one entitled *Economic and social development plans: Africa, Asia, and Latin America*, which appeared in 1964 and was followed in 1966 by another on a similar theme. Its *Bibliographical style manual*, 1963, lays down a procedure for standard practice in bibliographical compilation. In addition, the library's Documents Index Unit has a special task, that of ensuring the control and listing of the documents issued by the UN and the various agencies. This it does through its *Indexes to the UN sessional proceedings*, its cumulative *Indexes to the UN treaty series* and, most important of all through the tremendously valuable monthly bibliographical guide, the *United Nations documents index*.

The UN also has an archives library in New York and a library at Geneva which it inherited from its predecessor, the League of Nations. The Geneva Library's very extensive collections (over 600,000 volumes) are very strong in the social sciences and on economic and other questions relating to specific countries. It has a complete set of UN documents and a very strong statistical publications collection—the finest in Europe. Important from a bibliographical viewpoint are this library's *Monthly list of books catalogued* and *Monthly list of selected articles*, while it may be worthwhile to note that, although a dictionary catalogue is used, books are classified by the UDC. The UN economic commissions have libraries of some consequence too, although these are not nearly as gigantic as the ones in New York and Geneva. Their staffs have been quite active bibliographically; the *Library of the Commission for Asia and the Far East* has issued a *Select bibliography of economic planning*, 1959, for its region, the *Economic Commission for Latin America* produces *A monthly list of accessions and selected articles* and the equivalent *Commission for Africa* has *A monthly list of new acquisitions*. It is not possible here to mention more than one bibliography from each of the libraries of these economic commissions or to describe their work in more detail, but the student may find it of some significance to hear that the *Asian Commission Library* is classified by the UDC, but cataloguing follows the principles laid down in Ranganathan's *Classified catalogue code*.

If we consider the specialised agencies of the UN from the library viewpoint, we must note the library that is shared by the *International Bank for Reconstruction and Development* and the *International Monetary Fund*. This is housed in Washington. Its chief purpose is to provide its institutions with the publications needed to fulfil their programmes and it receives through purchase, exchange and, sometimes, donation the main economic and statistical works published in the member countries of the International Bank and the IMF. The stock, which is classified by a modified version of the Dewey system, exceeds 70,000 volumes and the library prepares various bibliographies and two monthly lists entitled respectively *List of recent additions* and *List of recent periodical articles*. The latter is prepared through the selective indexing of journals which this library takes in profusion, but these lists, like the other bibliographies of this library are not designed for external circulation.

The *International Labour Office Library* has already had its documentation programme reviewed. The library itself is in Geneva and its printed catalogue, published in 1962, and its monthly list *Selected acquisitions* are worthy of note. This library, too, compiles specialised bibliographies, an excellent example being the one on *Trade Union movements in Latin America*, 1965. The *General Agreement on Tariffs and Trade* is also served by a Geneva library, consisting mainly of journals, United Nations publications and trade statistics and, rather more peripheral to the sphere of economics, there are the libraries of UNESCO and the *Food and Agriculture Organisation*. That of UNESCO has, in its history, manifested some interesting vacillations between the Universal decimal and Congress classifications before finally opting for the former, while the FAO library also uses UDC and is extremely large. It has produced a *Select catalogue of books 1951-1958*, 1961, a *List of periodicals received*, 1959, and a number of specialised bibliographies in addition to its *Monthly list of accessions*.

MAJOR ECONOMICS LIBRARIES IN THE USA

It is possible to examine the library facilities offered to other inter-governmental organisations, but these hardly rival the resources of the best of the UN libraries. Nor can the present writer hope to do justice here to the more important libraries in the field in other European countries, although those of the *Institut National de la Statistiques et des Études Économiques*, the *Institute of World Economics* in Germany, which has recently made its magnificent catalogues available for sale, and the Dutch *Ministry of Social Affairs* must be mentioned by name. The great academic and other social science and economics libraries in the United States must be given considerable attention, however, for they represent some of the greatest collections within our specialised province. The stock of the *Library of Congress* itself, although of far wider range than the field of economics, cannot be ignored since it gives a tremendous amount of attention to the social sciences and has well over a million volumes (more than a sixth of the total stock) in its social sciences class H. The links of many of these volumes with economics and commerce will be admittedly somewhat tenuous, but there is obviously a vast range of literature on the subject to be found here and, to a lesser extent, in some other classes also.

University libraries in the United States cannot compete in size with the collections of their national library, but they provide some first rate examples of what can be achieved in large institutions serving undergraduates and research workers. There are so many of these splendid libraries, from the viewpoint of literature on pure and applied economics and economic and social history, that it is almost invidious to single out examples. The magnificent libraries at *Harvard University* must be mentioned, however, on account both of the depth and the range of their stocks. The Harvard Graduate School of Business Administration is served by the *Baker Library*, which has the world's most extensive collection of business literature, and is also very strong on many economic themes, especially those relating to labour problems and taxation. Economic theory is represented, but an associated library, that of *Harvard College,* is stronger in this respect. The Baker Library, apart from its resources on modern management is well endowed with historical and biographical material relating to business. Over the years, it has carried out much valuable work and has issued several publications; among the latter are *Guide to the Baker Library,* 1958; *Selected business sources,* 1963.

At Harvard also is the great *Kress Library,* which specialises in economic and business history. It was initiated some years ago by the generosity of the American businessman, Claude W Kress, who purchased for it a collection of rare material that had been formed by the bibliographer H S Foxwell. It is interesting to note in passing, that there is also a collection belonging to that nineteenth century scholar in the Goldsmiths' Library at London University and we are told that ' since the Goldsmiths' Library was formed fifty years ago, it does contain certain items which could not later be duplicated. On the other hand, we have the opinion of Mr John Maynard Keynes and of others, that the second Foxwell collection is superior in some departments. Probably there are enough rare and scarce books in each, so that each may claim superiority somewhere '. (A H Cole: *Harvard Library notes,* March 1940, *p* 4. Keynes, incidentally, once wrote an essay on Foxwell as a book collector.) The comment about rarity is certainly fully justified and today the Kress collections number over 30,000 volumes with a strong emphasis on pre-1850 material, and some outstanding special collections, such as the magnificent one on Adam Smith donated in 1937 by H B Vanderblue. The publications of the Kress Library include various booklets and reports and its curator, Mrs Reeves, compiled the Baker Library publication *Resources for the study of economic history,* 1961, which is mentioned in an earlier chapter. The published catalogues of the Kress Library have already been described as valuable retrospective bibliographies for economic literature prior to the twentieth century. At the time of writing, a new supplement is in preparation which will cover the entire period to 1848 recording accessions of recent years and incorporating the supplement to volume 1.

Other great library collections at various universities in the USA include the Commerce and Sociology Library at the *University of Illinois;* the *University of California's* libraries on business and economic and business history; and the 90,000 volumes on the general field of economics at the *University of Kansas. Columbia University,* New York has a very good business library and also contains the fine historical collection built up through the prowess and enthusiasm of E R A Seligman. A library of over 50,000 volumes, the latter is particularly strong on public finance. Universities mentioned previously, such as *Pittsburgh, Maryland, Cornell,* which recently published the huge catalogue of its industrial and labour relations library, and *Johns Hopkins, Baltimore* have been supported by good library resources, while comparatively recent years have witnessed the emergence of libraries concerned with economic development in various countries of the world, such as the one at *Yale University.* There are other distinctive libraries and collections at Yale too, including a special collection devoted to J S Mill.

The United States is also endowed with a number of special libraries in the economics sphere of interest, with a very active Special Libraries Association to unite them, while many public libraries have been sufficiently ambitious to establish good collections of economic literature. With regard to the public libraries, apart from the well known business collections at *Newark* and *Cleveland,* the magnificent stock at *New York* must be mentioned. This collection is, *in toto,* over 1,000,000 strong and economics material is very well represented. *Detroit,* too, has excellent collections and its social science department is very well endowed with volumes on labour economics in particular and with historical items relating to this and associated themes.

The reader who wishes to learn more about the great libraries in economics and commerce must necessarily turn to the readings which follow and to other published accounts of these superb collections. The study of major libraries in Britain and abroad is one which can have an appeal for its own sake, in addition to its undeniable value when the literature of a specialised branch of knowledge is being investigated. Some economists have been quick to appreciate both the value of libraries and the utility of descriptions of their resources; Palgrave included many years ago in his *Dictionary of political economy* an absorbing account of some of the then outstanding ones. Yet there are still many specialists, in this as in other subject disciplines, who do not fully understand the innate value of large repositories of literature, a value that cumulates with the continual extension of the collections. Apart from the provision directly of a good library and information service, the best way to make the subject expert in the social sciences aware of the distinctive and indispensable contribution of libraries to his research would be, were it only possible, to introduce him to the wonderful stock and services of the specialist collections that have achieved such great status and maturity.

SUGGESTED READINGS

Directories, handbooks:
1 Ministry of Defence: *Guide to government department and other libraries and information bureaux,* 1966, *pp* 43-56.
2 Irwin, R and Staveley, R (editors): *The libraries of London,* second edition 1961, *pp* 99-130 and 197-208.

Articles, papers:
3 Clapp, V W: 'The United Nations Library 1945-1961', *Libri,* part 2, 1962, *pp* 111-121.
4 Maizels, A: 'Use of the library of the Royal Statistical Society' (in Mallaber, K A (editor): *Conference on librarian-statistician relations . . .,* 1966, *pp* 9-18).
5 Mallaber, K A: 'Board of Trade Library services to statisticians and their staff, *Ibid, pp* 32-37.
6 Partington, L: 'Library of the Economic Growth Centre at Yale University', *Library Association record,* January 1966, *pp* 13-17.
7 Reeves, D D: 'The Kress Library of Business and Economics', *Business history review,* Winter 1960, *pp* 478-494.
8 Reynolds, M T: 'Economic development libraries: problems and prospects', *Special libraries,* December 1966, *pp* 701-705.
9 Vainstein, R: 'What's new in public library service to business?' *Library journal,* 1st March 1960, *pp* 913-918. (Includes a list of Canadian and United States public libraries that run a commercial information service.)
10 *Special libraries,* May-June 1964, is devoted to libraries and librarianship in advertising, marketing and communications media.

Library booklets:
The librarianship student should see as many as possible of the pamphlets and guides issued by principal libraries in this subject. They include:
The Library of the House of Commons, 1966, 56 *pp.*
The Board of Trade Statistics and Market Intelligence Library, 1965, 10 *pp.*
The British Library of Political & Economic Science: Notes for readers, 1966, 26 *pp.* (Its mss collections are well described in an article cited at the end of Chapter six.)
The libraries of the United Nations: a descriptive guide, 1966, 126 *pp.*

CHAPTER SIXTEEN

DEALING WITH TYPICAL ENQUIRIES

IT MIGHT BE thought that a large library having at its disposal many of
the bibliographies and other reference material described in this book
would rarely encounter difficulty in dealing with enquiries, but this
need not be the case. Even if there is no paucity of bibliographical
resources, and even if the staff make full use of the catalogue and
the benefits of classification and indexing, there are sure to be some
questions posed which give rise to problems and consume much time.
Requests for recent news items or for articles and books on the very
latest trends in, say, supermarkets make the library staff work
extremely hard to retrieve valid information simply because there has
been hardly time for it to find its way into print; again, some
obstacles may arise because the enquirer fails to state his needs
exactly, couching what is in fact a request for a specific piece of information in rather general and even vague terms.

There can be no doubt, however, that in the well equipped reference library where material is put to good use, a very wide range of
questions can be satisfactorily met; if the library does not have all
the items to which bibliographies and guides to the literature refer,
it should have a large proportion of them and others, if likely to prove
particularly valuable, may be borrowed. Caution must be exercised to
ensure in advanced reference work that the staff are finding information for readers and not interpreting it; economic statistics in particular may be traced but the value to be placed upon them must,
in most cases, be left with the reader. In commercial intelligence too,
there can be dangers in decoding for example, telegraphic messages
in a telephone conversation with the enquirer. If there is any doubt
about the meaning of a message, the reader should be urged to come
to the library and check the data for his own satisfaction. Some enquiries of a quick-reference type will be answered speedily, but
others take much longer. In some cases it will be necessary to telephone the information to the reader later or to ask him to call at

the library again; it is wise, in such circumstances to try to ascertain the urgency of the query.

Another point that must be reiterated is that there can be no fixed routine for the answering of questions on commercial, economic or management matters. The question itself often suggests that one category of bibliographical material will be more relevant than others or, perhaps, that the local chamber of commerce, a prominent society, or another library in the vicinity should be consulted for aid with the enquiry. A real difficulty in considering requests for information here and how they should be handled arises from the very varied forms which queries take. In the academic and, at times, in the public or special library, there may be a request for a bibliography or reading list to be drawn up on a certain theme; many demands in special and public commercial libraries are very different—they are essentially for precise and factual information that can be extracted from directories, yearbooks, trade journals, statistical bulletins and similar sources. Thus the word ' typical ' in this chapter's title is very hard to define; yet if we remember that at one end of the scale are advanced students and research workers requesting information and the compilation of bibliographies on a number of academic themes, and that at the other end are the specialist economist and the businessman demanding current information, we will be able to deal with a theoretical, but truly representative, range of questions in the remainder of this text.

It must be emphasised, before considering some possible enquiries at length, that the ability to cope successfully with most requests for information stems from a good working knowledge of the bibliographical services and other stock of a library, and the enthusiasm to scan current documents and remember interesting publications or articles, making sure that valuable items—especially those appearing in unlikely contexts—are indexed. In this way, for instance, we learn to turn with confidence to *Business periodicals index, Management abstracts* and similar tools for recent periodical articles on merit rating; to directories, government publications, trade journals, bank literature and so forth when helping businessmen engaged in overseas trade; or we would, if faced with a demand for literature on the prospects of the Scottish economy, either recollect that there was a 1966 command paper on this theme and that the *Stock Exchange gazette* issued a relevant inset early in 1967, or else trace them through our catalogue or indexes.

It will prove of value to consider at more length enquiries that are likely to prove fairly time consuming. If we were asked to compile a reading list on, for instance, the *Work and influence of Keynes,* or on the *Impact of the industrial revolution on various regions in Britain,* how should we proceed? To take the Keynesian query first, it would be wise to begin by searching the catalogue to see what books on this economist were in stock. Having listed these tentatively, it might prove profitable to consult biographical dictionaries like the DNB, and the articles in an encyclopedic economics dictionary such as that of *Palgrave.* These will certainly merit inclusion in the reading list and it is possible that their bibliographies may point the way to further useful items. We could then hunt for periodical articles of value and for details of books that were not in our own library by using important general and specialised retrospective bibliographies; the latter would certainly include, if available, the *London bibliography of the social sciences,* the *Index of economic journals,* the *International bibliography of economics* produced by UNESCO and, possibly, the *Income and wealth* bibliography. Some current bibliographies would reveal books or articles about the modern application of Keynes' ideas. Thus we might use, too, *Economic abstracts* or the *Journal of economic abstracts;* they could be supported by an actual examination of some recent issues of the scholarly journals. If we have the two series of the former *Economics library selections,* we shall certainly find reference to several writings of importance in the pages of series I and in one or two volumes in the second series.

Having consulted sources such as these and made a preliminary note of the items that prove useful, it would then be necessary to sift the material that had been traced. It might well be that the enquirer would prefer the reading list to consist mainly of items that were readily accessible, but there would be many articles not in stock that could be borrowed if likely to be of primary value. The question of the arrangement of the bibliography or reading list arises also. A long list of items relating to Keynes would certainly need to be broken down into systematic groups and the following is offered as a profitable outline, although to a large extent the arrangement should depend on the needs of the enquirer and the emphasis in his studies:

A Writings of Keynes prior to 1936 (sub-arranged chronologically).

B The *General theory* . . . and subsequent writings (sub-arranged chronologically).

C Biographical and critical writings giving a balanced or favourable account of Keynes' work (sub-arranged by author).

D Critical accounts of an adverse nature (sub-arranged by author).

E Accounts of the impact of Keynesian doctrines on government policy (sub-arranged first by country and then by author).

In a long bibliography, category C above would need further sub-division, but these groupings ought to serve many readers well and, naturally, they will accommodate the important writings on Keynes which were singled out in an earlier chapter.

When asked for a reading list on the effects of the industrial revolution on social and economic life in different areas, we would again find many key works in our own library catalogue. These might include the books of J L and Barbara Hammond, P Mantoux, H L Beales, T S Ashton, L C A Knowles, and others who have discussed the course and influence of the revolution in general terms, and possibly a volume or two which gives the attention to the regions that we require. The latter include *The industrial revolution in North Wales* by A H Dodd, 1951, H Hamilton's *The industrial revolution in Scotland,* 1932 (both of these have bibliographies), and from more recent times J D Marshall's *Furness and the industrial revolution,* 1958. If these and works like them were not in the library, we would certainly succeed in tracing them through guides to the literature, booklists and the extensive retrospective bibliographies mentioned in relation to the Keynes enquiry. Encyclopedias would again be useful and both *Palgrave* and *Seligman* could be consulted to advantage. The retrospective bibliographies would enable us to support references to books with some relating to articles in the historical and other academic journals. Having thus compiled a list of possible items, we would again need to evaluate them before deciding which ones are to appear in the reading list. Arrangement on this occasion would commence with the enumeration of general works included and then follow a geographical grouping, each major region being considered in turn.

The two requests considered above relate mainly to the history of the subject and it is natural to suppose that, while this type of enquiry will certainly be received, many readers will want information on pure and applied economics. With regard to economic theory, a representative enquiry in an academic or large public library is, for example, the extent to which the literature of the last decade favours the principles generally termed as ' welfare economics '? This necessitates the librarian checking on the welfare ' school ' of economists, unless the reader himself provided this type of background detail; information of this sort could be obtained through the use of a good guide to the literature (Lewis' *Literature of the social sciences* provides it), or by means of an encyclopedia or dictionary article, like those found in the *McGraw-Hill dictionary of modern economics* or J L Hanson's *Dictionary of economics and commerce.* Both of these mention A C Pigou as a prominent writer connected with this idea and the American work names some important texts relating to the concept. We would then be able to find out more about Pigou, through encyclopedia articles and biographical works of reference and could seek books and articles on the economics of welfare in our retrospective bibliographies. Our own library might well have some striking ones, such as *The economics of control* by A P Lerner and the reader should certainly be referred to I M D Little's advanced analytical work *A critique of welfare economics.*

An example of a task for the librarian in the realm of applied economics and contemporary economic problems might well be a reader who wishes help in tracing literature on prices, productivity and incomes in Britain within the last decade and with special emphasis on very recent material. Many of the categories of bibliographical material are used with profit in such an instance. Guides to the literature suggest some information sources to us and modern economics dictionaries outline the functions of major government organisations dealing with these important topics. Books and articles are traced by means of current and retrospective bibliographies and we should not forget the pamphlet bibliographies and reading lists, for Bakewell's *Productivity in British industry* and others are obviously going to be relevant here. Yet much of the literature is to be found in very recent periodical articles which will only be traced by scanning several journals, in pamphlets and cuttings and (most important of all) in government publications including statistical periodicals and annuals. There will be a wealth of detail in white papers and in departmental publications of the British government which can be traced through the HMSO bibliographies. Likewise, the *Monthly digest of statistics, Annual abstract of statistics, Economic trends* and other serials housing statistical tables, particularly of course the *Ministry of Labour's* quarterly *Statistics on incomes, prices, employment and production,* must be utilised.

The HMSO daily lists and the regularly issued accessions lists of other libraries must be employed, with a query of this kind to support the recent journals in the retrieval of current literature and trends. *Research index* gives a few useful references to very recent newspaper and periodical articles and news announcements as, indeed, may *Keesings contemporary archives.* This hypothetical enquiry illustrates well how many categories of material are often needed to satisfy fully some readers' requests; it brings government publications to the fore, but in the end it may even mean the consultation of directories for the addresses of productivity and other organisations. We must not forget that, if the reader is engaged in advanced studies or research on this subject, he may need to contact some of the specialist organisations; indeed, with any enquiry, the librarian and his staff must not forget that sources of information do not stop at bibliographical material and that it is often necessary to assist the enquirer further by providing him with the names and addresses of relevant societies and of government departments, or by seeking aid for him from local libraries and other institutions.

QUESTIONS DEMANDING A SPECIFIC ITEM OF INFORMATION

The enquiries so far considered may seem academic and remote to librarians in the commercial or management sphere. In the busy commercial information library, many questions do not involve the amassing of literature or the searching for references to build up a helpful reading list; on the contrary, a number of questions can be answered from a single source and the whole difficulty is knowing an appropriate publication, or publications, where a particular specific piece of information, like the name of an overseas manufacturer or the user of a particular trade name, can be found. It is impossible to outline a procedure for such enquiries in a text of this kind, but readers might well like to search on their own behalf for items of information and to try for themselves some queries of the kind already discussed. The questions below are offered with this in mind and each of them can be answered by the use of a source or sources mentioned in this book; they give due weight to commercial and some management topics as well as to economics and its various ramifications.

1 Where might a business executive find a good encyclopedia article on the impact of automation on modern industry?

2 Find statistics showing Britain's rate of unemployment in 1908.

3 Where would you look for details of recent periodical articles on profit sharing in industry?

4 Can you trace manufacturers of electronics equipment in Rotterdam?

5 Is there a map giving details of the distribution of the heavy chemicals industry in the USSR?

6 How often has the bank rate been altered in Britain since 1958?

7 Can statistics be traced relating to goods exported from Southampton in 1964?

8 What material has the British government published on the country's regional economic development?

9 What is the address of the British Oatmeal Millers' Association?

10 Where would one expect to find details of books and articles on economics and business that were published in the latter half of the nineteenth century?

11 To which specialist organisations in Britain might one refer a reader investigating the history of trade unions?

12 Can comparative statistics be found to show the exports of wood pulp from Canada over the years 1960-1965?

13 Is there a bibliography which indicates major sources of management information published in languages other than English?

14 Find details of cost of living increases granted to steelworkers in Britain in 1967.

15 Can the exact date of an article in *The financial times* on the development of commerce and industry in Peterborough be traced, if it is known that this appeared some time in the latter half of 1966 or early 1967?

16 Where can abstracts be found of periodical articles on the impact and effects of advertising methods?

The sixteen queries above are not intended to represent a comprehensive list, and yet all are typical of questions that might be posed in a social science or commercial library. Others can be constructed and pursued and, if this is done intelligently, the student of librarianship will find that the exercise is a profitable one and encourages a valuable direct insight into the use of reference material. With the questions above, one must first decide which category of bibliographical material is most relevant (this is often obvious from the wording of the question) and then select the most likely publication or publications from the category concerned.

CONCLUSION

It only remains to consider the future of economics and commercial documentation and its bibliography. Chapter ten referred to some gaps in the present bibliographical coverage, and it is clear that there is still work to be done, both in this respect and in the improvement of social science library collections and facilities. In the last few years the Library Association has held two conferences of interest within the province of the social sciences. The 1960 conference on the information methods of research workers covered the whole of the field, and the later one, mentioned in various parts of this text, was concerned with the library requirements of the economic statistician. But, if librarians are trying to improve their services, there is also a growing recognition in other quarters of the value of extensive repositories of literature in sociological fields. The recommendations of the British Academy report *Research in the humanities and social sciences*, 1961, have been supported and extended more recently by those of the Heyworth Committee on Social Studies, 1965. The latter document offers a useful explanation of what constitutes the social sciences, and stresses their increasing interdependence; it also supports the creation of a national lending library for them of the kind enjoyed already in this country for science and technology. One of this white paper's most interesting statements, however, is that to the effect that ' many economists still continue to find that the only practical needs for their work are a study and a library . . . '. This surely underlines strongly the case made in the present volume for an understanding of the problems encountered in economics and commercial collections, and the implied argument for the improvement of existing collections and the initiation of more such specialised services. When this quotation is endorsed and extended by one from Dr Urquhart to the effect that ' without literature, research in the humanities would be almost non-existent ' (see his article ' The needs of the humanities ', *Journal of documentation*, September 1963), one becomes acutely aware of the opportunity and challenge that lies before the library profession for the strengthening of the resources provided, and for better understanding of the requirements of the various groups of specialist workers in the socio-economic field.

The Heyworth committee recommended the setting up of a Social

Science Research Council and this is now in existence. It is obviously well equipped to initiate research and has made some appropriate grants for this—to the National Institute of Economic and Social Research and to the comparatively recently established UK Social and Economic Archive Committee for instance. It may be able also gradually to fill some of the gaps in economics documentation, such as the publication of an annual register of research work in progress. The extension of present services in this way, and the pursuit of social science research as encouraged by the Council, or by other British organisations such as OSTI, a body which has already shown a most active interest in economic and management projects, can only be favourable to the advancement of knowledge in a sphere which, because of the unpredictability of human nature, can never be as exact as the natural sciences, but nevertheless can and must offer a great deal to mankind's well being. Indeed, while the technological advance of the next quarter century is likely to be considerable, our material fortunes cannot be substantially increased unless the social and behavioural sciences receive their due share of attention. Economics is one of the most important of these and its principles pervade so many walks of life as to make the fostering of higher economic research high on any scale of priorities.

All this scarcely touches the professional work of the librarian, but he can make his contribution through effective knowledge and utilisation of the resources at his command. The growth of economics documentation nationally and internationally has been exceptionally rapid recently, and there are no signs of the rate slackening—indeed, if we use the word ' economics ' in a broad sense and include commercial materials, it is likely to assume even greater proportions. Increased research means increased documentation, but bibliographical control is necessary if the literature is to be harnessed for use. There remains much scope for the production of bibliographies and similar tools, by societies or individuals, on specialised branches of economic science, and for the librarian who provides a reference service to become more thoroughly aware of the literature needs of economists and businessmen and of the tools which can help us to meet these needs. The social science or commercial library depends upon the latter for its efficiency, but apart from the practical satisfaction given to enquirers, resulting from the proper use of bibliographical materials, there is—for many librarians—a great and justifiable personal sense of achievement in having taken the trouble to master their content and arrangement.

SUGGESTED READINGS

The reader may decide to refer to the report of the Heyworth committee (cmnd 2660:1965), and the British Academy report, and to seek evidence concerning the implementation of the recommendations of the former especially. In addition, he could consult:

1 Harvey, J M (editor): *Information methods of research workers in the social sciences,* Library Association, 1961, 28 *pp.* (Proceedings of the conference held in June 1960.)
2 Grose, D: 'A data bank: the social and economic archive centre, ASLIB *Proceedings,* May 1967, *pp* 126-128.
3 Guttsman, W L: ' The literature of the social sciences and provision for research in them ' *Journal of documentation,* September 1966, *pp* 186-193.
4 Lewis, P R: ' Present state of documentation services in the social sciences ' ASLIB *Proceedings,* February 1965, *pp* 40-49.

INDEX

THIS INDEX includes, in addition to personal and corporate names, entries under major economic themes and under striking titles—especially the titles of serial and other bibliographically important publications with no personal author. Alphabetisation follows the 'letter by letter' principle.

223

227

Everyman's dictionary of economics 25, 125
Exchange of publications, by libraries 159
Exchange Telegraph Daily Statistics Service 141
Export 89, 191
Export Credits Guarantee Department 99, 100, 191
Exporting
—bank material on 142, 185
—bibliographies 46
—government publications on 99, 109-110, 112-113
—guide to the literature 44
—journals on 89
—organizations relating to 185, 190-191
—statistical services on 109-110, 112-113
Export market 89
Export service bulletin (Board of Trade) 99

Fabian Society 188-189
Facet analysis in classification 168, 174, 176, 182, 204
Facts on file 39
Family expenditure survey (Ministry of Labour) 113
Fanning, D 46
FAO *see* Food and Agriculture Organization
Farmington Plan 163
Fay, C R 127
Fayol, H 13
Fenelon, K G 108, 181
Ferber, R 57, 58
Filon, S P L 161
Financial and company economics
—bibliography on 57-58
—reference books on 37-39
Financial statistics (Central Statistical Office) 112
Financial times 37, 83, 90, 138-139, 142, 180, 204, 219
Flexowriters, use of 81
Flinn, M W 68, 178
Follett, M P 13
Food and Agriculture Organization 101, 103, 117, 192
—library of 208-209
Food trades directory 34, 157
Ford, P and Ford, G 96, 167

Foreign Office 100
—Library of 203
Foreign trade (EEC) 117-118
Fortune 90
Foskett, D J 166, 168, 174, 183-184
Foxwell, H S 210
Franklin, B (publisher) 127, 128
Franks report 199
Fraser's Canadian trade directory 35
Fruit, flower and vegetable trades review 90
Fry, Edward—Library of International Law (London University) 52

Galbraith, J K 17
Gaps in present economics bibliography and documentation 131-133
General Agreement on Tariffs and Trade (GATT) 101, 117, 192
General index to the bills . . . 96
General Register Office 114
Geographia Limited 123
Geographical information 122-124
George, H 17
Georgi, C 48
Gibb, I P 161
Gide, C. 126
Gilbreth, F B 13
Gilpin, A 25
Glasgow University 72
—library of 199
Glass, D V 127
Godwin, R D 133
Godwin, W 14
Goldsmiths' Library (London University) 52, 66, 130, 199, 210
Gottfried, B A 27
Gould, J 23
Government publications
—bibliographies of 94-96
—cataloguing of 167, 179-180
—selection of 157-158
—use in commercial information work 137, 140
—value of 93
see also under Parliamentary papers, British; under the names of individual British government departments; and under individual international organizations and countries
Government records, preservation of 72-73

Government statistical services (parliamentary paper) 120
Government statistical services (Treasury) 107
Grandin, A 68
Gray, A 126, 127
Great Britain: Parliament see Government publications; Parliamentary papers, British; and under the names of individual departments
Greenwald, D 24
Gregg, P 17
Grigg report 72, 98
Grose, D 222
Groves, E B 190
Guides to official sources 107
Guides to the literature of economics and commerce, description of 42-45, 48-49
Guide to historical literature 56
Guildhall Library 72, 200
Guillebaud, C W 129
Guttsman, W L 222

HADIS see Huddersfield and District Information Service
Hall, H A 56
Hall, M 46
Hamburg Institute for International Economics 193, 196, 209
Hamilton, H 216
Hammarskjöld, Dag, Library (United Nations) 94, 132, 152, 164, 207
Hammond, J L and B 216
Hammond, R J 17
Handbuch der finanzwissenschaft 37
Hansard (Parliamentary debates) 97
Hansard catalogue of parliamentary publications 96
Hansen, A 129
Hanson, A O 149
Hanson, J L 12, 17, 25, 27, 217
Hanson, L W 66-67
Harbury, C D 17
Hardware trade journal register of trade names 140
Harrar, H J 163
Harris, R 187
Harris, S E 129
Harrod, R 129
Harvard business review 90, 195
Harvard College Library 210

Harvard University
—Business history review 88, 195
—Business literature for students 45
—Classification for business literature 175-176
—Harvard business review 90, 195
—Journal of economic abstracts 79-80, 87, 132, 195
—Quarterly journal of economics 88
for details of Harvard libraries see under Baker Library, Harvard College Library and Kress Library
Harvey, J M 120, 222
Haymarket Press 90
Hayward, E G 48
Hazlewood, A 57
Hazlitt, H 129, 130
Headicar, B M 198
Heilbroner, R L 15, 18, 126
Henderson, G P 32, 38, 141, 149
Her Majesty's Stationery Office see HMSO
HERTIS 47
Heyel, C 28, 124
Heyworth committee 131, 220-222
Higgs, H 24, 66-67
Hints to businessmen (Board of Trade) 99
Historical Association 74
Historical statistics of the USA 115-116
HMSO lists and catalogues 94-95
Holt, Alfred & Co (Blue funnel line), history of 70
Hopkins, Johns, University 58, 77, 155, 156, 211
Hopkins, K 44, 149
Horton, B J 24
Hoselitz, B 18, 43, 103
Houghton, B 149
House of Commons Library 200-201, 212
Howcroft, B 120
Huddersfield and District Information Service (HADIS) 163
Hutt, W H 130
Hyamson's dictionary of universal biography 125
Hyde, F E 70

Illinois University Library 210
Imperial Chemical Industries Ltd
—Dyestuffs division library 147

International Sociological Association 92
International trade (GAAT) 117
International who's who 125
Investors chronicle and stock exchange gazette 37, 89, 138, 156
Irwin, R 212
Istituto di Economia Internazionale 193

Jain, H C 174
James, G R 187
Jarvis, R C 75
Jefferys, J B 187
Jervis, F R J 187
Jevons, W S 17
Johns Hopkins *see* Hopkins, Johns, University
Johnson, A 22
Johnson Reprint Corporation 157
Jordan, R T 92
Journal of agricultural economics 188
Journal of commerce 138
Journal of common market studies 89
Journal of economic abstracts (Harvard) 79-80, 87, 132, 194, 215
Journal of economic history 88, 153, 194
Journal of industrial economics 89
Journal of the Institute of Bankers 89
Journal of management studies 90
Journal of marketing 82
Journal of transport history 72
Journal of world history 59
Journals
—range and examples of 86-91
—scholarly 87-88
—selection of 156-157
—tools for identifying and locating 91-92
—trade periodicals 89-90

Kansas University Library 210
Keesings contemporary archives 39, 138, 181, 218
Keith Business Library, Ottawa 85
Kelly's directories 31, 33
Kendall, M G 107, 108, 188
Kerchove, R de *see* DeKerchove, R
Kettle, A 128
Keynes, *Sir* G 129
Keynes, J M 14, 16, 52, 124, 128
—compiling a bibliography on 215-216

Keynes, J M
—critical works relating to 129-130
—discusses Foxwell collections 210
—special library at Cambridge 199
—work as editor of *Economic journal* 87
Keynes, J N 16
Kingsley, C 24
Kinloch, T F 126
Kish, G 123
Klein, B 32
Knowles, L C A 216
Kohler, E L 28
Kolb, W L 23
Kompass Register Ltd 33-34, 140
Kraus Periodicals Ltd 157
Kress Library, Harvard University 210, 212
—catalogues of 65, 67, 210
Kyle, B 133, 164, 167, 168, 170, 174, 176, 184

Labour economics
—bibliography on 46
—current awareness services concerning 80-81
—libraries 203, 211
—societies 188-189
—statistics regarding 111, 113, 114
Labour, Ministry of
—character and functions 99, 190
—*Directory of employers associations* 40, 100
—*Family expenditure survey* 113
—*gazette* 100, 106, 111, 113
—library 203
—Sectional list 94, 99
—*Statistics of incomes, prices, employment and production* 113, 114, 180, 218
—*Time rates of wages* 113
Ladenson, A 177
LADSIRLAC *see* Liverpool and District . . .
Lamb, J P 19
Lambert, R D 103
Langridge, D W 174
Larson, H M 69, 71
Laxton's building price book 34
Leeds University Library 199
Leicester University 72
—library 199

Marketing
—societies relating to 188, 194
—statistics sources 110, 113
Marketing (a journal) 89
Marketing guide (US Department of Commerce) 101
Marketing in Europe 190
Market research abstracts 82, 132, 174, 188
Market Research Society 82, 188
Marks and Spencers Ltd 147
Marshall, A 15-16
—critical works relating to 128-129
Marshall, J D 216
Martins Bank 142
Marx, K 15
—critical works relating to 128
Maryland, University of 45, 195
—library 211
Massie, J 67-68
Masui, M 57, 58
Mathias, P 74
Mathys, H R 75
Maunier, R 68
Meat trades journal 90
Medley, D J 56
Metal Box Company 147
Michalski, W 196
Microeconomics 16
Midland Bank 142
Mill, J S 15, 125, 198
—critical works relating to 128
—special collection at Yale University 211
Millard, P 39-40, 46
Mills, J 172, 174
Ministry of Defence *see* Defence, Ministry of
Ministry of Labour *see* Labour, Ministry of
Ministry of Labour gazette 100, 106, 111, 113
Ministry of Power *see* Power, Ministry of
Ministry of Social Affairs (Holland) *see* Social Affairs, Ministry of
Ministry of Social Security *see* Social Security, Ministry of
Ministry of Technology *see* Technology, Ministry of
Minute books, as business records 70
Mitchell, B R 109

Money, finance and investment
—bibliography on 57-58
—reference material relating to 37-39
Monopolies Commission 11, 71
Monthly bulletin of agricultural economics and statistics (FAO) 117
Monthly bulletin of statistics (UN) 116
Monthly digest of statistics (Central Statistical Office) 111, 112, 114, 117, 217
Moodies Investors Service Ltd 38, 141
Morgan, T 105
Morgan, W T and C S Morgan 63
Motor industry of Great Britain 115
Motta, G 29
Mukherjee, A K 43
Multi-lingual dictionaries 29-30, 138

National Association of Business Economists 194
National Association of Manufacturers 195
National bluebook . . . (Central Statistical Office) 112
National Board for Prices and Incomes 100, 201
National Book League 46, 48
National Bureau of Economic Research 194
National Central Library 160, 198, 201
National Economic Development Office 100
National income statistics (Central Statistical Office) 107
National Industrial Conference Board 39, 191, 195
National Institute of Economic and Social Research 89, 122, 187-188, 221
—library 134, 146, 173, 204
National Institute of Industrial Psychology 192
National Lending Library for Science and Technology 161-162, 164
National Lending Library for the Social Sciences and Humanities (proposed) 161, 163-164
National Provincial Bank 142
National Register of Archives 73
Nemmers, E E 24
Netherlands School of Economics 79
Newark Public Library 211

233

New books in economics (Pittsburgh University) 77-78, 152, 156, 195, 215
New publications in the Board of Trade library 152, 202
New society 89
Newspaper cuttings, value of 142, 204, 205
New York Graduate School of Arts and Sciences 78
New York Graduate School of Business Administration 88
New York Public Library 211
NIESR *see* National Institute of Economic and Social Research
Notes for collective subscribers (BIM) 191
Obituaries, as sources of biographical information 125
OECD *see* Economic Co-operation and Development, Organization for
OECD observer 104
OEEC *see* Economic Co-operation and Development, Organization for (formerly OEEC)
Office for Scientific and Technical Information (OSTI) 221
Oldknow, S 70
Ollé, J G 93, 96
Operational research, bibliography on 60
Ordnance survey maps 123
Organisation for Economic Co-operation and Development *see* Economic Co-operation and Development, Organisation for
Organisation for European Economic Co-operation (now OECD) *see* Economic Co-operation and Development, Organisation for
Organisations, economic, their value to librarians 185-186, 218
OSTI *see* Office for Scientific and Technical Information
Osaka University of Commerce 56, 57
Ottley, G 62
Outlier libraries 160
Overseas trade accounts (Board of Trade) 110, 112, 113, 114
Owen, R 17, 130
Oxford Centre for Management Studies 189
Oxford economic atlas 123, 190
Oxford economic papers 87, 153
Oxford University Library 199

Packe, M StJ 128
Paenson, I 29
PAIS *see* *Public affairs information service*
Palgrave, R H I 23-24, 27, 30, 125, 211, 215, 216
Pamphlet bibliographies 45-48
Pamphlet literature
—acquisition of 158
—use of in commercial information work 137, 140, 142
Pareto, V 17
Pargellis, S 56
Paris University 78
Parliamentary papers, British 96-98
Partington, L 212
Patent Office trade name slips 139, 163, 181
Peacock, T L 166
Pendleton, O W 174
Pennance, F G 25
PEP *see* Political and Economic Planning
Periodicals *see* Journals
Perry, F R 26
Physiocrats, the 13
Piggott, M 105
Pigou, A C 17, 128, 217
Pike, E R 127
Pilkington Brothers Ltd 70
Pitman businessman's guide 27-28
Pittsburgh University 58, 77-78, 152, 195
—library 211
Planning (PEP) 187
Plant, M 75, 119
Political and Economic Planning (PEP) 187, 189
Pollard, A W 63
Polyglot dictionaries 29-30, 138
Ports dues and charges 36
Ports of the world 36-37
Post co-ordinate indexing *see* Co-ordinate indexing
Power, E 68
Power, Ministry of, *Statistical digest* 114
Practitioners, wide range of using economics and commercial libraries 18, 118, 135, 140, 145-146
Prentice Hall encyclopedic dictionary 27
Prices and Incomes Board *see* National Board for Prices and Incomes

Sayers, R S 75
Scarcity, fundamental to economics 9
Schleiffer, H 55
Schuchmann, M 170
Schumpeter, E B 109
Schumpeter, J A 17, 126, 128
Schurer, H 46
Scientific and learned societies of Great Britain 186, 196
Scottish Economic Society 186-187
Scottish journal of political economy 87, 187
Sectional lists (HMSO) 94, 99
Seldon, A 25, 187
Selection of material in libraries 151-159
Seligman, E R A 22, 211
Sell's British exporters register 34
Sell's directory of registered telegraphic addresses 34
Servotte, J V 30
Sewell, P H 149
Shaw, W A 67
Sheffield Interchange Organisation (SINTO) 163
Sheffield Public Library 200
Shell International Petroleum Company 147, 182
Shera, J H 167
Shipping, reference material on 28, 35-36
Shipping world 37
Shopper's guide 46
Shops and stores retail directory 34
Shoup, C S 127-128
Simmons, G B 60, 155
Simmons, J 75
SINTO *see* Sheffield Interchange Organisation
Siting, of public commercial library 137
Skinner, Thomas Ltd 34
Sloan, H S 24
Smith, Adam 13-14, 199
—critical works relating to 127
—special collection on 210
Smith, A R 149
Smith, K 127
Smith, R E F 29
Smyth, A L 40, 76, 120, 136, 142, 149
Smyth, R L 46
Social Affairs, Ministry of (Holland) 79, 209

Social and Economic Research, Inter-departmental Committee on 107
Social science and humanities index (H W Wilson) 78
Social Science Research Council 131, 220-221
Social Security, Ministry of, Library 203
Societies *see* Organisations, economic
Society for Advancement of Management 195
Society of Motor Manufacturers and Traders 115
Source material for business . . . history (Harvard) 75
Southampton Public Library 200
Southampton University 96
Special classifications 173-176
Special libraries
—character of work in commercial 145-148
—major British economic and commercial 200-206
Special Libraries Association of America 48, 178, 211
Sraffa, P 127, 186
Standard industrial classification (Central Statistical Office) 176
Standard international trade classification (United Nations) 117, 176, 202
Standard periodicals directory 91
Statesman's yearbook 39
Statistical abstract of the United States 115
Statistical publications
—bibliographies of 106-108
—indexing of 180-181
—overseas 115-118, 202-203
—problems relating to 118-119, 213
—value and range of 106, 119-120, 123
Statistical yearbook (United Nations) 116
Statistics and Market Intelligence Library (Board of Trade) 35, 145, 202-203, 212
Statistics of incomes, prices, employment and production (Ministry of Labour) 113, 114, 180, 218
Statistics, sources of for Common Market countries 108
Statistisches jahrbuch 115
Statutes revised 91